College and University Student Work Programs

Implications and Implementations

Frank C. Adams *and* **Clarence W. Stephens**

Southern Illinois University Press   *Carbondale and Edwardsville*

Feffer & Simons, Inc.   *London and Amsterdam*

Contents

Preface

It is the major concern of this book to indicate the important role which work experience plays in the education of a great number of our high school and college students. We hope that we have placed student work experience in an educational perspective which will, at least to a degree, stimulate and encourage teachers, counselors, and financial aids officers to devote more time and research to this too frequently neglected aspect of education.

We further hope that this book will be a valuable source of practical information for financial aids officers and counselors in higher education. In addition, this book should be a useful aid to high school guidance counselors and others interested in occupational information.

The writing is the result of research and years of experience on the part of the authors. A listing of all those who have contributed to our work, directly or indirectly, in the compilation and composition of content, is virtually impossible. However, we do wish to direct attention to Chapter 5, "Self-Help Programs in Selected Colleges and Universities," where recognition is given to some twenty-five colleges' and universities' financial aids officers. Also, we want to recognize Professor Ronald Hansen, Director of Research and Projects, for approval of research funds necessary to carry out the study in Chapter 5.

We are grateful to Mr. James Moore, Chief of the United States Office of Education, Division of Financial Assistance, for his comprehensive information concerning the College Work-Study Program.

We wish to recognize Mary E. Adams, research assistant, Southern Illinois University, Carbondale, Illinois, for her editorial and secretarial services to the authors.

Frank C. Adams
Clarence W. Stephens

Southern Illinois University
Carbondale
February 1970

College and University Student Work Programs

Implications and Implementations

1 Philosophy of Student Work

THE WORLD of work is a continuous factor influencing the lives of most adult males. In fact, they are inescapably bound to it; it is a major portion of their way of living. Increasingly, according to statistical ratios in the labor force, work for pay is becoming a part of the lives of women. Since these are actual situations, perhaps it would be wise to take a closer look at this workaday world and to attempt to aid those who as yet have not entered it. Such an overview may provide the uninitiated with a knowledge of some of the frustrations and satisfactions which they may reasonably expect; it may, in turn, guide their activities so that the rewards far outnumber the penalties. Perhaps, knowing a bit more about the world of work would be helpful even to those who have already existed in it for varying periods of time. Certainly it is reasonable to assume that for this latter group, understanding the relationships between education and work will in many instances be informative and useful from a practical standpoint.

A common statement by too many parents is to the effect that they want their children to gain an education beyond that furnished in high school so that their sons and daughters will not have to work. Nothing could be farther from the truth. In reality, an education can provide an opportunity for doing a different type of work, possibly obtaining a position at one of the levels within one of the various "white collar" classifications. The number of hours worked will probably be comparable to those spent by persons in the so-called "blue collar" classifications, with the exception that as opportunities are afforded and accepted for moving into executive positions, the hours worked, on an average, will be considerably greater. It is likely that the educated individual will use his mental abilities considerably more than his physical faculties. The reverse is true for the non-educated person. Undeniably, the opportunities for advancement in positions are much greater for the educated than for the uneducated. Obviously, the assumption that an educated person with various kinds and levels of college degrees will not have to work is false; however, his work-satisfaction should be much greater.

A.
Worker Philosophies

Whether we want to recognize it, as previously stated, work for pay is a major part of living on the part of adult males and increasingly so on the part of adult females. If we accept this as true, and the authors do, then it follows that schools should be concerned that students have a background which includes work, either paid or unpaid, which will enable them to take their proper places in an adult society as contributing members to that society. In our increasingly automated world, opportunities for work at home are not available to students on the same scale as was true but a few decades ago. As examples, wood and coal have to be carried in daily in relatively few homes. With power mowers and the dangers of injury in usage, parents are fearful of turning over lawn-mowing responsibilities to children until they attain the young-adult state. The vegetable gardens of individual families seem destined to become a near-relic of the past. Basically, homes are becoming so structured that work opportunities for children are less available. Thus, far too many children now reach physical adulthood without having to assume somewhat comprehensive work responsibilities of other than perhaps those of a mental nature.

1. *Attitude and Responsibility.* The authors believe that meaningful work provides people with worthwhile purpose in life. Further, work can give a feeling of accomplishment, whether it is for pay or not. Individuals can gain a sense of fulfillment in that they are contributing members of the world in which they live. Also, work and work situations can be such that a genuine concern for the welfare of others is a natural result of effort. Some of these factors which influence attitudes will be presented in this chapter.

In essence, if a worker is to be most effective, he must truly want to work. A paycheck is important for the adult, but if this is his sole purpose in employment, almost any job can become boring, and the level of productivity may fall far below a desirable level. We believe that a worker should feel that work is a part of the overall responsibility of each individual, that his accomplishments are, even if minutely, changing the world for the better, that he is producing or helping to manufacture goods which are needed for living, or that he is performing a service required by the world in which he lives. If these attitudes are adopted by workers, then no job becomes inconsequential.

2. *Kinds of Work.* However, the problem of establishing the proper attitudes toward work is most difficult. In general, the problem is easier to resolve if the job of the worker is in the so-called "white collar" classification than if it is in the "blue collar" category. Working with the mind seemingly creates more prestige in the eyes of the average American than does labor of the manual order. Thus, the white collar worker receives more recognition from the general public than does the blue collar worker regardless of whether the former is employed in either the most repetitious or the most challenging of jobs. Another common type of distinction as seen by the general public evolves from whether a man does work which is basically physical in nature. If the work is primarily physical, the worker is considered to be a nonprofessional. If his employment is chiefly nonphysical, he is looked upon as a professional. In a status-conscious society, professionals are more highly regarded than are nonprofessionals. Irrespective of the feelings of the general public concerning the merit of various types of jobs, a man's attitudes can be changed by the reflected attitudes of his work associates, family, and friends. If these important groups will be ready to recognize and to praise him for his worthwhile accomplishments, his attitudes toward himself and his work will change. If respect is evidenced for human worth and dignity, no matter what the job may be, his attitudes will alter; if others recognize the real dignity of even the most menial of tasks, his attitudes will change.

It should be clear to the reader at this point that the authors of the book place great emphasis upon the importance of attitudes, and that they are concerned with establishing a proper set of attitudes as an element of significance in the background of each worker. We recognize, also, that the nature of work is such that the attitudes of workers will change, either to become better or worse; attitudes rarely remain constant. Furthermore, the establishment and continuance of a proper set of values and attitudes is a major task.

In the writing thus far, we have been concerned with the attitudes of workers in general, students or non-students, and part-time or full-time workers. Since we are primarily concerned with the student worker in this book, let us now focus our attention upon that individual, although it should be realized by the reader that most of the content to be presented would apply almost equally well to the non-student.

3. *Concepts of Student Work.*   Students need to be self-motivated if they are to be expected to change their attitudes in a proper direction or to acquire competencies needed for specific jobs. Also, orientation to a job is of vital importance, which implies that competent supervisors are perhaps necessary if students are to achieve at their best levels.

It has been the experience of the writers that when opportunities are afforded for advancement, students, both in terms of interest in position and pay, are more likely to be motivated and to acquire a proper set of attitudes, particularly when such advancement is based upon accomplishment.

Attitudes of students can be greatly changed in a proper direction through supplying opportunities for demonstrating initiative, followed by the recognition of initiative shown as expressed by fellow workers and supervisors. However, care must be taken to insure that initiative is not employed at the expense of the basic job to be done. Obviously, the basic task must be accomplished, but if better ways can be devised for performing the job, such is to be commended.

The element of self-satisfaction in achievement cannot be overlooked when one thinks of proper student worker attitudes. Not only does the worker need to feel that others believe his work is important, but he, himself, must sense that that which is being accomplished is useful and needful. It is helpful, too, in terms of attitudes for him to realize that if the work must be performed, it is significant. In general, being of service through the completion of a job engenders a feeling of personal worth within an individual.

4. *Home and School Philosophy.*   The role of the university in setting up and implementing work exxperiences for students is difficult. Society, in general, and the home, in particular, can help. Technological advances in the twentieth century have been tremendous and are continuing unabated. Accordingly, there is the resultant difficulty of establishing proper perspectives between the work which students per-

form while in school and the vocations following their college years. At the present time, an increasing proportion of students are coming from the urban areas of our country. This, in itself, creates a problem. Job opportunities for urban area students of secondary school age are markedly decreasing because of automation.

Thus, proportionately fewer and fewer college students have had previous work exxperience. The machine is taking over, and with this increasing automation, more technical knowledge and ability are required for work. Certainly, very few high school pupils have either the technical knowledge or the ability to handle capably the jobs which might be available in the community.

In addition, child labor laws and the unionization of labor tend to restrict out-of-town opportunities for high school students. We do not mean to imply that such restriction is entirely improper. It is most suitable in many instances because of the personal danger connected with certain jobs, the cost of machine repair if the job is not handled properly, and the lack of ability to function adequately in still other instances. Regardless, at the present time, fewer jobs are available. Such a situation is in diametrical opposition to that which existed until just the past few decades. Traditionally, we were for scores of years primarily an agrarian society; children were expected to work on family farms. In fact, family living was, in large part, dependent upon the work performed by children.

Where does the preceding discussion lead us? In the view of the writers, there has been a tremendous void in the lives of too many college students. Never have they been forced to assume worthwhile work responsibilities. The value of the dollar is nebulous; money for necessities and luxuries has been given to them by their parents. At any rate, they know very little, if anything, about the requirements of the world of work. Because of a lack of experience in working, they often have very little respect for the dignity of labor and for those men and women who produce goods or serve others. There appears to be the feeling that humanity exists to serve them, rather than that they exist to serve humanity. It is apparent that society, including the home, has a real responsibility for changing adolescent attitudes and values.

At the same time, society has a duty to furnish opportunities for correcting visible difficulties. Obviously, we must start with the home, if needed corrections are to be effected and to be made enduring. Parents of preadolescents and adolescents need to survey the home situation to determine the areas in which worthwhile work experiences exist.

The defining of duties needs to be followed by an assignment of work responsibilities to their children and a check-up to see that the responsibilities have been met, even though in many instances it may be easier and require less time for the parent to do the work.

Secondary schools, it seems to the authors, should be concerned with working with community business and industrial leaders to find worthwhile jobs which can be handled by adolescents, to be followed by placement of students on a part-time basis in such work. Care must be exercised that students are not placed in pseudo "Make Work" situations. To do this is nearly as bad as no employment because of the negative attitudes toward work which will be generated in the minds of the students. Work must have a genuine purpose, either in terms of producing or serving.

5. *Responsibilities of Student Work Supervision.* The authors believe that institutions concerned with education beyond the high school have a responsibility for furnishing work opportunities for students for various reasons, but perhaps most importantly for the purpose of changing attitudes and values. It is not thought by the authors that work can substitute for the academic background and skills acquired by students as they look forward to full-time work, but rather that employment can be a part of the total experience of students without diminishing the needed background and skills. To implement these beliefs, it seems that colleges and universities have the responsibility for finding and setting aside those jobs for students which can be performed as well by students as by full-time workers. Obviously, the costs of getting work performed by students should be comparable to the expense of having the same duties completed by full-time workers.

Adults sometimes forget, or perhaps have never realized, that persons who contribute toward making a better society or a better home and consciously realize that they are doing so, rarely get into trouble. Adolescents and other students are responsive persons, and they have feelings and acquire attitudes, just as do adults.

In work, as in education, we are concerned with change in behavior. An altered response can be brought about through the development of proper attitudes and abilities. Student workers acquire new skills which may or may not be needed for full-time work following completion of their education. At the very least, however, in the acquisition of skills, attitudes toward work are altered. Most important, perhaps, is the fact that student workers learn to work with others. They learn to cooperate with other students in completing a job, and, in some instances, they are placed in leadership roles where they supervise the work of others. In every case, if proper work relationships are maintained, students are working under supervision, whether in leadership or in group roles. Since this is true, we should recognize that good supervision can lead to respect for leadership. It can readily be seen from the discussion in this and other paragraphs that the authors believe that almost all work has educational values if we will but direct ourselves to a recognition and an implementation of the values.

Universities realize that friendship should not be a criterion for placing a student in a part-time job. In addition, it should be noted that, insofar as is possible, the economic position of the student should not be a major criterion for part-time job placement. If work is so structured that desirable changes in behavior can be induced, a philosophy which the writers endorse, we cannot do other than recommend that part-time work be a part of the program of every student. On the other hand, we are realistic enough to indicate that those capable students who could not attend college unless work opportunities are afforded should be placed first in jobs.

Over and beyond the fact that universities should know that individuals, in a major sense, demonstrate their worth through work, and that there should be a concern for the welfare of workers, is the factor that student workers need to be self-motivated if they are to change their attitudes and to acquire proper skills and capabilities. Such self-motivation may be induced by the introduction of a number of elements, in addition to those previously noted. Undeniably, an opportunity for advancement or promotion in a work area is an important factor. Likewise a chance for promotion to a better job in another work area with accompanying salary increments is a strong motivation. Students are also encouraged if they have the opportunity for merit increases while continuing in the same job. All of this means that universities should maintain job opportunities for students at various levels of ability and should at the same time have salary schedules with appreciable increase potentials, which can provide for recognition of differing student skills and abilities.

6. *Potentialities of Part-Time Work.* A strongly motivating factor is introduced when the jobs held by students are closely related to future

vocations. In fact, the authors believe that this is the most satisfying type of experience which students can know. Since they are acquiring experience and ability in the type of work which they will be performing on a full-time basis in later years, ordinarily increased interest and satisfaction will be evidenced in their prevocational duties.

Universities are just now beginning to move to any marked extent in creating such jobs on campuses. Within this job type area, the use of instructional aides seems to hold much promise. Most university and college professors can use such additional competent assistance. At the same time, it is believed that help received through the use of instructional aides should enable conscientious teachers to perform functions more efficiently, particularly teachers in those schools with rapidly increasing enrollments.

Perhaps, the job of an instructional aide should be thought of as representing the ultimate position for the student. However, it should be emphasized that these particular jobs are earned through performing well in other job assignments. Incidentally, the professors would benefit from this previous work experience since students who have worked in so-called menial tasks, such as janitorial or food service, and have performed well, assuredly may be expected to be even more competent and perhaps more conscientious when working assignments are in areas related specifically to major interests and background study.

It seems to the authors from their experience that the universities should exercise a maximum of caution in one respect. Students should be retained in employment in a given situation only if they are actually earning the money received. We are not interested in a "Give-away Program." It appears to us that it is unjust to award students, or any other worker, something for nothing because of the undesirable attitudes which will be established toward work. If a student's work record is such that he should be dismissed from a job, he should be discharged promptly and directed to report to the Student Work Office. After discussion and counseling, the work office may or may not recommend him for another student job, depending upon the circumstances involved.

7. *The Student Work Program: Foundation and Superstructure.* The work program structuring is of major importance in any school because of the many duties which should be performed. First, a work program should have strongly evidenced school support. Furthermore,

if referrals for placement are to be made in terms of comparative ability, if training programs are to be located appropriately and to be carried on efficiently, if testing of student ability is to be performed without prohibitive costs, if evaluation of student work is to be comprehensive, and, in fact, if students are to know where there are existing job opportunities, it seems that a centralized work office should be established.

There are varying philosophies applied to the setting up of a centralized work office on a university campus, as well as defining its delegated functions, when such a center is established. There is the position taken by the writers that there should be a centralized office and that its functions should be comprehensive, including those processes which can best be handled through centralization. However, there are those who do not believe that students should work at anything other than studies while in school, which would imply that no work office should be created. Naturally, varying positions between the two extremes are taken by individual schools, according to the philosophy of the university or college. Within schools, there may very well be particular programs which are emphasized.

An increasing number of schools are featuring cooperative programs, including those operating at Northeastern University in Boston, Massachusetts, the University of Cincinnati at Cincinnati, Ohio, and Antioch College in Yellow Springs, Ohio. In such programs, the students periodically apply the knowledge gained in academic study in off-campus work for a quarter or a semester, with the job closely related to the major area of learning. It seems to the authors that this type of program is very meaningful because students can readily see in a practical situation the relationships existing between work and school study through applying the knowledge gained.

Some schools believe that almost all work is educational in nature, as exemplified in the programs of Blackburn College in Carlinville, Illinois, and Berea College in Berea, Kentucky; however, others hold that student work downgrades the academic programming. It is interesting to note that with the provision of the new federally sponsored College Work-Study Program, many schools are changing their positions to include an increase in emphasis on work programs.

Paradoxically, even in programs which appear to be essentially parallel, there are differing philosophies as to implementation. For example, the philosophy of Blackburn College is to the effect that student workers should be supervised by student supervisors, the only exception being that of top-level supervision. In contrast, in Berea College, it is primarily believed that the supervision of student workers should be performed by competent full-time workers. Both programs, although similar in design but different in detail, have been successful.

The thought that the authors wish to stress is that there is no one and only way of conducting a work program; there are many good programs in which different philosophies have been implemented. We do, however, think that we have a duty to express our beliefs, based upon the experiences we have had in work programming in Southern Illinois University and upon the results of observations of other programs.

8. *Operational Procedures of Student Work Programs.* As previously indicated, we believe in a centralized work office, charged with responsibilities in line with performing those tasks which can best be accomplished by a centralized office. We do not believe that a work office can "be all things to all people" but, rather, that there are certain responsibilities which can be handled most efficiently through centralization and others through de-centralization. Perhaps our view can be expressed in part by stating that we believe in centralized administration and de-centralized operation.

a) COOPERATIVE PROGRAMS. In Southern Illinois University, we maintain and believe in cooperative programs of various types, but we have also initiated and encouraged the introduction of other programs in which we believe. There are opportunities for students to participate in programs involving college study for one or two quarters, followed by off-campus full-time work experience for one or two quarters, as previously explained. In addition, we operate an on-campus program which we believe to be cooperative in nature. As students move forward in their academic schooling, every effort is made to place them in part-time on-campus or in off-campus jobs directly related to their major or minor areas of study. In these situations, they work part time and study part time each day.

b) THE IMPORTANCE OF GOOD SUPERVISION. The writers, in most instances, favor the use of competent full-time supervisors of students in work which must be carried on for an extended period of time during the day. Continuity needed to complete the work is assured in these situations. In addition, there is greater confidence that work which has to be completed at a set time will be finished. We recognize that the opportunities for students to act in a major leadership capacity are not as great, if our beliefs are implemented, as when no full-time supervisors are used. On the other hand, the able, full-time supervisor will provide opportunities for students to assume leadership roles of a lesser nature. Where continuity is not needed for work completion, students should be placed in major supervisory roles if they are competent to handle the responsibilities. Under any circumstance, competent supervision is virtually an imperative.

c) WORK TRAINING PROGRAMS. The authors always have endorsed work training programs. Students should know what is expected of them and how to perform the job satisfactorily. If there is a wide range of work opportunities, the training program requires centralization if there is to be a referral of students to many different areas. For example, if the officials consider that secretarial help is needed in almost every operation of a university, it follows that centralized initial training is desirable. On the other hand, if the training is intended for only one operational function, such as janitorial service, we believe that the training program should be assumed by that function.

Further, we believe that the evaluation of work programs should be comprehensive and continuous. This evaluation should be assumed chiefly by the operating function, but it is cooperative to the extent that the work office assumes a leadership role if needed and assuredly should have the results of evaluation made available to it. If the results of the evaluations from the operating functions do not indicate that a satisfactory program is being conducted, the student work office should have the responsibility and the authority for making independent evaluations, followed by recommendations to the functions for program improvements. If improvement does not take place following the recommendations and the operating function cannot justify continuing as it has done in the past, the authority of the work office should be such that recommendations made to higher authorities in the line organization will be implemented. Every effort, however, should be made initially to resolve problems in a cooperative manner.

d) ASSESSMENT OF ACHIEVEMENT. The authors believe that students should be evaluated periodically while working in a particular job and particularly at the time when work in a specific job is terminated. Further, a composite of these evaluations should become a part of a student's permanent record in the University Placement Office. Good evaluations will be of great assistance to the Placement authorities and to the student in finding a rewarding full-time job. We believe that the evaluations should be made by the operating functions and directed to the Central Work Office. Also, we think that it is most important that supervisors in operating functions discuss student evaluations with the individual students concerned. Certainly, students who are doing poor work should be so advised by supervisors. If it is desired by the supervisor, the Student Work Office has a responsibility for counseling the student. We believe that students who have continued to receive poor work records in particular jobs should be released from duties by the operating function and referred to the work office. The resulting conference, together with cumulative past records, should determine whether students should be referred to other jobs. It is important to remember that forms used in student evaluation should not be so devised that an extended period of time is necessary for completing such evaluation.

e) TESTING PRIOR TO EMPLOYMENT. The writers have found that it is virtually impossible to carry on a comprehensive testing program of students, preceding employment. In theory, we believe such a program to be desirable, but, in practice, the very volume of students seeking jobs in a large, comprehensive university makes testing in many areas non-feasible. In small colleges, where there are not as many different job opportunities available, and where administration and operation are more or less centralized, testing can be conducted. As is true for full-time Civil Service testing, if examinations are to be given, they should include both written and performance acivities.

However, it should be pointed out that schools are not entirely unprepared for student placement in jobs if tests are not administered. Academic performance and various types of college placement test results are usually available and constitute valuable criteria for job placement. Also, previous evaluations of student workers furnish a sound basis in many instances for the placement of student workers. We do advocate that standardized tests of secretarial ability be given centrally to students in all schools since our experience with the placement of student secretaries, based solely upon high school grades, has not been too satisfactory. Usually, high school students will have acquired the speed but not the vocabulary needed for campus jobs. Further, an inability to spell seems to be another major hindrance to good job performance. Most of the present problems are not the fault of the business education teachers in high schools because personal typing has been emphasized; such training is highly desirable, but it does not generally prepare students well for office work.

9. *Experimentation and Research.* All of us are constantly reminded that the need for experimentation in academic programming and methods is both necessary and desirable in our public schools and colleges. Equally, the same concept applies in student work. In both instances, there are varying ideas as to the implementation of the concept. In Southern Illinois University, the authors have generally taken the position that experimentation should be conducted with a small "e," but that it should be continuous. In rare instances, major experimentation or experimentation with a capital "E" is necessary, but, as was true in Southern Illinois University, probably such emphasis is necessary only when a comprehensive program is initially established.

Similarly, research may be activated on a minor basis, "r," or on a major scale, "R," in student work. The writers have taken the position that, for the most part, if research is to be carried on simultaneously with the operational program, it should be conducted with a small "r," and be continuous. However, major research is possible, utilizing data gathered from previous experiences, if the data are historical in nature.

Earlier in our writing, it was emphasized that the university should never lose sight of the fact that the primary purpose of school attendance is that of obtaining an academic background. Obviously, this should never be forgotten in work program structuring and operation. However, this is one belief held by the writers which is seemingly in conflict with the purpose emphasized above. We feel that, insofar as is possible, students should be assigned time blocks for work prior to registration for classes. That is, if a student needs to work, e.g., two, three, or four hours in a particular job, these hours are to be worked consecutively. An hour of employment during several intervals of the day usually is not too effective in accomplishing the needed work. However, there are certain situations in almost any school which make the setting aside of a block of time for work virtually impossible. As students move toward higher undergraduate college work, even in a large, comprehensive university, fewer and fewer sections of the same required courses are offered. In fact, the courses may be scheduled during only one period of the day, or perhaps even only once **or** twice during the entire school year. Accordingly, the work schedule has to become secondary in such circumstances.

Further, it is much easier to use the block of time concept when the university is large and has various classes scheduled and distributed throughout a greater part of the day. For example, the setting aside of a block of time for a student to work is much simpler in a university which provides a comprehensive schedule of classes beginning at 8:00 A.M. and continuing through 10:00 P.M. than in a university or a college in which most classes are taught between 9:00 A.M. and 3:00 P.M.

B.

Philosophy Related to the Work Office Counselor

The responsibilities of the counselors in the centralized work office, as advocated by the authors, are all-encompassing. They must handle the myriads of details involved in the keeping of good records, and they should possess a considerable amount of ability in intake counseling. Above all, they must be able to establish rapport with interviewees. However, possessing ability in these areas is but a point of departure. Each counselor needs to be knowledgeable in the duties inherent in the many student jobs. Further, he must know or have information readily available to him in regard to the prerequisites for specific jobs. As may be inferred, it becomes a near imperative that a job classification plan be established, detailing each of the available campus jobs, particularly when a comprehensive program is in operation. Since rewards play an important role in the motivation of workers, information dealing with such matters as pay rates and opportunities for advancement also is necessary.

The work counselor has additional obligations and needs supplementary abilities over and beyond those indicated thus far. He must ascertain that students are placed in jobs which they can perform or learn to do readily. This means that there must be considerable interpretative ability, making use of available background data concerning the students. Academic grades and the subjects completed in school should be included in the student's record. The results of college entrance tests furnish indications which can be used in job placement. A review of recommendations and evaluations of the student is also helpful. Past work experience serves as a guide in many instances in anticipating possible performance in a new work situation. If the results of the tests related to potential jobs, both written and performance examinations, are available, they may be of considerable assistance. As can readily be seen, this "fitting" of students and jobs is not a simple task; mistakes will be made on occasion. The resultant adjustments of errors probably will indicate that the students concerned will need or should be relocated in other jobs.

Earlier in this discussion, it was pointed out that good files are required in work offices, with past and current information immediately accessible. The writers believe that opportunities should be provided for student workers to serve in a variety of situations, according to individual competencies. We need to remind ourselves constantly that the effects of automation are such that many former specialties are becoming outmoded and thus are of little or no value in finding and holding a job. It is better to become aware of and to recognize this fact of life as a student worker than to realize this truth after moving into the world of work as a full-time employee. An enrichment of job experiences can open new vocational doors, if one changes work areas, either by choice or by circumstantial demand.

C.
Philosophy Related to Supervisors of Student Workers

The success of the student work program will depend to a major degree upon the quality and the competence of supervisors of working students. The same statement can be made concerning the success of any industry or business. Since the roles of supervisors are so significant, it seems appropriate to detail some of the concepts and principles which are pertinent. First, it should be understood, almost without explicit statement, that supervisors, particularly supervisors of students, should be most competent in performing the type of work expected of employees under their direction.

Also, the ability to demonstrate and to describe many of the skills demanded for job completion is an invaluable asset in job supervision, especially in student work where individuals may not have perfected skills. An attitude which embodies the concept that it is constantly necessary to search for better ways of doing things creates a healthy work atmosphere. Better means may not be found immediately, but this emphasis by supervisors and the encouragement of employee initiative, followed by a personal recognition of the workers' accomplishments in supplying answers, creates an improved climate occupationally.

Good personal relations and specific personal characteristics can indicate the fine differences which distinguish supervisors doing a good job from those doing a poor one. Invariably, the writers have found that the good supervisor is loyal to his employees. We find that he is concerned with responding insofar as is possible to the personal and the physical needs of the student workers. There is a realization on his part that supervision cannot be cold and impersonal. He should be friendly and kind, but when the occasion demands, he must be firm. At all times, even at the risk of having his actions misinterpreted, he must be fair. To find supervisors who possess such abilities and personal characteristics is difficult; however, it is necessary to discover individuals with even additional qualities.

It was emphasized that supervisors should be kind, friendly, firm, and fair. Additionally, we feel that supervisors should be interested in and evidence a liking for people. They should be consistent in their behavior, regardless of personal feelings on any given day. Students and other employees must know what to expect in specific situations. Supervisors must be honest; otherwise, they cannot be respected by their employees. They must give recognition appropriately and be understanding as circumstances require.

In conclusion, there is one final factor in supervision which we feel should be underscored. A supervisor cannot become one of the employee group in his supervising capacity. If he attempts to do so, he will subsequently be treated as a colleague rather than as an executive. Yet, at the same time, if he is not to lose the respect of his workers, his words and actions should not imply that he feels that he is better than or superior to his unit. Indeed, the role of the supervisor is a difficult one; he must balance administrative ability with approachability.

2 An Overview of Student Work History

IN THIS chapter, the authors will briefly trace the evolution of student employment by calling attention to some major historical landmarks which influenced its development. It is to be emphasized that student employment in this country is a continuous work-experience operation, dating back to the founding of Harvard in 1636. Traditionally, the example of the poor boy working his way through college has been a symbol of initiative and ambition, cherished by the American people. Such academic perseverance might well be compared to the rugged individualism of our pioneers. The belief prevails with many of us that true maturation is developed through meaningful experiences which require the individual to overcome obstacles and to resolve problems confronting him in reaching his goal.

Additionally, youth does not acquire maturity by ignoring difficulties or by having other individuals solve perplexities for him. Therefore, the young man or woman who is capable of attaining a college education should be willing to expend much individual effort and earn a portion, at least, of the overall college expenses. Incidentally, the starry-eyed college graduate who believes that his degree will serve as a substitute for work will have a rude awakening when employed in his first job.

Today, in our economically affluent society, we have many parents who can well afford to provide all of the college expenses incurred in educating their children, yet they feel that their sons and daughters should be employed part time during the academic year, or work full time during vacation periods. These parents recognize that the maturational and the educational values attained in practical work experiences are not readily acquired in a classroom. In addition, many young people are equally aware of the worth of work. The authors have had direct contact and numerous interviews and counseling sessions with college students who wanted part-time work. Their reasons for seeking employment were different in nature; many needed employment in order to attend school, some felt that work experience was a valuable instrument in the learning process, others believed that parents were sacrificing too greatly in their behalf, and an appreciable number thought that their academic achievement would be higher if they were forced to budget their time. Essentially, the opportunity for students on or off campus presents infinitely more than monetary rewards. The actual benefit to the student depends upon many factors, tangible and intangible.

A.

The Colonial Period

In higher education, the student job came into being during the colonial period of our history by sheer necessity, not by design. Institutions of higher learning in the seventeenth century geared their curricula primarily to the preparation of ministers, teachers, and lawyers. Physicians were then acquiring knowledge mainly through apprenticeships. Then, as today, many students who desired a college education could not afford academic expenses. However, it is to be remembered that but a small percentage of the colonial population acquired a college education, nor did many need such schooling.

Nevertheless, among the group seeking higher learning, many students were young men of extremely limited means. Accordingly, it is not surprising that the future teacher of this time sold his services as a tutor. Although there is little doubt that the tutoring of students as a part-time work experience was beneficial to the colonial teacher's career, we cannot overlook the point that such employment was a financial necessity for personal maintenance. Ministerial students attended college through the week and conducted services on the Sabbath to earn funds to continue their education. Looking back through the past three centuries, we can see that in the colonial colleges, roots began to grow which brought to fruition the career-oriented work experience, although not specifically identified as such at that time.

We should not leave the colonial period without calling attention to the student financial aids philosophy of our early private colleges such as Harvard, Yale, and Princeton, all subscribing to the belief that a lack of financial resources should not constitute an insurmountable barrier to acquiring higher education. As a result of this tenet, Harvard College initiated the first student work program, identifiable as such. It is interesting to note the unique means employed to finance this early operation; administrators simply increased the tuition and fees of the wealthier students and used the surplus funds thus obtained to pay students of limited means to perform custodial work for the college. Today, through the efforts of Dean John Monro and Work Program Director Dustin Burke, the diversified work experiences provided by Harvard meet both the educational and the financial needs of the students.

B.

The State University

Following the Civil War, the state university, as we know it today, as a result of federal legislation, brought about curriculum changes which added to the overall diversity of institutions of higher learning in America. Our state universities are often defined as an eclectic combination of liberal arts from England, research from Germany, and service practicality from our own United States.

1. *The Contribution of the Federal Government.* Several historical factors have played dominant roles in the development of state universities. First, we have the federal government's contribution of land-grant funds provided by the First Morrill Act, passed by Congress in 1862, setting aside public lands for the establishment of colleges in new states, as well as in previously established states. From the standpoint of curriculum, the First Morrill Act provided instruction in agriculture, mechanical arts, and military science, without excluding traditional scientific and classical studies.

The Second Morrill Act of 1890 was generous and encompassing in that it provided for annual appropriations of money to each land-grant college. Original amounts allotted were increased by later amendments. It is significant that the land grants and the colleges supported by such grants were primarily created for the middle and the lower classes of society and were designed to provide a more liberal and practical education for these groups.

2. *Self-Help Programs.* Student self-help programs had fertile soil for development in state universities since many students with limited financial resources sought admission. In addition, a number of educa-

tional programs were structured specifically to meet the demands of the time, thus creating opportunities for earning money. However, there is but little evidence to indicate that any major effort was exerted toward organizing the work program or relating the work experience to academic study. In brief, early student employment was primarily oriented to providing jobs to enable the students to earn a portion of their college expenses. This was undeniably an important step in financial assistance, but it was only one phase of a highly structured work-study program, as we know it today. It is interesting to note that some of the largest self-help programs in today's institutions of higher education are located in state universities. Some of these institutions allot more than $4 million annually for their student work programs, which include a variety of jobs in keeping with the financial and the educational needs of students, extending from the entering class through the graduate school.

3. *The Space Age.* Undeniably, the Space Age with its demand for more scientific and technical knowledge has brought about wide-sweeping societal changes. Possibly one of the most significant results is the great migration from rural to urban locations. Although the economic advantages of technology can be recognized, there is little doubt that this progress has been purchased at the price of creating social problems of vast scope. One is acutely aware of the problems of unemployment, inadequate housing, slum conditions, juvenile delinquency, crime, and moral laxity.

Accordingly, the Space Age has grown into a giant of technological change, bearing with it the problems of automation, mass production, social welfare, governmental support, and subsidies ranging from farm production to educational grants.

4. *Free Higher Education.* There are those who think that the panacea for the problems and the conditions which endanger the health and peace of the world lies in our institutions of higher learning, with the state universities playing a prominent role. Regardless of what is conceived as the purpose of the American state university, we cannot deny that it embodies the concept of free higher education to the extent possible. Even today, with inflation and ever-increasing enrollments, there is evident resistance on the part of many state university administrations to increase tuition costs. Such an attitude reflects the

commitment of the American people to the principle of democracy with equality of opportunity for higher education.

In effect, the state university, charging little or no tuition, is affording the equivalent of a scholarship to all eligible students of the state. This benefit is frequently overlooked by parents and students who believe that the relatively small tuition which they pay is sufficient to serve as a fair share of operating a college or university. Another incentive furthering education is the effort of the state and the institution to provide scholarships to students of high ability and minimal financial resources, thus offsetting tuition costs, although such amounts may be relatively inconsequential.

C.
The High School

1. *College Preparatory.* Paralleling the development of the land-grant colleges and state universities and serving as a major contributory factor to college enrollment growth was the initiation of our tuition-free, tax-supported high school. Although we devote additional space to the program of the secondary school elsewhere in this book, a historical review is necessary to set the stage for work-experience programs on the high school level.

For many decades, college entrance was contingent almost exclusively upon the student's being graduated from high school, although per se, preparation for higher education was not the only important purpose of the high school. However, college and university influence upon the high school curriculum by the turn of this century forced the high school into virtually a one-function program—college preparatory. Such an emphasis, however, was contrary to the basic philosophy of the high school, that of serving the needs of all of the students, not merely the academically gifted. Consequently, students not planning to progress to higher education were exposed to few, if any, courses which would adequately prepare them for immediate employment following graduation or discontinuation of schooling.

2. *Curriculum and Community Planning.* It is not implied that general education courses should not constitute the heart of the high school curriculum, but rather than the needs of high school students cannot be met by a rather narrow selection of such courses. The more

complex our society becomes, the greater is the need for a broad and diversified curriculum in our secondary schools, supplemented by planned community services and experience in work and in play. It is the belief of the authors that neither parents nor community leaders are assuming the responsibilities which are necessary in the total education of our youth. Especially is this demonstrated in the instance of the adolescent who must develop wholesome attitudes toward a society of which he is an inseparable part, although he often feels, justly so, that he is an outsider.

Basically, the teaching of ethics, the "What's right and what's wrong," must be initiated in the home with the parents and the examples set for their children. Parental standards are often adopted by the children in determining individual behavior. The father who defrauds in reporting his income tax cannot justifiably chide his fourteen-year-old for cheating during an algebra test. The community, also, must be aware of the responsibilities with which it is charged. An area which offers many opportunities for adolescents to perform part-time work under adult supervision after school, on Saturday, or during summer vacation periods is playing a significant role in the total education of our youth.

Further, the community which affords supervised playgrounds and parks for children is keenly interested in the development of wholesome personalities. While great emphasis is effected in Washington to strive for The Great Society, it is incumbent upon the church, the parents, the community, and the schools to work together in a mutual concern for The Good Society.

3. *The Smith-Hughes Act.* The Smith-Hughes Act of 1917 provided a favorable milieu for a growing emphasis upon the teaching of agriculture and home economics by providing federal funds to help pay the salaries of teachers in these academic areas. Such a breaking away from the former high school curriculum, centered upon the purely academic and general education subjects, to the inclusion of courses of a more practical nature was truly the first major step in making high school theory a practical reality. It is evident from the foregoing historical sketch that we now have a subject base established to which we can relate career jobs, at least in the areas of home economics and agriculture on the high school level.

Despite the fact that the work experience of students often took the form of projects in the home or on the farm, we cannot discount the educational value of the experience. An important element was added to the work experience of the agriculture and home economics students, that of supervision. In the instance of high school students, the supervision was provided by the teachers, thus assuring the students, parents, and the school board that the work experience was educationally oriented by design. The importance of supervision and of supervision in the vocationally oriented experience will be discussed later.

D.
The Co-op Program

To maintain our historical development of student work experience in its proper chronological perspective regarding the higher education movement, we must digress from World War I and the Smith-Hughes period and retrace our steps to 1906. At this time, Professor Herman Schneider was a member of the engineering faculty of the University of Cincinnati. While serving in this capacity and making many contacts with students, he arrived at two conclusions, destined to be a far-reaching importance.

His first observation was based upon experience and his discernment as a faculty member. He noted that every profession for which students prepare demands certain elements not readily taught in the classroom; these prerequisites must preferably be learned through on-the-job experience from professionals in the field. He further observed that most of the college students in this country found it necessary to obtain part-time work, often in jobs which bore but little relationship to their future vocations. Such self-help, however, was necessary to help finance all or a portion of their college education. Based upon these two observations, the concept of cooperative education was developed by Dean Schneider.

1. *Theory and Practice.* From its inception, Dean Schneider's goal of a work experience for the college student was one which would provide a practical experience blended with classroom theory. Further, he was well aware of the need of many college students to earn money to supplement or to supply the educational expenses. Since the teaching of Dean Schneider focused upon the School of Engineering, it was a logical approach for him to initiate the cooperative education program in conjunction with industrial establishments.

2. *The Co-op and Higher Education.* Today, the Co-op, as it is usually termed, has been adapted to most, if not all, of the academic programs in higher education. In business, industry, and governmental agencies, some forty-five thousand students annually devote part of their time to study and a portion of their hours to work. In their working capacity, they earn upwards of $60 million. Colleges located in twenty-seven states and in Canada participate in the cooperative program currently.

One of the nationally recognized spokesmen for the program of Cooperative Education is Dean Roy Wooldridge of Northeastern University, Boston, Massachusetts. He says of the Co-op:

> Many informed persons believe that cooperative education will play an important role in the future expansion of higher education in the country. There is a strong conviction that the system of education can make a significant contribution to the education of youth in a period when the concept of work in this society is undergoing substantial change. In this age of scientific and technological expansion and automation, employment and the choice of a vocation becomes increasingly difficult for young people . . . Cooperative education, by frequently exposing the student to a real work situation, not only gives him a basis for a more intelligent choice, but serves to lessen the psychological shock of entry into a profession after the completion of his educational program.[1]

3. *Career Work Experience.* We concur with the views of Dean Wooldridge in considering the Cooperative Education plan, both in philosophy and design, as a career work-experience program. However, this does not indicate that all students and all jobs can be so aligned that each student achieves the ideal placement in a work experience definitely related to his major field of study. Rather, it emphasizes that the total program is basically structured for such a purpose, insofar as is possible. It is to be remembered that the work experience in a program of cooperative education can supply the vocational guidance which reinforces the career choice of the student or provides him with the necessary evidence to select or to alter his vocational goal.

---

[1]   Roy L. Wooldridge, "Cooperative Education, an Evolving Educational Pattern" (Address delivered at the Annual Fall Conference of the Eastern College Personnel Offices, Lake Placid, N.Y., October 4, 1964.)

Although cooperative education relies primarily upon establishments in business, industry, and government to provide the work experience of the work-study program, there are a number of institutions today which have applied the Co-op principles to their own on-campus student work programs. In these instances, the institution provides and supervises both the work and the study aspects of the program of cooperative education.

E.

The National Youth Administration

The next major landmark in the history of student work experience was established with the formation of the National Youth Administration Student Work Program, or the N.Y.A. Program, as it is commonly called, initiated in 1935. This service was also the first financial assistance program sponsored by the Federal government, directly aiding high school and college students. The N.Y.A. Program, like the present College Work-Study Program, was administered by individual institutions, operating within fiscal guidelines and directives supplied by the federal government. The submitting of required reports to the central agency is a characteristic of the programs, both past and present.

1. *Institutional Program Design.* However, each institution was permitted an amount of latitude, with the government allowing individual design and development of a program to meet particular needs. Schools were encouraged to consider the student's interests and aptitudes, and whenever possible, relate the work experience to the student's academic field of major study. From its inception, the N.Y.A. Program emphasized the importance of work projects which would supplement the student's regular school work. However, it must be emphasized that each institution supervised its own specific program, and, as one would anticipate, considerable variations in work projects and job assignments developed.

2. *Work Experience—Misunderstood.* In a summary report on the N.Y.A. Program, the span of the operation is shown in the following quotation:

Since traditionally, the American school and college plan was designed primarily to meet academic needs, it was natural that school officials in devising work assignments under the first N.Y.A. allocations met with difficulty. Job assignments went to two extremes, from the highly academic on one hand, to the more menial or "leaf raking" type on the other. Academically minded teachers and professors, failing to see the guidance and training values of work, often insisted that only the most mentally capable youth be assigned to their supervision. The less capable, as judged wholly by academic standards, were often shunted into jobs lacking both in purpose and supervision.[2]

So, in spite of the fact that funds to develop career-oriented jobs in institutions of higher learning were available during the N.Y.A. years, 1935–43, institutions, on a national scale, did not take full advantage of the opportunity. This does not indicate that most of the work experience for students was not educationally worthwhile, but rather, it suggests that better use could have been made of the opportunity to utilize work as a career-oriented experience.

3. *Contributions of the N.Y.A.* Nevertheless, there is little doubt that this program had a profound and lasting effect upon higher education. Many of some six hundred thousand students who participated in the N.Y.A. Program could not have acquired a college education without the financial assistance of this agency. Much important institutional work would not have been accomplished, had the program not been in force. It is significant, too, that the N.Y.A. students achieved academically as well or better than did the college students as a whole.

Although we cannot say that the N.Y.A. Work-Study Program was truly a career-oriented program as such, we can say that it directed attention to the educational value of work experience as a contributing factor to the overall schooling of our youth. Further, we can say that this program provided the work experience based upon which institutions through ingenuity and experimentation could develop career-oriented work-study projects. In addition, it called attention to the important status of supervision, both the direction of the program totality, emphasizing such overseeing as a key factor in career-oriented work situations. The N.Y.A. also gave encouragement to potential

2   Federal Security Agency Manpower Commission, *Final Report of the National Youth Administration, Fiscal Years 1936–43* (Washington, D.C.: Government Printing Office, 1944), p. 59.

students with limited financial resources, providing the means for continuing education. Finally, the N.Y.A. College Work-Study Program was the forerunner of our present tripod of federally sponsored Financial Aids Programs in higher education, offering assistance in the areas of work, loans, and grants.

F.

World War II

The N.Y.A. Programs conducted in institutions of higher education and in secondary schools were at their peak when the United States entered World War II, following the attack upon Pearl Harbor on December 7, 1941. The concept of self-help had expanded far beyond the N.Y.A. expectations to the point of estimating that between one-third and one-half of all college students were earning a portion or the total amount of their college expenses.

With the swift change from times of peace to conditions of war, everyone was affected, directly or indirectly. In the instance of college-age youth, almost overnight, ways of life were changed from reporting to class to answering to reveille. The scourge of unemployment which had plagued the country through the great depression of the thirties was virtually eliminated in a matter of a few months as the great industrial companies of America retooled for wartime production.

Another transition came about when women by the thousands joined the labor force in the manufacturing of war materials in defense plants across the land. With the pressing need for manpower in the armed forces and industry, there was little need for the N.Y.A. Program, and it was discontinued in 1943. During the World War II years, college and university enrollments declined to the extent that they were only a fractional part of the prewar educational registration.

1. *The Veterans Return.* With the conclusion of World War II in 1945, literally millions of GIs returned home to resume civilian life. The GI bill, Public Law 346, and the educational opportunities which it provided for the World War II veterans had far-reaching impact. During the twelve years that it was in force, more than 7 million veterans took advantage of the educational and employment benefits, at a governmental cost of some $14 billion. College enrollments spiraled, and institutional physical facilities were taxed to the limit during this period.

2. *The Veterans and Institutional Change.* In addition, the influx of returning veterans introduced campus family housing on a large scale. The GI brought purpose, experience, and maturity to the classrooms, and they were more serious and definite in their desire for education than was formerly true of students. Many of the veterans returned with saleable skills which were marketable in the institutions which they were attending or in local communities. The fact that the typical GI was older and more capable of assuming responsibility contributed greatly to the development of institutional part-time jobs for students. Educationally, they disapproved any preconceived thought that only a select group could benefit from higher education; the GI students were truly a cross-section of our democratic society.

G.
The Need for Multiple Programs of Financial Assistance

Not only were the American people deeply grateful to their military personnel during World War II, but they did not forget their sons and daughters when military hostilities ended. Perhaps the greatest national monument as a recognition of service in the history of the United States was a small piece of paper, the GI bill. This document contains the expressed appreciation, patriotism, and generosity of the American citizenry.

As previously indicated, the bill provided the financial resources required to maintain educational opportunities for some 7 million veterans. So, the philosophy established by the private colleges of the Colonial period of our history, emphasizing that a lack of finance should not constitute a barrier to higher education for capable American youth, became a reality for our returning service forces.

1. *The Capable, Needy Student.* However, many young people who had both the ability and the desire to further their education were not eligible for the benefits provided by the GI bill; neither did they have other sources available for funding higher schooling. The result was an ever-mounting number of capable, needy high school graduates who were forced to terminate formal education with high school graduation. Such an apparent educational loss of human resources grew into a matter of national concern, noted by educators in the postwar years.

Despite the efforts of private and state institutions to increase the scholarships, loans, and student employment programs, an increasing number of high school graduates could not hope for higher education because of financial reasons. The magnitude of the problem reached such proportions that President Harry S Truman appointed a commission to study the extent and nature of the situation. The report of the committee in 1947 indicated that the number of capable high school graduates who did not enroll in college because of limited family income was equal in number to the high school graduates who advanced to higher education. As important as the findings of the committee report were, however, they did not stimulate Congressional action to provide any assistance upon a national scale.[3]

2. *Enrollment Increases and Inflation.* Both private and public institutions renewed their efforts to obtain additional support from alumni, business, and industry for gifts, grants, and endowment funds in the postwar period. In general, the benevolence of the alumni and agencies external to institutions helped to keep the college portals open. The success of fund raising campaigns, although well above institutional expectations of securing funds to meet academic goals in many instances, was far short of solving the financial problem as it existed on the national level. The two major reasons were the inflation taking place and the increasing numbers of capable, needy students seeking enrollment in institutions of higher learning. One might compare institutional financial aid efforts at this period to the strenuous attempts of a good swimmer struggling against a strong current; he holds his own, but he does not actually make progress.

3. *Tuition Costs and Operational Needs.* The authors would like to emphasize the fact that it has never been the philosophy or the practice of private institutions of higher education in the United States to rely solely upon student tuition and fees to provide the total funds for the educational operational budget. The capital outlay for new buildings and equipment has depended almost entirely upon gifts and endowments. Revenue from endowed funds and gifts has been used traditionally for operational purposes.

3   President's Commission on Higher Education, *Higher Education for American Democracy* (Washington, D.C.: Government Printing Office, December 1947), p. 1.

However, the inflation of the dollar in the fifties was reflected in the necessity for private schools having to increase tuition costs to parallel operational demands. Incidentally, the problem of increasing tuition costs is still with us today. The impact of increasing the basic cost of education for students from affluent families was negligible; however, middle-class families were realizing the financial pressures, and students from lower-income families, even those fortunates receiving scholarships, found private college costs prohibitive. Financial aids officers were aware that the increasing budgets for scholarships and grants were quite inadequate, permitting the accommodation of no more students than previously because of the ever-expanding circle of inflation.

4. *Scholarships for the Elite.* Another contributing factor, most discouraging to students, was the criterion maintained for selecting recipients of scholarships. Usually, requirements stipulated a talented or high academic potential and a great financial need. Accordingly, the high school graduate with a good solid achievement average, but not excellent, who had a greater than 50 percent probability of succeeding in college was not likely to be selected for a scholarship. Such a high school graduate could possess the desire for an education, have the proper attitudes toward society, be responsible, demonstrate leadership qualities, and good character, yet not be selected. With these qualifications, he could well benefit from a college education and make a meaningful contribution to society, but he would not be eligible for assistance by means of a scholarship. We do not criticize the financial aid policies of the institutions, but we indicate the limited scope of financial resources then available for assisting the worthy, needy youth.

5. *The President's Committee on Education Beyond the High School.* There was a rising awareness of the great need for multiple programs of financial assistance in the 1950's. Realizing the problem, President Dwight D. Eisenhower appointed a committee to study the area of concern. One of the findings of the group was most significant. An excerpt of the summary follows:

> Present student financial assistance is available very unevenly. For instance, one-half of all scholarship funds in the United States in con-

centrated in fifty institutions. Very few states have scholarship programs, although more than half have one or more kinds of categorical programs for limited numbers in limited fields.[4]

The release of the committee report had a salutary effect upon educators and state government officials. It is to be recalled that this was the beginning of the "Sputnik" period when programs of our high schools were subjected to considerable criticism. Additionally, institutions of higher learning were not exempt from severe scrutiny as the nation recognized the imperative need for scientists to fight the cold war with Russia, especially in satellite competition. The necessity for academic excellence and education expansion, serving as instruments of survival, was emphasized with each news report from Washington.

The schools of the nation picked up the challenge with alacrity as society was apprised of the financial demands upon our educational systems on all levels. Local, state, and national administrators responded, directing efforts to meet the crises at hand.

6. *The National Defense Education Act.* Upon the national level, the National Defense Education Act, signed by President Eisenhower in 1958, had far-extending effects. Especially we are interested in the impact of the Act upon programs of institutional financial assistance. Title II provided for student loans on a national scope by allotting sums among the states in accordance with their enrollments in institutions of higher learning. Institutions within a state agreed to supplement each $9.00 of the federal governmental funding with $1.00 of their own financing budget. Students who borrowed sums agreed to pay the money due over an eleven-year period after termination of their educational programs at an interest rate of 3 percent on the unpaid balance. A special feature of the loan program, encouraging students in colleges and universities to enter the teaching profession, was the provision that up to 50 percent of the loan would be cancelled at the rate of 10 percent for each year in which instructors taught fulltime in a public elementary or secondary school. The NDEA Loan Program had a $30 million budget established for 1959. A decade later the budget exceeds $190 million.

4 President's Commission on Education Beyond the High School, *Needs and Resources* (Washington, D.C.: Government Printing Office, 1957), p. 53.

7. Self-Help Program Recommended. It is interesting to note that the NDEA Act which made provisions for the Student Loan Program did not include funding of a College Work-Study Program. However, such a project was in the thinking of the President's Committee on Education Beyond the High School, as noted under the title of Work-Study or Self-Help Programs of the Committee Report.

> Most institutions employ some of their own students to do various kinds of work directly connected with the institution's educational mission. These work opportunities encourage and assist the ambitious student to assist faculty members in certain of their varied duties.
>
> The critical financial situations of most institutions prevents them from providing more student assistance of this sort, and work which could and should be done by students is frequently left undone. A program which provided greatly expanded on-campus work opportunities at fair wages financed by the Federal Government could have at least four advantages.
>
> *1)* It would contribute in the growing need for student financial assistance.
>
> *2)* It would enable institutions to obtain the benefits of useful and needed work which they cannot now afford.
>
> *3)* It could be applied equally as well to private as to public institutions without raising the legal issue of "church-state" relations.
>
> *4)* In areas of labor surplus, it would help keep students from competing with the local labor force.[5]

Actually, the recommendation of the committee was not adopted until some seven years later with the passage of the Economic Opportunity Act of 1964 during the administration of President Lyndon B. Johnson. Thus, in spite of the weighty evidence in favor of multiple programs of work, scholarships, and loans on a nationwide basis, this financial aids tripod did not materialize on even a minimal basis until the enactment of the Higher Education Act of 1965. This legislation added the educational opportunity grants to the existing Loan and College Work-Study Program.

8. Factors Contributing to the Need of Multiple Programs of Financial Assistance. During the past two decades, attention has been directed to the ever-growing number of high school graduates who were financially unable to enroll in institutional programs of higher

5   *Ibid.,* p. 52.

education. Local, state, regional, and national authorities were and are concerned with the matter of making higher education possible for qualified individuals. The authors, too, have been concerned with the problem and consider the following factors as major contributors in the justification of multiple programs of financial assistance.

a) The increase in population, especially during the World War II period, is undeniably one of the chief elements. The increased numbers of pupils is reflected throughout the elementary and secondary schools, resulting in teacher and classroom shortages within many communities. The vast scope of enrollments anticipated has caused higher education officials to predict the number of college students to double in the decade 1960–70, rising from approximately 4 to 8 million in a ten-year span.

b) There is no evidence in our economy to indicate that the percentage of children from low-income families change. Neither is there substantial evidence to conclude that the parents of these children will increase their earning power sufficiently to make appreciable financial contributions toward the mounting costs of college education for their children.

c) The cost of obtaining a college education continues to rise; not only have many institutions necessarily had to increase tuition and fees to offset increased operational expense, but the costs of room and board continue upward.

d) A constantly increasing percentage of high school graduates is pursuing higher education. Our changing world of work proffers job opportunities in the areas of the professional, preprofessional, managerial, technical, and skilled fields of employment. Simultaneously, there is an ever-decreasing proportionate demand for unskilled workers and trainees. Further, the earning power which accompanies a college degree cannot be denied. The natural desire of parents for their children to acquire additional education as insurance of a better way of life must be acknowledged. Also, the demands of technology to provide the needs of the nation in the space age is an educational goal.

H.
Student Work — A Revival

Being well aware of the multiplicity of pressures for advanced schooling, the financial aids officers of an increasing number of higher education institutions accepted the challenges. They reviewed the ways and the means of assisting students with financial problems and perceived a neglected possibility, student employment. As previously indicated, part-time employment which flourished during the depression as the N.Y.A. Work Program was incorporated in the secondary and higher educational levels.

However, during World War II, the Federal Government discontinued the N.Y.A. With the disappearance of the program, both student work emphasis and program organization diminished. This should not be interpreted to indicate that one could not find students working on most, if not all college campuses, but rather that many institutions had allowed the work program concept and concomitant values to be filed away with the concluding N.Y.A. Report of 1943. Institutional student employment in too many schools became a decentralized operation, administered by financial aids officers who frequently had little control in the functioning of the program. Additionally, many financial aids officers had neither the training nor the time to administer a structured student self-help program. There were a number of other reasons for such an unfortunate situation.

1. *Self-Help and Adverse Conditions.* First, a large percentage of personnel trained during the N.Y.A. period who were well-grounded in the educational concepts of work experience had left the financial aids scene with the discontinuance of the N.Y.A. Program. Second, the staff, in terms of numbers, in financial aids offices was woefully inadequate to perform the duties of their assignments. Administrators of financial aids programs were often compelled to delegate important self-help responsibilities to graduate assistants or to full-time personnel who were not sufficiently trained to assume the duties and responsibilities incumbent in supervising such a complex operation.

Third, the chief administrators, both in private and public institutions of higher education, were confronted with financial problems of such magnitude that the operational budgets could have only negligible or no provisions for funding self-help. Even now, the operational budget for student work is invariably cut when priorities are established. The institutional consideration for work programs can usually be measured by an allotted slice of the total budget which is available. Meager allocations are most unfortunate if we accept the belief that the institution exists for the students primarily and that the majority of students can benefit from educational work experiences. If work in combination with academic training produces a better rounded, more integrated individual, students deserve such an enriched education.

It should be noted that the institutional potential for student job diversity is in proportion to the variety of academic programs of the school. To deny the student a work experience which could better prepare him for the world of today is to defeat one of the basic purposes of the institutions' existence.

Fourth, student employment officers and work programs did not receive the recognition and status merited by such an important service. Although students in general were most appreciative of the efforts and assistance of student employment personnel, neither the academic community nor the administration appeared to recognize the genuine contribution to higher education which a properly staffed operation could make. Needless to say, personnel were underpaid; the employee turnover was excessive.

Fifth, the student employment personnel had neither a regional nor a national association in which they could meet and discuss student employment problems common to almost all institutions.

Sixth, more recently, the NDEA Loan Program was receiving the focus of attention, both on a national and regional level, as constituting the major financial aids program assisting the capable, needy student. However, evidence steadily mounted that such a single operational plan could not compose a well-rounded program.

2. *The Work-Oriented Schools.* However, it should be indicated that some institutions, rather than decreasing their self-help programs during the 1950's, actually expanded student work operations to aid the increasing numbers of qualified high school graduates. Such programs flourished primarily because they had the support of the institutional administrations. Some exponents of the worth of work are President Delyte W. Morris of Southern Illinois University; President David Dodds Henry, University of Illinois; President Robert Ludlum, Blackburn College; President Elmer Ellis, University of Missouri; Dean John Monro, Harvard University; and Dean Roy Wooldridge, Northeastern University, all of whom were influential in the movement. These

outstanding administrators believed that the educational value of part-time work experience for students fully justified the expenditure of money and effort to provide an organized student work program.

3. *Self-Help Advocates Organize.* In the interests of coordination of program planning and communication of thought, in November 1960, John Griffin, Director of Student Employment, University of Illinois, sent invitations to the student work directors of "The Big Ten Schools," the University of Missouri, and Southern Illinois University to convene at Urbana on March 23, 1961, to discuss a regional organization concerned with the problems of student employment on the college level. The representatives attending the conference were enthusiastic as to the possibilities, and a committee was appointed to draft a constitution and by-laws to be considered for adoption at the next session. It was decided to title the organization "The Midwest Association of University Student Employment Directors."

In the subsequent meeting, April 10, 1962, held in Urbana, the association adopted a resolution, which was to be recorded in the Congressional Record in Washington, D.C. Much favorable publicity was given by the press regarding the revitalization of student employment. The Resolution of the April 10, 1962, meeting follows.

RESOLUTION *of the Midwest Association of University*
Student Employment Directors

WHEREAS, Great publicity is being given to the fact that a significant percentage of the upper twenty-five percent of high school graduates are not going on with college work, and further that the reason given for not continuing their education is financial limitation; and

WHEREAS, Considerable emphasis is being placed upon scholarship and loan programs to entice talented young people to enter college; and

WHEREAS, Comparatively little publicity is being given to the significant virtues of financing a college education at least partially on a "do-it-yourself" basis of summer and/or part-time employment; therefore be it

RESOLVED, That the Midwest Association of University Student Employment Directors, whose members represent years of experience in dealing with working students, go on record by attesting to the fact that many students today, through a combination of savings, summer employment, and part-time employment while attending school, are paying a major portion of their college expenses. Some earn all of their expenses. The Association also testifies to the fact that although the academic records of working students vary as much as do those of non-working students, studies indicate that the academic standing of working students surpasses that of non-working students; and that some of the superior records are made by students who are employed between twenty and even more hours per week during the academic year. The working student finds it necessary to organize his time and to develop effective study habits, and he is encouraged to accept greater responsibility.

It is the conviction of the membership of the Association that during the education period there are definite and important values in work and practical experience. It grants that there are likewise values in certain extracurricular and social activities. Even so, there are times when it is highly desirable for students to limit their involvement in the social activities in order to facilitate the achievement of important educational goals.

Too frequent and too diversified by source to be discredited are statements that many of the current generation of college-age youth are soft and lacking in self-dependence, motivation, determination, ingenuity, and application—qualities which have contributed so much to the greatness of our nation. Counselors of young people find every day evidence to substantiate these claims. It cannot be expected that ingenuity will be developed if there is not the need nor the opportunity to use it; that maturity will be achieved without experience in facing and solving day-to-day problems, as well as the long-range problems such as the setting up, planning, and realization of career objectives.

The Association urges, in the interest of our society, that more attention be given to the guidance of young people in such a way that they will be sufficiently motivated toward an education, to be willing to labor to attain desirable educational goals, and that talented students who do not enter college because of financial reasons be made more fully aware of opportunities of achieving the educational opportunity through one's own efforts and earnings. Educational institutions and governmental agencies are urged to direct their efforts toward assurance of adequate opportunities for part-time employment of the increasing numbers of college students.—

Urbana, Illinois, April 10, 1961

4. *Multiple Support.* Another major organization lending its support to revitalize student work as financial assistance is the College Scholarship Service of the College Entrance Examination Board. Rexford G. Moon, Jr., Director of the College Scholarship Service, released a re-

search study on institutional financial aid support in institutions of higher education, based upon the 1959–60 period. His study revealed that institutions were providing some $98 million for scholarships and an equal amount for self-help programs.

In addition, the College Scholarship Service emphasized student work in its regional financial aids seminars, and gave special coverage to the subject in its newsletter, *Financial Aid News.*

By the time, the momentum of the student work movement had reached congressional attention to the extent that a bill (H. R. 3000) included a special consideration for student work programs as Title I, Part C. The Advisory Committee on National Student Financial Aid Programs of the College Scholarship Service gave their support to this bill as did the American Council on Education and the Midwest Association of University Student Employment Directors. Although the bill (H. R. 3000) did not become law in its original form, aspects of the bill, including the College Work-Study Program, were incorporated into President Johnson's Economic Opportunity Act of 1964.

I.

Current Views of Student Work

The trends in student work today include the provision of work experience for more students, wider job diversity, expanded student services, and a range of job complexity capable of accommodating the work experience needs of students, spanning from the potential high school dropout to the college graduate. Sponsors of such student work include higher educational institutions, business establishments, industry, and local, state, and national governmental agencies, in addition to the school districts.

1. *Federal Programs.* Recent federal legislation, the Economic Opportunity Act of 1964, made provision for a number of programs. One such operation is the Neighborhood Youth Corps for high school students from low-income families. This program, if properly supervised by the high schools and supported by the cooperation of the community, could be both an educational work-experience program and a significant control in the prevention of high school dropouts. The authors believe that the program possibly would enjoy more success if the control were to be moved from the Department of Labor to the United States Office of Education, with the specific management assigned to the Department of Health, Education, and Welfare. Such a move would

make educational work-study experience on the secondary school level parallel college work-study experience and thus provide the opportunity for more continuity in program planning, operation, and evaluation upon the two school levels. With the passage of the Elementary and Secondary Education Act in 1965, there is a definite trend for increased cooperation between secondary schools and higher educational institutions as they work together to implement programs funded by the federal government.

Another program created by the Economic Opportunity Act is the Job Corps, managed by the Office of Economic Opportunity. This project consists of training centers where underprivileged youth from sixteen to twenty-one years, boys and girls, are provided with a combination of general education, vocational counseling and training, some part-time experience, and instruction in constructive social living, the program designed to prepare them more adequately for employment and citizenship. As worthy as the objectives of this program are defined to be, the project itself at this writing has been marred by riots, problems of discipline, and dropouts from training. The trend in Washington is inclined away from educational institutional management and toward industrial management in Job Corps Centers, and we suspect that some drastic changes will occur before the predicted three hundred thousand enrollment is reached.

Because of the problems in control which are likely to be persistent, we believe that there is some justification in recommending that a special branch of the military be created to accept the responsibility of conducting an educational program which concerns itself with reschooling these young people so that they can be employable and contributory to our society. It is clear that advisory personnel from all facets of our society should be consulted, particularly school personnel.

Although the College Work-Study Program was originally a part of the Economic Opportunity Act of 1964, it is now included in the Higher Education Act of 1965 as Title IV, and it is administered by the Higher Education Division of the United States Office of Education.

At present, some 1,400 colleges and universities participate in the College Work-Study Program which provides part-time work experience for some hundred thousand college students. The project is financed on a matching fund basis at the rate of one dollar of institutional money to nine dollars of federal funds, the federal budget providing more than $100 million for the 1966–67 program.

Although the program exists primarily for students of low-income families, other students who must work to earn a portion of their college expenses are also eligible. The College Work-Study Program is structured to be adapted to the on-going institutional student work operation; accordingly, all institutions of higher education may qualify for having College Work-Study students, assuming certain criteria are met.

However, institutions cannot reduce their financial support of their already activated programs. Thus, College Work-Study funds are primarily to be used to provide additional jobs for students, to supply additional services for the faculty, and to afford counseling of students seeking assistance. The essential point is that the College Work-Study Program should be so constituted that it is not only a means of helping a student financially, but by educational experience through work. In conclusion, the goal of the College Work-Study Program is based on the principle that the participants who are graduated from college achieve a more enriched education than they would have acquired had they not experienced both physical and mental work in receiving their degrees.

2. *On-Campus Programs.* The criteria employed to determine the scope of a given institutional on-campus self-help operation are substantial in number. Examples of the salient factors are: how many students are working, how much money do they earn, and what is the job diversity?

In a recent study released by the United States Office of Education for the 1963–64 school year, preceding the College Work-Study Program, the results tabulated from 1,854 colleges and universities showed that these institutions employed 438,019 students at a cost of $144,574,306.[6] If we compare the number of students working as listed in on-campus jobs, 438,019, with the total institutional enrollment, approximately 4.4 million for the year of 1963–64, we can conclude that one student in ten was employed in campus work throughout the higher educational institutions of the United States. As would be anticipated, considerable variations can be found both on an institutional and regional basis.

6   Richard C. McKee, *Financial Assistance for College Students, Title I* (Washington, D.C.: United States Department of Health, Education, and Welfare, 1965), pp. vi–vii.

For example, a composite report from the Midwest Association of University Student Directors, derived from figures supplied by the member schools, gave the following averages for the year of 1961–62: Enrollment, 21,000; Working Students, 4,000; Self-Help Expenditures, $2.6 million, and Wages per Working Student, $650. We can conclude that for these schools, during the school year of 1961–62, approximately one student in five was working on campus.

In general, large state universities are more generous in providing student work opportunities than are the smaller schools; however, some of the liberal arts colleges with lesser enrollments are known for their unique work-study programs. The diversity of student jobs in a given institution is contingent primarily upon the following two factors: the size of the institution, and the organized effort of the institution's administration to provide a variety of work opportunities. We usually think of institutional size as the total number of students enrolled on a full-time basis of study and the number obtained by converting the enrollment of part-time students to a full-time basis. Thus, a university of twenty-five thousand students with multiple degree programs, service organizations, and business operations could be expected to maintain a job and occupational diversity among the faculty and staff, ranging from the top class of the listings by *The Dictionary of Occupational Titles*, i.e., professional, semiprofessional, and managerial, to the entry jobs requiring insignificant or no training.

Ordinarily, institutional increases of enrollment constitute the major factor in the creation of more employment opportunities upon all levels in institutions of higher learning. The students deserve and should receive their equitable share of the job opportunities so created because of their educational and financial needs. It must always be remembered that if it were not for the enrollment of students, there would be no employment for the many types of full-time staff members.

A significant point, at times overlooked by some faculty members, engrossed in research and writing, is that we forget that the institution exists basically because of the students. Teaching, therefore, must always be the foremost of the several functions of the institutions.

The writers believe that the colleges and universities should make maximum utilization of their own career laboratories. For example, if financial resources are available, should not the future teachers have experience as teacher aides in individual major fields of study before assuming student teaching? What faculty member is there who cannot well employ and wisely use some clerical assistance? What better opportunity exists for faculty and students to know each other than through the medium of work?

There should be no misunderstanding by the student as to his principal purpose in attending school. The classroom should always take precedence in the learning process; nevertheless, education can be made much more encompassing than that received only in the classroom. Other activities can supplement the assigned study and exert great influence; possibly, work experience should head the list of such complementary pursuits. The authors believe that the scope of student work opportunities should extend throughout every academic, administrative, business, and service division of the university. The job diversity should range from the unskilled service jobs to work situations requiring advanced college training, with job descriptions listed for all of the specific student jobs.

In retrospect, we have known far too long of the educational values of Cooperative Education not to have expended more time and effort in adopting its principles to on-campus jobs. In truth, institutions with underdeveloped work programs are in that unhappy state because they have not recognized the educational potentialities of work experience and because they have relied too much on other forms of financial assistance. Too often, they believe that part-time employment of students is too expensive and that the student cannot work and simultaneously achieve well academically in college. Some, we sadly believe, do not appreciate the worth and the dignity of work; in effect, they deny the principle upon which our nation was founded.

3. *Factors Affecting Program Budgeting.* The authors have emphasized that institutions of higher education by their nature and design have an inherent responsibility to provide on-campus jobs for students, both for educational and financial reasons. The problem posed is how a given institution can arrive at a justifiable budgetary figure sufficient to support its self-help program. The writers know of no infallible process which will provide the solution, but several factors such as the following should be considered in decision making.

First, the location of the institution is an important consideration. Institutions in metropolitan settings will find that there are many part-time student job opportunities off campus because of the business and the industrial establishments within the city. Accordingly, fewer on-campus jobs may be needed in this instance. In fine, such an institution's on-campus program must be developed in conjunction with the off-campus operation. Large state universities in towns and cities under 25,000 in population will surely have greater need for structuring well-developed student work programs than those located in metropolitan areas.

Also, institutions located in regions of high unemployment rates and conditions of poverty should concentrate more time, effort, and money in their self-help programs. More money will be needed for jobs and additional professional staff will be required to direct experimental studies and to maintain program operation. Institutions in such underprivileged locations should be allocated the maximum amount of College Work-Study federal funds and also be given support and encouragement from Washington to combat poverty through the combined programs of work and education.

For analysis, a given institution can compare its self-help costs in terms of dollar per capita expenditures with colleges and universities, either on a regional or a national basis. For illustration, if we review the report of the United States Office of Education, *Financial Assistance for College Students,* by McKee, for the year of 1963–64, we find that the 1,854 institutions spent $144,574,306 for self-help. *The 1964 Book of the Year,* published by Encyclopaedia Britannica, Inc., lists the higher education enrollment in this country at 4.4 million for the 1963–64 year. By simple division of total enrollments into total dollar expenditures, we find an average of $32.85 per student enrolled, as the cost of institutional student employment in higher education in the United States.

On a regional basis, we can take the figures from the previously quoted report of the MAUSED for the year of 1961–62 in "The Big Ten Schools," Southern Illinois University, and the University of Missouri. Again, by dividing the enrollment average, twenty-one thousand, into the $2.6 million average expenditure for each school, we find the per capita cost of self-help to be $123.80. The range between the two figures, national and regional, could be used by a given institution as a guide or index to determine the desirable financial level of its own operation.

We may draw yet other conclusions, including the following: If the institutional potential for self-help programs in the United States could be developed to approximately 80 percent of that of the Midwest region, previously mentioned, then an allocation of $100 per enrolled college student, as an average, could be achieved nationally. The effect of such an expenditure could well be tremendous. If we take the enrollment figures for 1963–64, 4.4 million multiplied by $100 per student, we arrive at a national self-help potential of $440 million. Since institutions nationally spent only $144,574,306 that year, we see with clarity both the need for additional funds and the untapped possibilities for the federal Work-Study Program. We can further reason that if institutions could financially approach the above hundred dollar per student average, there would be no need for the federal government's College Work-Study Program.

The trend currently in force is that the federal government contributes more money and individual institutions are attempting to keep expenditure of internal funds constant, which is, in a way, saying that the schools probably will be contributing proportionately less to program development in the future.

Students work off campus either part time or, during vacation periods, full time; such employment does not lend itself well to record keeping. Few institutions know how many of their students are engaged in off-campus jobs or how much they actually earn; therefore, we are but speculating upon the number of students who work off-campus during the academic year. Estimates, however, would lead us to believe that as many students work in such off-campus jobs as are employed on campus. This employment would be over and above the Cooperative Education Program where the work experience is arranged for the student off campus, but it is under the supervision of a college or a university.

About 1 percent of the college enrollment, or between forty-five and fifty thousand students are participating currently in Co-op Work-Study Programs. There is little doubt that the trend of the Co-op is toward the participation of more students and the addition of institutions in this worthwhile career-oriented work experience program.

Summer employment has been one of the main sources of funds for college students in the past, and it continues to be so today. Usually, business, industry, governmental agencies, resorts, and camps have been generous in providing such summer work for college youth. Nevertheless, the supply of college students seeking summer employment is in excess of the employers' demands.

There are several significant trends in student employment which provide additional financial and educational opportunities. First, more educational institutions are maintaining year-round educational programs to accommodate enrollment increases and to make maximum use of their physical facilities, which, in turn, creates more need for student on-campus employment. Also, the continuous scheduling of educational programs permits students to leave school for one term, other than during the summer, to work in a full-time job. Thus, there is a trend toward more student employment during other seasons in the year than in the traditional summer vacation time. For example, students in some institutions could attend school during the spring, summer, and fall terms and find vacation jobs during the winter quarter in southern resorts.

Second, the College Work-Study Program, sponsored by the United States Office of Education, has provision for full-time employment for qualified students either on campus for the institution or for certain governmental agencies and nonprofit institutions such as hospitals, precollege schools, park boards, etc., off campus. With these possibilities and some foreplanning by financial aids officers, the principles of the Co-op Program can be applied to place many students in work which relates directly to particular academic programs. This specific aspect of the College Work-Study Program potentially makes it superior to the earlier NYA Program.

However, the success of this phase of the College Work-Study Program rests nearly exclusively with the efficiency of the institutional financial aids officers who must realize the educational value of the program for the student, in addition to the financial benefits accrued.

Third, an increasing number of business and industrial establishments are recruiting qualified students, usually in their junior year, for summer employment jobs for their companies. Such firms have highly developed training programs and reimburse the students well. However, their major interest in the student is to determine his employability following his graduation. In other words, they have three months in which they can observe the student in a work situation; this period is usually sufficiently long to decide if they want the student to become a permanent employee following his graduation. This effective screening device is often referred to as early placement. With the competition increasing for the qualified college graduate, we can expect the early placement trainee programs for the undergraduate to increase in popularity.

The occupational and job diversity inherent in summer employment is nearly boundless; however, few institutions can provide the staff personnel or the guidance necessary in a career-oriented placement to capitalize on the summer employment educational potential.

The net result is that most students, on their own initiative or with the help of parents and friends, take summer jobs primarily for the salary received. Regardless, the value of summer employment should not be minimized since it usually takes place under full-time employment conditions, which, in itself, is a worthwhile educational experience.

4. *Additional Trends.* Attention should be directed to some trends pertaining to programs of work, scholarship, and loans, other than those previously discussed. Trends which we think are significant predictions of future program direction follow:

a) The Emerging Profession
b) Cooperative Education Expansion
c) Increasing Job Opportunities
d) Student Job Classifications

One of the more prominent trends which may well have a profound effect upon higher education and programs of financial assistance (work, scholarships, and loans) in the future is the transition of financial aids work from a clerical occupation rank to a professional status. Several factors are operative currently to encourage this change.

First, the role of the federal government in the organization, development, and expansion of multiple programs of financial assistance is prominent. Program expansion alone has created a demand for trained financial aids personnel far in excess of the present supply. Also, the emphasis of the federal government upon counseling for both the individual and selected groups, e.g., students from low-income families, calls for personnel with specialized training acquired primarily in graduate programs in higher education.

Second, expanding aid programs call for a greater staff, which, in turn, will encourage the application of the principles of manpower structuring. Thus, the Financial Aids staff of a large university may have an organization consisting of administrators, counselors, personnel assistants, clerical employees, graduate assistants, and part-time student employees. It is clear to the writers that such an organization will upgrade in performance and prestige the role of the financial aids program in our nation's colleges and universities.

Third, more consideration is being given to a national organization for financial aids personnel.

Fourth, one of the marks of the professional in higher education is his contribution to research and writing in his particular field. As more faculty members with doctoral degrees are retained or recruited for financial aids positions, the greater is the possibility of producing much-needed research in our neglected field of financial assistance.

One of the more pronounced trends at the present time is the movement toward additional cooperative programs. A number of institutions of higher education such as those at Antioch, Northeastern, and Cincinnati have been carrying on extensive programs for a considerable number of years. However, a majority of universities and colleges have, in the past, taken the position that almost their entire concern should be with increasing the academic background of students. This attitude is now changing in a substantial number of institutions. There is still a concern for the academic background of students, but it is thought that the background becomes more meaningful as it is related closely through work experience to the type of work which students will enter following graduation from school. At the same time, an increasing number of students are questioning the value of their academic experience, except as it is related to a work experience.

The above factors, among others, are causing some educators to look at and alter traditional programming. The scope of cooperative programs at the present time is narrow enough that there would be little difficulty in placing students in work situations in business and industry. Many business and industry leaders, traditionally, have worked closely with universities and colleges. However, an increasing number of these leaders is beginning to view the situation in a different light. The supply of competent employees is not meeting the current demand. Seemingly, under optimum circumstances, the rate of new employee turnover is high. Too many employees resign from their services at the end of only one or two years, just at the time when they are becoming ready to make valuable contributions to the company. The Cooperative Work-Study Programs help to alleviate the preceding situation.

Under the programs, an opportunity is afforded the employer to assess the capabilities of students and, thus, to determine whether full-time employment after graduation is desirable. At the same time, student workers are assessing the opportunities within the company while on the job to decide whether they are interested in returning to full-time employment with the firm, following graduation. The point of importance is that the trial period is completed for both employer and employee prior to full-time, continuing employment. Also, forward-looking business and industrial leaders are cognizant of the fact that they are minimizing the problem of supply and demand. Competent full-time college graduates are at hand and in sufficient numbers to meet the usual demand after the program has been in operation for a period of time.

Another major trend related to the number of students working in on-campus jobs is the increase of available jobs in colleges and universities. Basically, the number of on-campus jobs open to students is increasing more rapidly than the proportionate increase in student enrollment. This is traceable to a number of factors or lesser trends. Initially, it can be said that students, in general, are working a fewer number of hours per week and month than was formerly true. More exacting academic requirements in many institutions of higher education have brought about this situation, in part. Students have found it more difficult to carry, for example, a so-called normal academic program of study and at the same time work ninety to one hundred hours per month. An example in arithmetic shows what is happening. If two students worked a total of one hundred hours per month but now are each working sixty hours per month, or a total of one hundred and twenty hours, there is an eighty-hour-per-month job available for a third student.

Also, students are working a fewer number of hours and, thus, creating additional jobs for another major reason. For those students who necessarily are self-supporting or nearly so, the "packaged program" has been a boon. The program of federally sponsored loans, plus state, other agencies, or individually sponsored scholarships has been greatly expanded recently. These sources of funds along with work possibilities have given university financial aid functions the opportunity to develop packaged programs in the following manner:

If a student needs $1,500 for the academic year, he can perhaps receive a scholarship, award, or educational opportunity grant, depending upon individual need and academic accomplishment for $200 or $300 per year, work in a student job assignment for approximately $600 per year, and borrow the remainder of the money, assuming in these latter provisions that his grades are sufficiently high to qualify. With the packaged program, even though it may include only work and a loan, he needs to work a lesser number of hours than was formerly ture. Accordingly, such a progarm creates a condition whereby an additional student has the opportunity to perform the needed work.

A substantial impetus has been given to the number of student jobs on university campuses because of the federally sponsored Work-Study Program. A condition for receiving federal funds has been that of requiring participating schools to increase the money expended for student work from that which was the case in the previous year. The money received has automatically been directed into new job situations. Another condition of the federal program has influenced the thinking of university and college officials. Students are permitted to work in the program a maximum of sixty hours per month while attending school. With the substantial number of jobs created at the sixty-hour-per-month level, there has been a tendency to move to the sixty-hour level in other student jobs on-campus.

The expanding use of instructional aides on campus has led and is continuing to develop toward an increased number of student work opportunities. It seems that a considerable number of institutions are beginning to realize or to take advantage of the capabilities of their students. With the increasing number of students, the student-faculty ratio is going up, even though, on the average, the number of classes taught by a faculty member is remaining constant or being reduced.

Because of this increasing ratio, it is becoming more and more difficult for teachers to help individual students who need assistance, and also to handle simple office routine matters, and to take care of some of the matters related to the classroom and laboratory teaching. Since students do have multiple capabilities in many instances, they are being employed to ease, to a degree, the teacher loads. Students are handling more and more tutoring responsibilities both for individuals and for small groups. They are typing and filing materials, taking roll, proctoring or helping to proctor examinations, collecting materials which can be used for teaching, and preparing materials and equipment for demonstration and laboratory purposes. As can be seen from such student assignments, as teacher aides, they are doing many of the things for which they will have a responsibility in their full-time work following graduation. Basically, it can be positively stated that instructional aides' positions are truly career oriented.

Beyond a doubt, the increasing emphasis being given to student job classifications constitutes another major trend. As more jobs and a wider diversity of work becomes available to students, it becomes virtually impossible to make proper referrals, except as job responsibilities and student abilities are matched. If such articulation is not done, employers become dissatisfied and students become frustrated. Obviously, poor referrals lead to employer requests for full-time employees who have been screened and tested, prior to referral. Also, job descriptions are basic to work-experience evaluation, student promotions, and rates of payment. An emphasis on the need for job classifications is shown in the encouragement by the federal government in the College Work-Study Program.

In conclusion, it should be noted that the preceding discussion includes but a portion of the major trends discernible. As student financial aids programs in institutions of higher education are given additional emphasis, it is to be anticipated that the composite thinking of a greater number of university faculty-administrative staff members will evoke more views and new vantage points which will lead to yet further trends and sophistication in our future programs of financial assistance.

3 Vocational Planning

THE PERSONAL, social, educational, and vocational problems of high school youth have focused attention on a greatly needed addition to the high school curriculum, guidance services. An important aspect of guidance services is providing the necessary occupational information and vocational counseling to assist the student in making a wise career choice. Our youth of today are confronted with a multitude of challenges and choices. Perhaps, however, no more crucial decision faces them than that of judiciously selecting a future vocation.

Therefore, definite attention is fixed upon the importance of vocational choice and career planning in this chapter and in subsequent sections of this book. Determining a life's occupation is a weighty judgment and should be decided only after due consideration is given to many factors. Personal preferences, potentialities, and latent talents should be assessed. In addition, beginning with the immediate family circle, there is a sphere of advice available, including the classroom instructor, the guidance counselor, and community consultants. No longer is it necessary that the teen-ager simply fall into a line of work, perhaps to flounder and to sink in failure; he can avail himself of the sound evaluations and judgments of adult minds and rise to fulfill his true potentialities.

However, the ultimate decision rests with the student. He may wish to ignore the wise counsel of parents, teachers, counselors, and consultants because he wants to express his independence and direct his own life. He may wish to drop out of high school and obtain immediate employment. If so, he should know the facts. Employers want youth with salable skills, initiative, and a dedication to hard work. Most high school dropouts do not measure up to the employers' criteria. If they matched work standards, unemployment in this age group would not exceed 10 percent while the average of unemployment in all age groups would be less than 4 percent.

A.
Vocational Choice — A Problem

1. *An Overview of the Problem.* One of the major problems of high school students is determining a vocational choice. Precisely how significant is this problem? Professor Harold Hand of the University of Illinois, in testing some seventy-five hundred high school students, using the *Mooney Problem Check List* [1] found this area second only to the problem dealing with adjustment to school work. Even the fact that students are aware of difficulties does not assure that they will develop a plan of action to solve or to improve the situation. One needs but to interview at random a small percentage of a high school senior class to draw conclusions concerning their indefinite plans following graduation.

Not infrequently, graduates confronted with the need for immediate employment have failed to make application for work; nor have they been interviewed for a possible job. Often, they have had no part-time work experience as a basis for knowing the value of employment. In our affluent society, it is a sad commentary upon adult guidance that many high school students learn to drive cars much earlier than they learn to work.

Also, it is disillusioning to realize that many students planning to attend college consider matriculation as a type of temporary career. However, a saving grace lies in the additional years of schooling provided in college, offering greater information through study and, hopefully, through work experience, before a final vocational decision is made. It is rather unfortunate that too many high school girls consider marriage an immdiate solution to all present problems, including career planning. As nearly every bride knows, with the exception of the high school bride, teen-age marriages, like teen-age drivers, have had insufficient experience to cope with the critical problems encountered on the road of life. Accordingly, many adolescent marriages are destined for destruction. Today, the educational oppor-

---

1 *Mooney Problem Check List* (New York: Psychological Corporation, 1950). The checklist consists of 330 problems in eleven areas; these problems are common to the high school age group.

tunities beyond the high school level for girls, as well as boys, with above average intelligence, are all but boundless. Also, an increasing percentage of women helps to make up our total employment force; in fact, in some of the clerical and professional occupational groups, the demand for women employees far exceeds the supply. Even girls who do not seek a college education but prefer employment following graduation can receive adequate high school training for work, providing that proper guidance has assisted in selecting the appropriate high school course of studies.

2. *The Dropout, a National Problem.* A problem of national concern is the incidence of the high school dropouts. In particular, authorities are concerned with the numbers of boys terminating education before graduation. For such youth, employment opportunities, even in unskilled entry jobs, cannot match the number of adolescents seeking employment. So narrow in range is the job selection for the school dropout in the 16–21 age group that unemployment statistics soar as high as 25 percent. Unhappily, there appears to be no evidence to indicate that youths leaving high school usually possess either the work experience or have developed suitable work attitudes which might cause an employer to recruit from this category for mere trainee employment. The non-graduate rarely, if ever, has developed a sufficient skill to interest an employer. Accordingly, if the adolescent is hired, he must be trained if he is to become an asset to the firm.

Since the dropout should be gainfully employed, society must train him suitably, equipping him for work; or must retain a type of work which he can perform; or if necessary, must virtually create a job in keeping with his capabilities. Almost daily, automation and technology eradicate hundreds of previously existing jobs, tasks which required but little or no training. The high school dropout is a singularly twentieth-century problem; society must search out the answer.

One possible solution to the adolescent employment difficulty might involve the designing of a new branch of the military services, charged with the function of preparing young people, boys and girls, educationally for military careers or for work in business and industry. Because of limited financial resources few, if any, high schools have the curriculum diversity to accommodate the needs of all the students, although this objective is theoretically endorsed by secondary education throughout the United States. Further, with the exception of business training and diversified occupational study in vocational education, most secondary schools, by tradition, are not vocationally oriented toward terminal education which prepares one to earn a living following graduation. In essence, it is too often true that our secondary schools are primarily concerned with but one type of education, that of learning from the printed page. It is easily discernible that other measures should be adopted in addition to admonitions to stay in school, when one notes the number of dropouts in secondary education.

However, this does not suggest that many drastic changes in the schools should be effected, but, rather, that some additions and variations should be made in curriculum planning. For example, some potential dropouts might be retained in the academic system if a daily program of two school courses and four hours of supervised work experience in any one of many types of employment were provided. Such an experimental project could be an individualized study plan with perhaps most gratifying results. Supervised work experience in the community not only takes best advantage of community resources but offers the students an education which is action-centered. All adolescents want to be considered mature; particularly do boys wish to be thought of as adults. They want, indeed they need, a day partially filled with activity.

For example, what boy does not hope to achieve success in athletics? It appears that there is not sufficient adventure within the classrooms for many boys; equally, there is a lack of contact with the community of adults. Making a man of a boy is a challenging responsibility for the parents, the school, the church, and the community. Frequently, far too much of the maturation process has been delegated to or assumed by the schools.

Since ours is a period of progress and constant change, a perspective appropriate to the times must be assumed. In times past, our society expected every able-bodied individual to work and to earn his own way. It was also believed that anyone who wanted a job could obtain work if he really had the proper initiative. However, the depression of the thirties changed these concepts markedly. It appears that a new principle of work is in order, a tenet more in harmony with present industrial and social patternings.

Such a concept could presuppose that the *opportunity* to work should be a guarantee of society. Work, in itself, although a necessity for a livelihood, is equally essential in maintaining the respect, dignity, and worth of the individual. This principle does not hold that society owes an individual a specific job cut to his own liking, but rather that it owes him the opportunity to sustain his own esteem and recognition of worth, as well as subsistence, through the medium of work.

B.

Vocational Choice — A Beginning

1. *The Problem.* One would rarely embark upon a long journey or even a brief vacation without some definite planning and preparation for the trip. If the agenda includes a vacation trip by automobile beyond the immediate community, road maps or an atlas of state highways and secondary roads would be consulted. With the complexity of the new interstate highway systems, it is equally important for business and pleasure to gather the most recent information concerning construction in progress. Overnight stops require a knowledge of suitable motel and hotel accommodations and, many times, advance reservations. Even the routine task of packing the automobile to carry all of the necessities takes planning; sometimes, a trailer must be rented or purchased.

Accordingly, it would seem if one devotes so much time, thought, and planning to the details of a small trip, what infinitely greater preparation and evaluation should precede a *vocational* trip which starts in youth and terminates with retirement. When one considers that a vocation is not merely an important part of an individual's life, but that it lends significance and meaning to life itself, it is obvious that priority should be placed upon the essentiality of education-focused planning and preparation for our youth.

2. *Early Childhood.* Children learn very early in life that one parent and, not infrequently, both the mother and father, spend a great portion of the day away from home in an activity called work. They soon learn to associate the importance of the parents' work with the family's needs for food, shelter, and clothing. However, children are not inclined to learn a great deal about the actual nature of the parents' occupations. Actually, the information which children may inadvertently acquire concerning work by means of parental conversations might well be more of a negative than a positive value.

Since early childhood is a magic time of nearly boundless imagination and unrealistic aspirations, youthful vocational goals are often defined in terms of fancy and fiction. There is a strong possibility that if one asked a ten year old questions concerning his future plans, his answers would often be in the space realm, ranging from an astronaut or space cadet to an interplanetary pilot. Should one carefully explain to the youngster that in the United States that there are some 60 million citizens working in forty thousand different jobs, and that the astronaut program was limited to a few dozen assorted participants, his vocational choice would not likely alter. Should he be urged to make a second selection, the occupation would probably be that of a colorful, action-centered figure, such as a cowboy, detective, or professional football player. The influence of television cannot be denied!

3. *The Community—A Resource.* The community is an excellent source of job information for children who learn much from seemingly casual observation. In truth, they often learn more in this manner than through any project or study supervised by school or parents. Accordingly, it is our belief that the community is a prime laboratory of learning and can be a very fruitful source of job information, regardless of the age of the youth searching for work opportunities.

Undeniably, the larger communities which support employment opportunities in business and industry have advantages over rural communities since the job diversity of the former usually includes a wider span of unskilled and semiskilled job opportunities, as well as managerial, technical, and professional jobs.

However, despite the many opportunities for youth to learn much concerning the world of work through community resources, there is sparse evidence that our schools have found the time or the inclination to develop learning projects in this important area. Such a lack of provision in vocational information is not surprising, since few school curricula, particularly those preceding the junior high school level, relate subject matter to future employment in a meaningful manner. Also, it is to be remembered that teacher preparation in our institutions of higher learning rarely, if ever, includes a course in vocational information and even less frequently does it have a practicum offering. Unless the teacher through financial necessity or through a personal interest has been employed in other occupations prior to serving on the school faculty or during his school service, he might not be of much assistance to the student seeking career information.

In contrast, let us consider work experience on the college level, assuming that such experience has not been previously acquired, as a requisite in the total educational preparation of future teachers. The opportunities for part-time work experience on college and university campuses or in local communities are usually available if the student has the need, desire, and initiative to look for such employment. It is our belief that teachers with knowledge and experience in occupations other than merely in their own areas can supply a more adequate professional service for students and parents than can instructors whose activities were limited to rather narrow professional academic confines.

C.
Vocational Choice — A High School Function

1. *Vocational Emphasis.* It is our belief that the most appropriate school years for basic career planning and preparation are those within the period of secondary education. However, this is not to exclude the benefits of prior planning and orientation available in the junior high school. Nevertheless, the more formalized career programs should be a function of the high school administration. Again, we are not ignoring the significant role of higher education and the evident need for vocational guidance and counseling on the college level, emphasizing the multiple and diversified programs of technical, liberal arts, and professional training. We recognize, too, that vocational choices may change in some instances at the higher educational level, even when there has been good planning.

Such extensive explorations into the various general areas of employment are not merely desirable; they are essential. One needs but little experience with the typical college-age youth to perceive the unrealistic goals and naïve concepts of many such students regarding career choice and occupational fields. However, the question persists as to where to level the major emphasis upon occupational choice, i.e., the age and school graduation, to achieve the maximum benefit. A point of worthy consideration, at times underrated, is that despite the status placed upon higher education and with college enrollments exceeding all predictions, we are still enrolling only about 50 percent of the high school graduates of the nation in institutions of higher learning. In addition, we cannot discount statistics concerning the large number of students who enter high school but drop out some time before graduation. Accordingly, there is evidenced a justification of our conviction that vocational information must be presented and guidance services provided throughout the entire educational process, and that the major emphasis should begin at the high school level.

In order to disseminate such information as a part of the student's educational experience, a highly organized program of vocational guidance services is required to provide the knowledge and the enlightenment which young people need concerning work in our society, including necessary worker qualifications for the variety of opportunities in business, industry, government, and labor. Obviously, our youth require much more than a cursory glance toward the many avenues of vocational opportunity to make intelligent decisions which will frame their future lives.

However, the necessity for knowledge, so stressed in the twentieth century, is also an age-old requirement. Some five centuries before Christ, Socrates is reported to have admonished his Athenian students, "Know thyself." Meander, a century later, revised the axiom, believing that, "In many ways, the saying, 'Know thyself,' is not well said. It is more practical to say, 'Know other people.' "

From our vantage point, such classical advice is equally applicable to the youth of today. Further, our complex society requires that our youth learn all possible things concerning the world in which they live. Anyone who has ever counseled a sixteen year old, who is determined to discontinue his high school education, is aware of the youngster's lack of comprehension and dearth of knowledge as to his future vocational opportunities and how an academic background fits into capitalizing upon education. Such naïveté concerning potentialities and limitations can well be disastrous. Information must be given early and continue on an accelerated basis during the adolescent years.

2. *Broad Preparation.* This is not to indicate that every student must select a specific job; rather he should be supplied through guidance services of various kinds with job occupational information pertaining to present and predictable trends, to curricular preparation needed, and to work experience required. Such an overview will assist him in scanning and wisely selecting at least a vocational field appropriate to his abilities and interests. Qualifications should be well outlined, both general and specific, in many different vocations.

For example, if a high school sophomore thinks that he wants to become a mechanical engineer, there are definite points which he needs to know and academic directions he must take.

a) OCCUPATIONAL AND EDUCATIONAL REQUIREMENTS (ACADEMIC). First, engineering degrees require a minimum of four years of academic preparation in an institution of higher learning, certified by an accrediting association.

Second, the admission to engineering schools is usually restricted to high school graduates ranking at least in the upper third of their class. In the instance of students attending junior colleges and four-year colleges which offer a preengineering program, the student must be rated as in good academic standing and show promise for further work before he can expect to be accepted as an engineering student by transfer.

Third, the engineering profession, as is true of other professions, wants candidates to be well-informed in general education, both in high school and in college.

Accordingly, a student hoping to become a mechanical engineer should achieve well above average in his total high school program of studies. He should rank as superior in mathematics and science courses. Four years of high school study in each are generally required. If the student believes it would be acceptable to receive good grades only in his preferred field and achieve poorly in English courses in institutions of higher learning, he should put away his engineering plans and slide rule permanently. Further, a good command of English as a means of articulate communication is essential for engineers and, in fact, for all professions.

b) TESTS AND MOTIVATION. The sophomore student should receive high scores on appropriate tests in spacial relationships and in engineering aptitude. High percentiles, above 75 at least, in these examinations indicate that the student has met the basic potential to become an engineer. Such aptitudes, however, cannot guarantee that the student will be successful in college or that he will become an engineer; rather, it shows that he is not likely to achieve his goals if he lacks such potentiality.

Again, our sophomore student should show an active interest in the actual work which engineers perform. Interest inventories and tests are most helpful in revealing a preference for one classification of work above another. However, interest evidenced in itself, does not promise sure success; lacking necessary ability, only frustration and near-certain failure can be anticipated.

Another very important factor in successful progress academically, as well as a primary element in job satisfaction, is motivation. Unless there is the desire, initiative, drive, and perseverance to overcome obstacles and to withstand disappointments, all other skills, abilities, potentials, and interests are negated and wasted.

In illustration of this point, we in counseling and teaching could produce books of case studies of students, apparently possessing all of the qualifications pointing to school success, but who were failures in reaching their potentialities. Frequently, they do not only underachieve; they are complete failures. Why? Seemingly, the answer lies in some intangible quality within the individual which inspires him to accomplish something truly worthwhile, to concentrate his attention upon the problem, and to have the determination to achieve. Probably most of us as teachers and counselors have searched our books, reviewed and evaluated our experiences, and sought the advice and counsel of older, more experienced colleagues to determine how we can help such students. Too often, we receive such answers as: "He has to grow up." "She is still immature." "It takes time." "Keep encouraging them." "I wish I knew." "You are only wasting your time."

c) THE PARENTS. It is essential that our high school sophomore should discuss fully with his parents his vocational choice. It is necessary that they be well aware of his vocational plans, if for no other reason than that he will need their encouragement and possibly their financial support. In the event that the family income is such that little or no resources can be made available to finance a college education, he should recognize this fact while still in high school. At this time, his guidance counselor should know or be able to acquire for him a listing of institutions of higher learning, able to assist with the financial problem. At the present time, with federally sponsored financial aids programs on the college level, all high school students who are academically capable can include some good college in their future, if they so desire.

As added information about education beyond the high school, it is good to know that junior colleges in a number of states are rapidly becoming established and will be well within commuting distance of many high school areas. In brief, the youth of our time should initiate vocational planning in high school. Should their career choices require formal education beyond high school, ways and means are at hand as assistance in financing such educational programs. Today, there is no valid reason for a high school student achieving poorly in academic work because he believes college is beyond his financial grasp.

d) THE PROFESSIONAL ENGINEER. It is important that the sophomore should make the acquaintance of some established engineers in his community or area and direct specific questions to them. He should determine some of the advantages and the disadvantages of the profession on a first-hand basis. No one should be in a better position to give accurate information and advice to the would-be engineer than the practicing engineer. As a caution, it should be pointed out that although the high school sophomore has in mind mechanical engineering as his future vocation, he should question and get answers from engineers in as many fields as possible. He may well find it appropriate to change to another specialization later. At this age level, the student should chart his career plans for the high school level, so that they are geared more to the broad field of engineering. His college training will first be general engineering, ideally, and then he can specialize in mechanical, electrical, chemical, aeronautical, civil, or another branch of the area. It should be realized that currently there is a trend toward broad engineering background degrees rather than narrow specializations. Thus, choices may well change within the next few years.

Essentially, his college curriculum will aid him in selecting a focus of study which would probably range within the scope of his greatest strengths. Equally, the same generalization can be applied to other professions, such as the medical and the teaching fields.

e) THE TEACHER. Most assuredly, the student should discuss his vocational plans with his teachers. This is not to indicate that they are all-knowing and able to supply answers to every question, but frequently instructors can direct the student to others who can be of further assistance. For the high school sophomore, mathematics, science, and industrial arts teachers should be of great aid because all have had some college courses common to the engineering curriculum. Therefore, the chemistry teacher can provide information concerning college chemistry requirements, including specific courses in organic and inorganic chemistry; the industrial arts teacher knows something about the mechanical drawing and design courses which the student will need; and the physics teacher will probably be versed to some degree in the basic courses required for the physics field. Possibly the most important outcome of discussing educational plans with the teacher will reveal the instructor's willingness to assist.

It is the mark of a dedicated teacher to make every effort to help a sincere student with problems, significant or trivial in nature. If the teacher can offer only friendship and give encouragement, students will seek out such an instructor. A teacher who thinks of himself as merely a purveyor of academic information has a narrow concept of his profession and himself, as well. Unless he has the total welfare of his students at heart, he is but a technician and not worthy of the title, teacher.

Further, teaching is a service profession; only those who are willing to give of themselves should remain in the instructional ranks. If a young teacher enters the profession and cannot take a private moral oath to spend lavishly of his time and talents, he should consider a career elsewhere. If it is important that our physicians take the Hippocratic oath, assuming all of the duties and the obligations of their calling, it appears equally imperative that teachers, who spend far more time with our youth, assume their particular responsibilities and be aware of the influences which they exert upon impressionable and responsive young people.

f) THE GUIDANCE COUNSELOR. The high school student must avail himself of the total resources of his school and community if he is to accumulate the essential information required in making an intelligent decision regarding his future vocation. Nevertheless, despite all of the available information which he can gather, our typical high school student will encounter periods of indecision and frustration in determining his lifework. This is as it should be since there is no easy solution to complex problems; choosing a career is indeed a decision which calls for thoughtful planning and evaluation as the student prepares for his ultimate vocation, step by step.

One resource of the school, the guidance counselor, has not as yet been adequately presented. It seems appropriate to present some information at this time regarding his background, responsibilities, and overall role. The student can find a ready reference and objectivity of view by consulting a qualified guidance counselor on the school staff. Generally, the guidance counselor is a teacher who has completed at least one or more years of academic training above the bachelor's degree, with his postgraduate study focused on guidance and counseling. Such specialized training enables him to serve as the chief coordinator, bringing together the student, teachers, community, and family in providing a program of student personnel services.

A comprehensive guidance program, as it is commonly called, is a relatively recent addition to the overall school program. Many of the specific responsibilities of the department are not new to the good teachers, who have always performed services for students, far beyond mere classroom instruction. But such assistance in no way conflicts with the responsibilities of the guidance counselor who works closely with all of the faculty in a given school system, directing his efforts in the best interests of the students.

Although the counselor's role is not one of pure authority, his is a function which must be administered by a professional specialist. He must be well acquainted with the secondary school curriculum in order to assist students in wisely selecting academic programs which will establish a maximum contribution toward the students' career plans. He must have sufficient training in adolescent psychology and counseling if he is to be of effective assistance to students, who present many personal as well as academic problems. He must be most knowledgeable in statistics, tests, and measurements if he is to administer and to evaluate tests for diagnostic and prognostic purposes. In fact, he must be equipped to administer a variety of examinations, such as intelligence, achievement, aptitude, and interests, and to interpret skillfully the results. All this is necessary if he is to assess truly the students' academic progress and to appraise the students' vocational goals realistically in the light of individual capabilities and inclinations.

g) OCCUPATIONAL INFORMATION. The guidance counselor is charged with the responsibility of procuring, maintaining, and interpreting occupational information for the students. If he performs his duties well, he provides an invaluable service. Occupational literature is constantly changing, as is work in our society. Much material is available in the form of books, pamphlets, periodicals, bulletins, films, and graphic displays. Texts and brochures should be on file in the library as well as in the guidance office for frequent use by students and teachers. Instructors frequently use occupational information to supplement instructional materials, making individual courses much more practical and meaningful.

Motion pictures and film strips illustrating jobs and occupations are especially helpful to beginning high school students as a means of orientation, prior to career selection. Some schools offer a ninth- or tenth-grade orientation course to acquaint the student with the school curriculum and its provisions. Such an early, introductory course is extremely practical and beneficial to the ninth or tenth grader since he learns early in his high school career precisely what his school offers.

Also, students should be encouraged to borrow occupational information for home review and discussion with parents. The work experience and education of many parents can prove to be of great influence in charting the child's future. Unfortunately, many of the problems of teen-agers never reach the discussion level in the home since the adolescent prefers to talk over particular problems with friends who have similar difficulties and evidence more sympathy in a common plight.

However, jobs, occupations, and vocational choice are often brought to parental attention. There is, of course, an inherent danger here; parents can set very unrealistic goals for their children. It is but natural that they should want their sons and daughters to achieve high personal ambitions and social recognition. It follows also that parents are eager for their children, regardless of abilities, to have a college education and to prepare for a professional career. Here lies another in the framework of duties assigned to the guidance counselor. It is his responsibility to arrange conferences with the student and parents to give objective overviews of individual capabilities and limitations.

In many instances, it is necessary for financial reasons that students obtain part-time work while in school or secure full-time work during vacation periods. For such needs, the good guidance counselor maintains an employment office, offering a practical service, mutually beneficial to students and community employers. Disregarding the money received, work is valuable to the student because of the experience which he receives. Also, regardless of the future plans of the student, a variety of work experiences while in high school is most beneficial in career planning.

One of the greatest values of work experience for high school students, at times overlooked by teachers and parents, is the self-esteem gained by the student. The teen-ager is constantly striving for independence, feeling this qualifies him as an adult. Actually, the student can legitimately employ work experience to identify himself with the adult world. Motivation and meaningful experience lead to maturation in its true sense.

Unfortunately, parents frequently assume the task of solving too many of their teen-ager's problems; overprotection is a hindrance at times, not a help. Problem solving is an essential part of the adolescent's life and is closely related to his search for independence and identification. As adolescents resolve problems, they gain the confidence and ability to accept more challenging responsibilities. The extent of the maturity of the teen-ager can be gauged by assessing the responsibility he can and will assume, as determined by adult standards.

Although parents must allow their children to assert individuality, a definite value system must be established early to guide them through the crises of adolescence. Teen-agers need both praise and reproof in activities, both in and out of school. Further, teen-agers must learn respect for others and have a genuine regard for the rights, privileges, and responsibilities of society. Optimum conditions for acquiring social and emotional maturity can be provided by parents who establish limits upon teen-age behavior and require honest effort in school work and extracurricular activities. The overly permissive parents or the overly solicitous parents who cater to the whims of their children are not building character but creating chaos.

Ideally, whenever possible, the counselor should attempt to place the student in a work situation relating to future vocational plans. Work experience in such instances should either reinforce his choice or give him a valid reason for changing his contemplated vocation. A high school girl who plans a career in nursing can gain greatly from work experience by serving as a nurses' aide in a community hospital. Should she discover while in high school that hospital work is not her forte, career plans are much easier to change at that point than if she makes the same discovery during her first year of formal training in nursing.

Another responsibility of the guidance counselor is the maintaining of an employment record of all working students. Such data are valuable to students seeking immediate employment after graduation, if the information is properly compiled and disseminated. In addition, college-bound students having verified work experience will usually encounter little difficulty in obtaining part-time work in conjunction with higher learning, especially if clerical skills (typing, shorthand) are well-developed.

Today, the problem of meeting the financial needs of students has been greatly alleviated. High school students of low-income families are provided with work opportunities in many communities through the Neighborhood Youth Corps, a work experience program sponsored by the Federal government as part of the Economic Opportunity Act. Again, the guidance counselor must cooperate with the community in the referral and the placement of these young people. Such a program, well administered, can serve as a restraint against the potential high school dropouts who plead the need to work to assist their families financially as the basis for leaving the classroom. Such young people can be placed in the program of the Neighborhood Youth Corps and receive financial assistance while remaining in school.

4 Institutional Financing of Self-Help Programs

THE WAYS and means of financing self-help programs in institutions of higher learning, as one would anticipate, depend upon a number of factors such as institutional size, location, objectives, source of operational funds (private, public), and institutional awareness of student needs. Also, the history of higher education in the United States reflects the diversity of educational programs; thus, we would expect a similar patterning of diversity for financial aids programs.

Even in institutions with highly sophisticated financial assistance programs, there appears to be more variation in the administering and the financing of self-help programs than in other forms of financial assistance. Differences in budgeting practices and payroll procedures are common; in fact, our visitations of a number of institutions over a three-year period revealed more institutional differences than likenesses.

However, it must be recognized that difference does not necessarily indicate that some programs lack organization or that one way of doing things is much superior to another. Usually, there are several ways to accomplish a purpose meaningfully. That which may be considered a successful practice in program financing in School X could be a dismal failure if conducted in School Y. In this chapter, we shall give consideration to some of the purposes, means, methods, and problems encountered in student work program financing.

A.

Purposes of Student Work Financing

1. *To Provide Institutional Funds for Work Done by the Students.*
Most, if not all, higher educational institutions afford some part-time
employment for their students. Institutional administrators recognize
that some of the institutional work lends itself well to part-time student employment. For example, maintenance units, cafeterias, libraries, and housing units have work to be done which is virtually impossible to schedule within an eight-hour day or in eight-hour shifts,
the normal working arrangements for full-time employees. Additionally, at various times of the day more help is needed than normally
utilized, such as in cafeterias at mealtimes and in libraries, during
the day and evening, for checking and shelving books.

Thus, it can readily be seen that if for no other than economical
reasons, institutions can well afford to employ students on a part-time
basis at reasonable rates. Obviously, both the students and the university can benefit from such arrangements. How well the individual
student fares depends primarily upon the institution's placing its interest in him as a student above its interest in him as an employee.

Institutions which are interested first in the welfare of the student have policies, rules, and procedures regulating the employment
of the workers. Such control serves to assure the students and the
university staff that the educational goals of the students and the
academic program of the institution are foremost in institutional planning and operation. Lacking such controls, both the student and the
university as the employer, too often lose sight of the student's ultimate goal. The net result may be that the student, for financial reasons, will undertake to work more hours than needed and consequently have too few hours remaining to devote to attaining proper
academic achievement.

How well the college or the university fares in its part-time employment operation depends to a great extent upon the institution's
willingness to develop training programs for students, to provide
proper supervision, and, in general, aim toward graduating good
employees, as well as good students. Such consideration for the welfare of the working students probably will, ultimately, cost the institution as much financially as would the employment of full-time personnel. This is a point not always recognized by working students or

financial aids administrators when they place pressure on the administration of the university to increase the current hourly rates of student employees.

2. *To Add Flexibility to an Overall Financial Aid Operation.* One way in which this can be accomplished is through the "Package Program," so termed by financial aid administrations, with the program consisting of varying amounts of financial assistance from work, loans, and gifts (scholarships, awards, and grants). The quantity of each depends primarily upon the financial need and the academic ability of the student. Thus, an attempt is made to use the resources in a comprehensive program to meet the individual needs of the students. From a financial aid point of view, student work, long unrecognized in many institutions as a monetary aid, provides additional flexibility so necessary in arranging package assistance for individual students.

However, a very important point, often overlooked by college and university presidents, is that financial aids administrations must have control over student jobs if the "Package Program" as described is to become a successful operation. Not infrequently, the administrator of institutional student employment has little voice in determining the finances to be used and how such funds are to be utilized. When such is the case, the administrator becomes little more than a clerk and is not deserving of the title of director. The writers believe that the financial aids administrator should have the authority and responsibility to direct the student work operation. It further follows that the director should have the necessary qualifications to perform the job well.

Participation in the College-Work Study Program of the United States Office of Education lends flexibility to the institution's program, but such participation also requires that those student jobs which are financed on a matching basis with the federal government be part of the total financial aid operation. It should be recognized that to qualify for this program, a number of institutions have had to reorganize their financial aid operations so that the scholarships, loans, and student employment services are coordinated by a single office.

If the student's part-time job is a part of a package program, he should work for the university under the same conditions as does the non-package program student. Thus, student employment rules and regulations should apply equally to all working students, regardless of the kind and the amount of work assistance required and received.

3. *To Provide Work Experience Which Will Make a Positive Contribution to the Education of the Student.* Institutions which subscribe to the above philosophy recognize that the financing of such a student work operation may be an expensive undertaking, and they can see that the work performed by students on a part-time basis, when compared with that accomplished by full-time personnel, can be just as expensive or even more so than if full-time employees are hired.

However, the writers' knowledge of institutions which finance such work operations indicates that when the institutions' first consideration is the education of the student, the relatively expensive student work program is justified on the basis of work as a part of the total education of the student.

Although such institutions acknowledge that working students are naturally interested in the financial returns from their efforts, nevertheless, in the best interest of the students' education, it is recognized that a variety of work experiences can supplement the overall academic program and make a positive contribution to the total educative process.

Such work programs, to be successful, must have the support of the faculty and the administration, both recognizing the value of part-time work in supplementing the academic program. When such programs are given the academic and administrational approval and the financial support to carry out adequately the design, the employment service is usually efficient and successful.

4. *To Provide Funds for New Program Development.* Enrollment increases undoubtedly will be the major factor contributing to expanded institutional employment at all levels in the future. Increases in positions in academic and nonacademic areas usually will contribute to the occupational diversity of the institution. A decision which the administration of the institution must make is to determine which jobs are to be filled by full-time personnel and which are to be delegated to student work. In view of the fact that the growth of the institution can be attributed primarily to increased numbers of students, it would seem reasonable that a fair and consistent proportion of the jobs be allocated to students for part-time work, in keeping with the skills and the abilities required for satisfactory job performance.

Another factor which should contribute to student job diversity is the addition of new operations and programs. Additionally, the formation of new departments and operations should make a major contribution to the number of student jobs in a given institution.

Also, new programs could be activated by the acquisition of research grants. It is possible that the United States Office of Education, which finances the research in many academic areas, or one of the many great foundations similarly interested, would supply funds for student work as a part of the grant. Generally, it should be recognized that as institutional research relating to student work becomes more productive, there is an enhanced possibility of obtaining financial aid for student work from resources outside of the institution.

The most recent program development, accompanied by the financial resources for implementation, is the College Work-Study Program, originally Title I, Part C, of the Economic Opportunity Act, later becoming a part of the Higher Education Act of 1965. Not only will this program assist institutions immeasurably in putting into practice their mutually shared philosophy of assistance to the worthy, but, operationally, the institutions will be able to accomplish a considerable amount of work which has been neglected previously. (See Chapter 1 for more information on the College Work-Study Program.)

5. *To Provide Part-Time Help in Understaffed Operations.* In a great many departments in most, if not all, instiutions, the amount of work which needs to be accomplished does not justify the employment of a full-time person. This situation is not temporary; it is continuous. An example would be that of an academic department which has too few faculty members to justify the employment of a full-time secretary. Accordingly, one or two students working on a part-time basis can take care of the secretarial needs of the department. Actually, the utilization of student-help to bridge the gap between the requirements of some additional help and one full-time employee is one of the main justifications for using students in a variety of jobs. An illustration would be the case of a bibliographer in a library which does not have sufficient need to employ another full-time employee, but demands more work than one bibliographer can do. In such an instance, a student or several students could well be employed on a part-time basis.

Probably if a job analysis were to be made in any given institution, one would find a considerable number of the faculty and administrative personnel performing daily a number of tasks which could be accomplished by students. In such situations, a $14,000 a year professor who spends one to two hours daily in clerical tasks which could be performed by $1.45 per hour student workers reflects an institutional defect. The time of the professor could be better utilized in additional teaching, research, writing, or counseling his students. If the above is not sufficient justification, it should be remembered that a number of the institution's students need funds for college expenses and that they could profit educationally from such a work experience.

B.

Means of Financing Institutional Student Work Programs

Student work operations do not differ greatly from other institutional programs in that both the quality and the quantity of a given operation frequently depend upon the financial resources which can be made available for the operation of the program. However, it does not follow that institutions with more than adequate financial resources will be generous in allotting funds for self-help programs.

Some institutions may place their self-help programs at the bottom of their priority listings. Usually, this means that if any money is left over after all other departments have received their allocations, the remaining funds are placed in the self-help budget. Naturally, it is difficult for financial aids administrators in such institutions to develop work programs when they do not know the minimum and the maximum amount of money available from year to year on which they may depend to carry out their programs.

In discussing the topic of work-program financing with a number of employment directors over the past few years, the writers were made aware of the small role which most employment directors play in the financial aspect of student work programming. In fact, prior to the implementation of the United States Office of Education College Work-Study Program, few student employment directors could give accurate answers to such questions as the following: How much money does your institution spend for self-help? How many students are working on campus? What are the hourly rates for student workers in your institution? Who determines the maximum hours which a student may work? Who controls the budget for student help? Where do the funds come from to cover the expenses incurred? Because of the lack of answers to some of the questions raised, the authors are particularly interested in pointing out the major source of revenue.

1. *State College Funds.* State colleges and universities receive the major portion of their financial support from allocations made available through the legislative body of the state. Of course, the primary source of state funds is taxation. In Illinois, the government sales tax provides the major portion of tax funds used to finance higher education.

Higher educational institutions usually have two major budget divisions, one concerned with capital allocations and the second with internal operating allocations. The capital budget provides funds for such purposes as the purchase of land, site improvement, new buildings, and the rehabilitation and renovation of buildings. The operating budget provides the funds to underwrite the on-going affairs, business affairs, student affairs, and area services. Within the operating budget is a subdivision usually called Personal Services, which provides the funds for the employment of personnel, academic and nonacademic.

Frequently, the funds to pay the part-time student employees are a part of the nonacademic budget. At other times, funds are included in both the academic and the nonacademic budgets. Regardless, unless an administrative policy specifies the amount of funds or the percentage of the allocation which will be spent for student help, there is no assurance that the fair share of the budget will go for that purpose.

2. *Private College Funds.* Private colleges and universities rely more upon gifts, endowments, grants, investments, and student tuition for operating funds than do public institutions. Financial aids administrators are well aware of the importance of private gifts or grants in maintaining a good scholarship program. Unfortunately, gifts or grants to institutions are rarely designated to help support a student work program.

Exceptions to this general rule apply in institutions such as Berea College, Berea, Kentucky, and Blackburn College, Carlinville, Illinois, where work experience is considered to be a part of the educational experience. In recent years, a considerable number of smaller private liberal arts colleges are finding it increasingly difficult to finance their academic programs, to say nothing of student work programs. Increasing tuition as a means of acquiring more institutional operational funds not only prices a college education beyond the

reach of a higher percentage of high school graduates, but it also has
the effect of decreasing the amount of institutional financial assistance because the employment of teachers must be given first consideration. Even with the United States Office of Education College
Work-Study coming to the rescue in the area of self-help programs,
the outlook for enrollment increases in many small and even some
large nonpublic colleges is anything but encouraging. Comprehensive
scholarship programs, underwritten on a state or national level, seem
to be one possibility. Certainly, the GI bill as presently written will
not encourage student attendance in nonpublic colleges and universities.

3. *Auxiliary and Service Enterprise Funds.* The financial means for
the operation of enterprises and services in colleges and universities
such as dormitories, cafeterias, student unions, centers, and textbook
rentals comes primarily from the students through designated pay-
ments and fees. The management of these services and enterprises
usually becomes a responsibility of the administration of the institution.

Since most of the cost of maintaining such operations is borne
by the students, directly or indirectly, and because internal operating
funds from tax sources are not available, the business attitude of the
institution is that such services and enterprises should be on a self-
liquidating basis. There is also a tendency to employ as many students as possible, chiefly for two reasons; to help keep operating
costs down wherever student help is less expensive than full-time non-
student work, and to provide employment for financially needy students.

In fact, the writers have observed that most institutions rely
heavily upon these jobs in auxiliary and service enterprises to make
the major contribution to their self-help programs. Putting it another
way, without such jobs, many institutions would have limited part-
time employment opportunities to offer to their students. This is rather
unfortunate because a greater potential for worthwhile part-time employment lies in providing more employment opportunities in academic and nonacademic departments. This potential, when developed,
can provide more diversity and structure an experience bearing a
closer relationship to the vocational objectives of the students.

Incidentally, it is one of the purposes of the United States Office
of Education College Work-Study Program to develop the part-time

employment potential in academic departments. Of course, it is to be remembered that the Federal Government N.Y.A. Program recognized the same educational potential some thirty years ago but gained little permanent success in institutional development.

4. *Federal Funds.* At present, a major source of student work-program financing is the fund set aside for the United States Office of Education College Work-Study Program. This program has had tremendous growth since its inception early in 1965. Funds are made available to both public and private institutions on a matching fund basis with the governmental share at 90 percent and the institutional share at 10 percent, at the present time. The institutional share of the total is expected to increase in the future which, in turn, may create financial problems for some institutions.

Although the major purpose of this program is to provide financial assistance for needy students, it is also readily recognized that institutions can afford to participate in terms of benefits received. For example, even with the matching ratio changing to $1.00 of institutional money for each $4.00 of federal funds as of July 1967, the College Work-Study Program still enables the institution to get work accomplished which probably would otherwise not be undertaken. The United States Office of Education regulations which permit students to work full-time during vacation periods not only help the student solve his financial problems but give the institution an additional source of labor.

It is more feasible now for institutions which formerly had underdeveloped self-help programs because of a lack of finances to structure their resources in well-organized, functional operations.

c.
Methods of Financing

1. *The Departmental Method* (*Division, School, or College Unrestricted*). A common method of financing institutional student employment is to make funds available to all using functions, both academic and nonacademic. Although the sums of the department, division, school, or college allocations are frequently determined through recommendations by the dean, chairman, and director, the decision in reality to the total funds made available for a part-time employment usually rests with the president and his vice-presidents because they

make the recommendation as to the distribution of funds to the governing board of the school.

Even though the office of the president may make adequate funds available for a seemingly good student-work program, this, in itself, does not assure that such a program will develop. To illustrate: If the functions have unrestricted freedom in employing students, then one can readily imagine that there would be as many small student-employment operations as there are functions in the institutions. There is little reason to believe that students with great financial need and high academic potential will receive any special priority in employment consideration. One reason for the above statement is the difficulty confronting the function heads in knowing who the capable, needy students are. Also, students with training and experience who could be an asset to the function are not properly placed because neither the functions nor the students know the others' needs. The results of such an ineffective student employment practice is a disorganized operation, in which neither the students nor the institution benefit adequately in relationship to the expenditure of funds.

2. *The Controlled Method.* The controlled method differs primarily from the unrestricted one in that school policy requires the using functions to employ only those students referred by the student employment section of the financial aids office. The writers favor the controlled method because they feel that without such an arrangment, it is all but impossible for financial aids administrators to work out package programs for needy students. Also, with the adoption of such an institutional policy, it is possible for financial aids officers, in cooperation with the admissions and academic offices to recruit academically capable, financially needy students, permitting at the same time financial package commitments to be made to students.

Financial aids officers usually know the extent of their scholarship and loan funds, but in the past there has been little control allotted to their institutional student employment operation. This situation is now changing to a marked degree because of a recent development.

The role of the financial aids officer has been strengthened considerably in institutions which participate in the United States Office of Education College Work-Study Program when the officer is institutional representative for the program. It should be noted, of course, that the United States Office of Education requires that the instituional representative be engaged in financial assistance work because the representative will be deeply involved in finances related to the Work-Study Program and will have to consider money received in terms of the financial aspects of the school work program in its entirety. The writers feel that the result will be that he will accordingly be concerned in other financial matters relating to student employment, regardless of the source of funds. Further, we feel that the net result will be good.

D.
Problems involved in Self-Help Program Financing

1. *Pay Rates for Students.* In institutions permitting the individual departments to set the hourly rates for students in employment, one can expect problems. One great difficulty is the wide variation in hourly rates given to students with similar training skills, and experience, who perform the same or parallel work. Such a situation is not only difficult to explain to the students but equally hard to justify to a budgetary review committee. A second problem is unnecessary competition among departments for student help and funds for student workers. A department with a generous budget can become a very popular place for students to work if the hourly rate is, for example, ten to fifteen cents per hour more than most other departments can pay for the same type of work. Departments with limited budgets can find themselves in the position of training students for the more affluent departments. We also find departments exerting undue pressure upon the administration or the budgetary committee for additional funds to conduct self-help projects. A third problem may be called departmental partiality. This is a common practice in academic departments and consists mainly of employing only those students who are majoring in that particular department. To illustrate, the department of English may employ only those students who are English majors, regardless of the kind of work to be performed.

2. *Evaluating the Use of Funds for Student Employment.* Assessment can constitute quite a problem, be it an individual or a committee that attempts to evaluate the use of funds for self-help. It can readily be seen that academic departments will not be inclined to look on evaluation with favor if the evaluation group is from a nonacademic area, such as Business Affairs, Student Services, or Student

Employment. Also, the reverse of the above statement is true.

Probably a committee appointed by the president of the university, a group which represents the major functions of the university and includes faculty members, would encounter the least resistance in any plan to evaluate the use of funds for self-help. Of course, any attempt of an institution to evaluate the use of funds for student help must continually keep in mind the philosophy and objectives which the institution has for its work program.

For example, the goals of a self-help program in a large metropolitan university with many off-campus job opportunities may differ considerably from that of a college or university located in a rural area where few out-of-school employment opportunities exist for students. An institution with a highly developed cooperative education program may give negligible time or attention to its own on-campus self-help operation because of its institutional philosophy and educational objectives which tend to emphasize off-campus work. An institution with a self-help program which is an integral part of a total program of financial assistance may have different goals for student employment than does an institution which relies primarily upon scholarships and loans as the base for its financial aid program. We conclude with the opinion that the efficient use of institutional funds in a self-help program depends primarily upon the goals of the institution and expected accomplishments in the expenditure of such funds.

3. *Contingency Funds for Self-Help Programs.* It is the experience of the writers that few financial aids administrators have access to contingency funds to initiate new student-work projects, to expand existing operations, or to meet emergency needs. Also, although departments may have control over original allocations for student help, they rarely have contingency funds because such financial resources are usually controlled on the presidential or vice-presidential level of administration.

However, where institutions aspire to have student work operations which serve both the needs of the students and the institutions, it would seem expedient to the success of the program that contingency funds be made available to the director of the program. For example, with such funds at his disposal, the director would be in a position to initiate new projects during the year and not be compelled to wait until the next fiscal year for funds. It is understood, of course, that the budget committee or one of the president's line officers would review and recommend each project for approval before the actual release of funds. Basically, the writers take the position that the financial aids director should have the competencies to assure the wise use of contingency funds made available to the program. Further, if wise use is not made of such funds, the director should be replaced by an individual having the necessary ability to do so.

5 Self-Help Programs in Selected Colleges and Universities

ONE OF THE universally recognized distinguishing features of higher education in the United States is diversification. This salient characteristic is evident not only in academic programs, organization, and administration, but it is noted also in financial support, whether the students are engaged in a work program or whether it concerns college facilities, providing instructional staff and physical facilities.

There are those who believe that the strength of our American higher educational system is keyed to its diversity. This principle provides a fulcrum for institutional experimentation and operational freedom in keeping with student needs and institutional goals, furthering the best interests of our democratic society.

In discussing the importance of the element of diversity in our higher education systems, John S. Brubacher and Willis Rudy state:

> American educational diversity and localism certainly helped to broaden and democratize higher learning by opening college doors to large numbers of people who otherwise would not have been able to enter. . . . For many Americans in varied economic circumstances, it was not really a question of going to Harvard or Yale or to a small college, but rather of going to that small college or getting no higher education at all.

> Obviously, higher education could not well have been organized in any other way in a country as vast and heterogeneous as the United States, and one can agree with the committee of the Association of American Universities which held that this situation had basic value since it reflected "the characteristics of a free society and of the role of higher education therein." Diversity had furthered equality of educational opportunity, with all that this meant for American social

mobility. It had made it easier to maintain freedom in general and operational freedom in particular. It had afforded the opportunity for original and fruitful experiment, for the serving of the public need, with a multiplicity of institutional types and academic programs, for a healthful competition which might never have existed under a more authoritarian and centralized system.[1]

We feel that the emphasized factors of diversity will help the reader to understand not only *why* but *how* certain elements and events contributed to unique student work programs in a number of American colleges and universities. In some instances, the leadership came from the founding fathers of the institutions; in other examples, the presidents of the institutions provided the necessary direction; and again in others, the location of the institution was influential in the distinctively different program development.

The major purpose of this chapter is to provide the reader with some organizational, operational, and philosophical aspects of work-experience programs in selected colleges and universities. The choice of the institutions is intended to include both private and public higher educational schools—small liberal arts colleges and multicampus universities, urban colleges and universities, and rural colleges and universities, institutions known for their work-study programs and others, unique in their own right, giving special emphasis to work as financial assistance. Although we furnish the reader with a commentary on our study, including recommendations, it is to be hoped that the reader will examine the summaries of the various colleges and universities. These précis list not only information about work experience programs but also afford additional information concerning the institutions.

A.

A Field Study of Student Work-Experience Programs

1. *The Nature of the Study and Acknowledgments.* The material for this study was primarily acquired by personal interviews with financial aid directors and their assistants in some twenty-five colleges and universities. The material was collected over a two-year period (1966–68) and required some ten thousand miles of travel. The office of Re-

---

1   John S. Brubacher and Willis Rudy, *Higher Education in Transition* (New York: Harper & Brothers, 1958), pp. 376–77.

search and Projects, Southern Illinois University, provided most of the necessary travel funds through an institutional research grant. The major purpose of the study was to find answers to the following questions:

a) What is the nature of student work experience (student jobs) in American colleges and universities?

b) Do the institutions have qualified and a sufficient number of personnel to administer and supervise their work-study programs?

c) What is the impact of the federal government's College Work-Study Program on institutions' financial aid programs?

Before we attempt to answer the above questions in our commentary, or through the interview summaries, we would like to acknowledge the cooperation and/or the contribution of the following financial aid officers:

Allan Purdy, *University of Missouri, Columbia, Missouri*
Charles J. Sheehan, *University of New Mexico, Albuquerque, New Mexico*
H. W. Kennedy, *Kansas State University, Manhattan, Kansas*
Milton D. Schroeder, *Northern Arizona University, Flagstaff, Arizona*
John Hagerty, *Antioch College, Yellow Springs, Ohio*
Elton G. Davis, *University of Oklahoma, Norman, Oklahoma*
Donald S. Coby, *University of South Florida, Tampa, Florida*
H. H. Harbison, JR., *Wayne State University, Detroit, Michigan*
George C. Fix, *University of Wisconsin, Milwaukee, Wisconsin*
James E. Ingle, *University of Kentucky, Lexington, Kentucky*
Grant E. Curtis, *Tufts University, Medford, Massachusetts*
Carroll L. Beardslee, *Fort Hays Kansas State College, Hays, Kansas*
Vinson A. Watts, *Berea College, Berea, Kentucky*
Wilson Evans, *Berea College, Berea, Kentucky*
Robert E. McKay, *Bowling Green State University, Bowling Green, Ohio*
Wallace H. Douma, *University of Wisconsin, Madison, Wisconsin*
Robert B. Kimmel, *Florida State University, Tallahassee, Florida*

Donovan Allen, *University of Indiana, Bloomington, Indiana*
John Griffin, *University of Illinois, Urbana, Illinois*
Guy Spitler, *Miami University, Oxford, Ohio*
Mabel Irwin (Mrs.), *University of Colorado, Boulder, Colorado*
Dustin Burke, *Harvard University, Boston, Massachusetts*
Charles McCombs, *Ohio State University, Columbus, Ohio*
Howard Moffitt, *University of Iowa, Iowa City, Iowa*
John G. Danielson, *Princeton University, Princeton, New Jersey*
Glenn McConagha, *Blackburn College, Carlinville, Illinois*
Peter Mousolite, *U.S. Office of Education, Chicago, Illinois*

2. *What is the Nature of Student Work Experience?* The single word which best describes the nature of student work experience is diversity. The term could apply in analyzing the kind and variety of student jobs on a given campus or when comparing one institutional program with others. Although the work program summaries in this chapter will verify the above point, we shall highlight the summaries by brief illustrations.

Frequently, students, faculty, and financial aid officers use college work-study, student work program, self-help, student employment, and cooperative program as synonymous terms. Actually, we found that two of these terms identify work experience as an important part of the institution's curriculum, contributing significantly to the students' academic programs. First, the term, student work program, at Berea College, Berea, Kentucky, involves all sixteen hundred students in this liberal arts college. Student work is considered an integral part of their educational program. It is a philosophy at Berea that, "One does not come to Berea College to get away from work but rather comes to learn to work and to live on a higher level." We find it difficult to improve upon this philosophy.

Also, at Blackburn College, Carlinville, Illinois, all students who enroll are workers. In both schools, the students work primarily on campus in projects under the supervision of their colleges. The two institutions illustrate work as education in its true sense since work is included in their curricula and required for all of their students.

The term, cooperative education, refers to a work experience that differs markedly from that of Berea and Blackburn, yet it is a part of the curriculum at Antioch. Antioch is internationally known as a leader in cooperative education. The Co-op, as it is commonly termed, places the student in an alternating work-study situation. Customarily, the student is in full-time employment for the duration of a term or semester in a business or industrial establishment and then returns to the classroom for an equal period of time. The work experience is primarily for upperclassmen, juniors, and seniors.

The other three terms, student employment, self-help, and college work-study, appear to identify programs more closely related to financial aids. In fact, the College Work-Study is one of the multiple financial aid programs (work, loans, and grants) sponsored by the federal government. We do not intend to indicate that students who participate in a self-help, student employment, or College Work-Study Program may not receive an invaluable educational experience through work. Rather, we note that such an educational experience is not programmed as a part of the student's education. One might say that work experience is established on a schematic scale, extending from pure education at one extreme to pure finance at the opposite end. However, in practical situations, educational and financial returns overlap. In rephrasement, it is possible for the student to obtain his educational experience and be financially reimbursed, simultaneously.

Some schools superimpose a student work program upon their student employment operation. Both Harvard and Princeton have established institutional student employment operations in which students work in a variety of on-campus jobs, including food service and maintenance. However, they also conduct a special student work program through their institutional business agencies. One of the prime values of this program is the amount of responsibility which students are permitted to assume in operating the agencies.

Some schools use a satellite approach, incorporating a special type of summer work program administered by the college but supervised in communities remote from the campus. Again, such programs are supplementary to the institution's student employment operation. The Universities of Colorado and Missouri have both developed extensive summer employment operations in conjunction with the college Work-Study Program of the United States Office of Education.

Institutions located in metropolitan areas usually capitalize on the job opportunities, diversified in nature, afforded by most urban areas. Wayne State University at Detroit and the University of Wisconsin at Milwaukee rely on their counseling of placement service to assist students in locating educationally related off-campus jobs. An interesting note about these two universities is that some 75 percent of the enrolled students are employed on a part-time basis at least.

If our study is a cross section of American colleges and universities, it is clear that this generation of youth is not only willing and able—they work! Further, we can say that higher educational institutions are directing concentrated effort to provide a variety of financial and educationally related work experience, either on campus or in the community. Also, we believe that the combination of work and study graduates better citizens and employees who can contribute meaningfully to a better society.

3. *Do Institutions Have Qualified and a Sufficient Number of Personnel to Administer and Supervise Their Employment Operations and the College Work-Study Program?* We should point out that our study was made at a time when the United States Office of Education Work-Study Program was in its first or second year of operation at a number of colleges and universities. One would expect a staffing problem. However, it was not only the area of College Work-Study, but whole financial aid operations that were undermanned. We did not find a college or university adequately staffed to carry out the duties and responsibilities necessary to administer properly their operations.

We did find, without exception, at least one or two well-qualified persons in each school which we visited. It did appear to us that too much of the counseling, referral, and placement of students was conducted by clerical employees and graduate assistants. This is not a criticism but rather an observation. It should be noted that personnel with adequate education and training, plus experience in the various aspects of financial aid counseling and administration are a scarce commodity. Another problem, the one that has persisted over the years, is insufficient funds to employ additional personnel for financial aid program administration. This problem could be partially resolved, at least, if the United States Office of Education would authorize for the administration of the College Work-Study and Educational Opportunity Grant Programs, a financial arrangement similar to what now exists for the National Defense Student Loan Program. Actually, the thinking of most of the financial aid officers we contacted was that some 3 percent of Federal Financial Aid Program allocations could be justified for administrative purposes. Important as these programs are to both institutions and students, we do not foresee in the immediate future college administration removing much needed funds from academic budgets to allocate additional funds for financial aid program administrators.

4. *What is the Impact of the Federal Government's College Work-Study Program on Institutional Financial Aid Programs?* FIRST, ORGANIZATIONAL IMPACT. Prior to the implementation of the federal government's College Work-Study Program, financial aids in many of America's colleges and universities consisted mainly of scholarships and loans. A United States Office of Education regulation placed the College Work-Study Program for institutional administration in the financial aid operation. This regulation stated that the institutional representative for the College Work-Study Program should be one responsible for other institutional financial aids, the rationale being that the National Defense Student Loan Program and the College Work-Study Program should be administered by the same office. This was a very important organizational step toward the development of multiple programs of financial assistance. It is to be remembered that institutional student employment operations were seldom administered by the financial aid office. In fact, it would be difficult to establish a pattern of student employment administration in the hierarchy of American colleges and universities. Some institutions used their placement offices to house their student employment offices, others relied on their business office, and probably an equal number used the institution's personnel office or the dean of student's office to supervise their student employment offices.

Because the United States Office of Education required that the College Work-Study Program be administered by the financial aid office, the principle of a single office to administer multiple programs of financial assistance was established.

It has been the thinking of some of the leaders in financial aid that institutional student employment, as well as the College Work-Study Program, should be administered by the financial aid office. Our study revealed a definite trend to consolidate the self-help and financial aid operations. Probably few organizational changes would do more to establish the operational importance of financial aids.

SECOND, FINANCIAL IMPACT. Implementation of the College Work-Study Program was not only a financial means of helping students, but institutions as well. In previous chapters, we pointed out the lack of institutional funds to develop student employment operations. The willingness of the federal government to provide funds on a 90 percent federal and 10 percent institutional basis (the present matching is 80 percent and 20 percent) meant that institutions could expand and diversify student work experience. It also meant that the faculty and staff could be relieved of some of their clerical and para-professional duties since the students could be trained to perform these tasks.

THIRD, EDUCATIONAL IMPACT. The College Work-Study Program provided an opportunity for financial aid officers to administer an educational as well as a financial program. Financial aid officers now had the responsibility of placing students in meaningful jobs. Not only could they have a feeling of gratification in helping a student to attain a goal but they contribute directly to his education and experiential growth. Also, the working relationship between the faculty and the financial aid officer increased the stature of financial aid officers since this level of performance was taking on a professional role instead of clerical. However, the student is the real benefactor of the provisions of the program.

Conclusions. From our study, we conclude that not since the National Youth Administration Work-Study Program of the thirties has such a large percentage of our college youth, through their own efforts, contributed so much toward the cost of their education. When a student participates in a student work-study program, he is not only helping himself but helping others. If the basic purpose of a college education is to prepare oneself to serve society in a meaningful way, then the working students are progressing steadily toward achieving this goal.

B.
Programs in Specific Colleges

Student work programs differ to a marked degree in direction and implementation, even in those colleges and universities which have well-recognized programs. So that the reader will realize the above and in turn, if he is in a counseling situation, give good advice, the following programs are presented for review and informational purposes.

ANTIOCH COLLEGE, YELLOW SPRINGS, OHIO

Antioch College was founded in 1853 with Horace Mann, the educational reformer, as its first president. From the date of its development, admissions to the school were granted with no discrimination as to color, sex, or religious affiliations. Today, Antioch College is universally recognized for its emphasis on cooperative education. All members of the student body, numbering approximately eighteen hundred, participate in the institution's work program.

The diversity of the employment program is extensive with some six hundred employers involved in the operation. The scope of the cooperative education design is not merely state-wide and nation-wide, but it also extends to foreign countries.

At any given time, some two hundred students are employed in the Antioch Education Program in positions abroad. Customarily, the students are away from the campus for a period of one year to fifteen months. The Domestic Student Body averages sixteen hundred with eight hundred students attending campus classes and eight hundred off campus, working. The college operates on a basis of one six-month and two three-month quarters, is in session twelve months yearly, the majority of the students being employed for half of the academic year. Ordinarily, the program requires five years to earn a bachelor of arts or a science degree, although some exceptional students can be graduated in four years. There are occasional waivers in the usual cooperative hour units but not in the academic requirements.

The student is an integral part of the overall college policies with the campus regulations controlled by a nine-member Community Council consisting of six students and three faculty members. Individuality and self-responsibility are emphasized, each student being personally obligated for his own behavior.

The philosophy of work which undergirds the basic structuring of the Antioch College curricula and programs is that work in real situations constitutes the educational value often overlooked by other institutions. It is the purpose of Antioch to provide a series of work opportunities, to offer varied employment opportunities, and to promote exploration in differentiated fields of work. At the beginning of the third year, the student selects a major field as his academic focus. However, the students are encouraged to move horizontally through an entire spectrum of activities before proceeding vertically to a chosen career. Often, there is as great a sequence of rejection of ideas regarding a vocational choice as there is an acceptance of an occupation.

When the student is actively engaged in off-campus employment, he is encouraged to learn virtually as much through observation of his new surroundings, of the community, and of those about him as he does while actually employed. This is an important point of the training; all the potentialities of the situation are to be exhausted. Further, the firm which employs the student must always be willing to serve as an instrument of education.

The Antioch College administrators do not actually evaluate the job performance of the student workers. While students are employed, supervisors submit ratings of work productivity, and students also write reports to the Antioch College office. Upon returning to the campus, the student spends several hours with his advisor, reviewing the educational value of the work experience. The institution is not chiefly concerned with the amount of salary received since the basic principle of the program is not merely financial assistance but rather the educational values derived from employment situations.

The Cooperative Education Program was initiated in 1921 and has grown steadily in dimension since its inception. The entire faculty of Antioch shares concern for the students' development, always stressing the educational values of work, coupled with academic achievement. Antioch might well be called a cosmopolitan campus, with members of its student body employed during the academic year throughout the United States, Europe, Asia, Africa, and Latin America. The student body is equally representative of varying communities and countries, including students from every state and the major continents.

It is significant that in the ultimate decision on a work assignment, the Antioch student makes the final choice of the area of his employment. He must arrange his own transportation to the initial interview, find his own lodging, and be self-sufficient. This, in itself, constitutes a valuable learning experience. The philosophy of Antioch College is that a student should not be retained by one employer on a single job, but rather that he should be "stretched" vocationally through the opportunity of a variety of contacts.

Paramount in the administrative thought is the horizontal approach made to the work experience initially; this later changes to a pyramid system. The extent of the growth of cooperative education has been most apparent in recent years. It is estimated that during the academic year of 1966–67, some sixty-five thousand students engaged in cooperative work at 103 different schools in varying levels of employment. Antioch College, however, incorporates its administration and faculty members in the overall program as active participants. The concept of higher education in Antioch is that of experiential and academic education. There is no divorcement from the classroom, with the contribution from the cooperative program supplementing and enriching the academic studies.

As a part of the preparation for citizenship, Antioch College stresses leadership and development of initiative. While in college, students assist in faculty selection and have a voice in all collegiate affairs. The student body is a world-wide campus, and members live and learn in such disparate areas as Saudi Arabia, London, Paris, and Tokyo. As participants in the cooperative education plan, the students are representatives of Antioch College, but simultaneously they possess individual rights which they may assert, while recognizing and respecting the privileges of others. All bills, fees, and grades are issued to the students, not directed to the parents. Such an arrangement further promotes a sense of maturity and self-reliance.

Initially, the students identify the two areas of occupation which are of greatest interest. Although the individual student receives counseling from the staff and advisors of the college, the student makes the final choice of a work assignment. The extramural cooperative division of the faculty of the college makes field trips each quarter, observes the accomplishments of the students, checks the educational potential in work areas, and makes recommendations for the following term. Large metropolitan areas are always included on the staff visitations since many students are employed in large cities at a variety of occupations, ranging from sales work to semiprofessional positions.

The plateaus of job complexity and difficulty increase as the student progresses academically and occupationally. This is a needful process in a truly complete education, including lessons in theories and practicalities. Since man is confronted with a most complex civilization, the educative process must match the demands of society. Antioch College pioneered in the philosophy that students could benefit most greatly by alternating study periods with full-time work, and this tenet is increasingly being adopted by other institutions of higher learning.

BEREA COLLEGE, BEREA, KENTUCKY

Berea College, founded in 1855, is unique in its practical self-help program, designed to provide higher education to some sixteen hundred students, more than 90 percent of whom are selected from the 230 mountain counties of eight southern states. No tuition charges are made; however, every member of the student body participates in the work program of the institution. No student works less than ten hours per week or in excess of fifteen hours per week, thus undertaking a forty to sixty hour monthly employment. Every student earns a portion of his college expenses, and the diversified work programs are organized for the benefit of the student and the college. It is possible for a student to enroll in Berea College, work twenty-four hours per week and be self-supporting. However, he must register for a reduced academic program of study.

Academic study receives priority, with the work providing the means of acquiring an education and as education itself. Voluntary work outside college activities is not permitted, and all employment is performed under the direction of school authority. Berea College seeks highly motivated students and is highly selective in its admissions, with only one-third of the applications accepted by the institution. Berea extends its services also to the secondary school, with some two hundred students participating in the work-study program operated by the college.

Berea College affords the opportunity for ambitious, qualified students to develop employment potentialities while acquiring a higher education. The entering freshmen have choice of work only within certain areas, generally in service operations such as caretaker work in school buildings or in food preparation assignments. As the student progresses in his studies, many openings are available, including the college operated bakery, candy kitchen, printing shop, needlecraft, broomcraft, and woodcraft industries, weaving, dairy, farms, and hotel service. All of the work is performed by the students under supervision of the faculty or the departmental superintendent.

Berea College is located in the foothills of the Cumberland Mountains, and the campus spans a picturesque ridge. The campus proper encompasses some 140 acres, and the lands used for instruction in farming, dairying, and animal husbandry cover more than 1,000 acres, with approximately 6,000 acres of forestland adjoining.

The faculty and staff number approximately 175, providing a most desirable student-staff ratio. Berea is a private, non-denominational school, receiving no church or federal support, with the exception of the College Work-Study Program and provisions made by the Economic Opportunity Act.

The philosophy of Berea College is stated simply: "One does not come to Berea College to get away from work, but rather one comes to learn to work and to live on a higher level."

Living expenses are kept to a minimum, averaging approximately $605 to $620 for room, board, and fees. The average student can earn approximately $300 to $350 during the school year, carrying the prescribed number of courses as a full-time registrant, while participating in the college work program.

The worth of work is emphasized throughout the year, and an annual observance, Labor Day, is held the first Tuesday in May, recognizing student work in Berea's Labor Program. Berea College looms large as an institution of significance in its encouragement of self-reliance, independence, and the learning of skills, as well as providing an excellent college education. The student body represents democracy in its true sense, as all those enrolled in the institution take active and equal parts in the diversified industries directed by the institution.

Scholarship funds are available, but no state funds are allocated to the school. To carry on educational functions, Berea College depends upon endowments, labor grants, and gifts from alumni and friends. The cost of teaching a student for one year is approximately $2,000, and assistance is received from private sources to meet this amount.

As a member of the Association of American Colleges, Berea is accredited by the Southern Association of Colleges and Secondary Schools and the National Council for accreditation of Teacher Education. Also, the Department of Nursing is accredited by the National League of Nursing.

Founded as a strong liberal arts college, Berea today offers a B.A. degree in twenty-two major subjects, and it awards a B.S. in Agriculture, Business Administration, Home Economics, Industrial Arts, and Nursing. Its Foundation School provides a college preparatory course and a specifically designed course for those who wish to terminate their education upon high school graduation.

The student work program of Berea College has been in existence for more than a hundred years. Before the implementation of Federal aid to education, approximately $240,000 was budgeted for wages. It is anticipated that this figure will be doubled in the 1967–68 academic period.

The philosophy of Berea is work-oriented, both in the physical and the intellectual areas. The institution has a historic principle, that of improving the level of living in its area of the country. Such a tenet is evidenced in the academic courses, campus climate, and demonstrated acceptance by faculty and students. Berea College holds closely to the founding doctrine of providing sound liberal arts and vocational education for residents of the Southern Appalachian area, and approximately 90 percent of the students are of this section.

Today, Berea emphasizes its original objectives, established more than a century ago, but is equally twentieth-century oriented, expanding its goals to match the demands of a changing world.

BOWLING GREEN UNIVERSITY, BOWLING GREEN, OHIO

Bowling Green State University, located in Bowling Green, Ohio, is a state supported institution enrolling approximately ten thousand students in 1966. The importance of a school-sponsored work program is recognized and supported by the university officials, and nearly one student in seven or eight is employed during the academic year.

Scholarships, loans, and employment are all under the direction of a single office, providing continuity in the administration of student assistance. Student workers are located in virtually every department of the university and provide valuable services for the school, at the same time receiving much-needed funds for academic expense.

Every department head of Bowling Green is advised of the amount of the allocation granted by the administration, and the departmental official is charged with the necessary budgetary details. Proper supervision of all students is provided by the various divisions of the university to assure that desirable work standards are maintained and that individual students work during the assigned periods.

Bowling Green emphasizes academic achievement as well as the learning of adjunct skills. No student is permitted to work more than twenty hours per week, and the College Work-Study students are employed a maximum of fifteen hours weekly.

The process of making application for employment is specifically detailed. On the initial interview, students are screened on the following points: comparative need; attitude; appearance; general impression; type of work desired; previous experience and training. A Student Employment form card is filed in the Student Financial Aid Office, and data is recorded monthly, listing time and wage received. Only one card is required throughout a student's college career, and the form is filed permanently in the Student Financial Aid Office as a record of performance.

Each student receives a Personnel Report, which is submitted to the supervisors or department heads, who rate the student worker in the following categories: Attitude to Work and to Supervisor, Initiative, Dependability, Courteousness, Cooperativeness, and Accuracy. The rating scale ranges from Excellent, five points; Good, four; Average, three; Fair, two; and Poor, one point. The year-end ratings are kept confidential and are recorded on the permanent Student Employment Form. The student is aware of the significance of such appraisals and realizes that a commendable work record can be of significant value while in college and following his graduation.

There is a definite line of demarcation drawn between the granting of scholarships and awards, with awards given at the third level of grade points. Scholarships are granted on an index, weighing the relative measure of need. There is a differentiation established in the granting of scholarships beyond the freshman year, with first year students receiving upwards of $400 and scholarships on the sophomore level and above being limited to $200.

There is also consideration given to those students who rank below scholarship level, with some sixty grants and aids available to students who require assistance to remain in the university.

Academic excellence is recognized by the annual award of six scholarships to freshmen, regardless of financial need. Students are carefully selected and must rank in the top 10 percent of their class. Possibly forty or fifty are initially chosen, and from this group, about eight boys and girls are selected. Invitations are sent to these students to attend a meeting on the first or second Saturday in May. It is indicated that they are being considered in recognition of outstanding scholarship. Following an interview period, the students are asked to write an impromptu paper for further evaluation. Based on a faculty committee's evaluation, six scholarships are given, amounting to $400 a year.

Nearly 700 scholarships and awards are administered, with some set aside for departmental units, such as music, debate, athletics, forensics. When superiority is demonstrated, it is the belief of the administrators that recognition should be given in the form of a grant.

The Economic Opportunity Grant is employed in the operation of the program of financial assistance. It endorses the basic tenet of Bowling Green State University that the capable, needy student be provided an opportunity to further his education and to develop his capabilities to the maximum. Perhaps, most important, the student is encouraged to realize the value of the work situation and its concomitant merits which stem from meaningful, developing initiative, resourcefulness, and conscientiousness.

THE UNIVERSITY OF COLORADO, BOULDER, COLORADO

A diversified program of financial assistance is provided for qualified, capable students at the University of Colorado. Particularly emphasized is the College Work-Study Program as an integral part of the overall services of the Office of Financial Aids. Approximately six hundred students currently (1967–68) participate in the function, as administered by the university.

The significance of the growth of the College Work-Study Program in the University of Colorado is evident in contrasting the relatively small group of students who were employed in 1965 with the present scope of the service. Officials maintain detailed records as to the eligibility of students for such assignment, the hours of part-time employment performed, placement in departmental or service units, and the rates of wages. No more than fifteen hours of campus part-time employment are permitted each week, in conformity with federal regulations. During the academic year of 1966–67, approximately $750,000 was disbursed in wages under the provisions of the program.

In addition to the regular on-campus work opportunities during the school sessions, students in the College Work-Study Program are encouraged to seek summer full-time employment. The Office of Financial Aids is currently initiating pilot programs in the areas of Rifle and Montrose, Colorado, listing work potentialities for the vacation months. All summer employment payrolls of the College Work-

Study Program are issued to students so placed by the University of Colorado. Upon returning to the campus in the fall, students are requested to show their bank savings passbooks to indicate that they have saved approximately one-half of their vacation time earnings. Also, high school graduates may be referred to such full-time employment, with the stipulation that they register for regular student classification in the fall session of the university.

The customary university on-campus employment has expanded greatly within the past few years. To a major extent, the regular school student-work program is under the direction of the various departments of the colleges of the University of Colorado. Frequently, departmental officials select specific students to meet the requirements of job assignments. Although there is a degree of latitude in student placement, the rates of pay must be consistent with the standards estimated by the Personnel Office. In addition to individual selectivity, many departments consult the Office of Financial Aid to obtain students for part-time employment.

The minimum and maximum rates of pay range from $1.25 to $3.11, with the higher rates applying to graduate research assistants. The Program is functional, designed to meet the requirements of the students concerned, as well as to fulfill the needs of the employing university department. At any given time during the academic year, the total employment figure is twenty-five hundred. A survey recently conducted by the University of Colorado indicated that approximately 50 percent of the student body is employed during the course of the school year, including the divisions of the College Work-Study, the regular university employment program, or in positions obtained independently by the student.

Although there is flexibility in the operation of the regular non-College Work-Study Program, vouchers are filed by the various departmental offices and the same standardization and classification of types of employment are maintained. Internal auditors review the work programs periodically for any possible inequities in rates of remuneration.

Excellent cooperation with off-campus agencies has been evidenced in matching the 15 percent of funding required to meet the the federal fund allocation of 85 percent, specified by the College Work-Study Program. During the 1966–67 academic year, sixty students were employed in the Boulder Valley School as teachers' aides. Great enthusiasm is expressed concerning this work detail, with teachers and students mutually endorsing the experiential employment opportunity as truly meaningful.

A comprehensive index to the student's actual financial need as well as his job performance is provided through the voucher approval of the Office of Financial Aids and the master-card system, codified to indicate individual placement, proficiency, and academic standing. Such a process permits a true evaluation of the overall operation of the program. There is only one major difficulty encountered in off-campus employment, in that there is an occasional time lag in acquiring approved vouchers by the date they are due in to qualify for payroll processing. A new payroll system has been instituted whereby students are paid every two weeks and this has improved the time lag situation. Currently, there are thirty-four off-campus Colorado agencies participating in the College Work-Study Program.

Personnel of the Office of Financial Aids oversee Work-Study jobs in the Grand Junction area, Colorado Springs, and the Denver Center, with all employment coordinated through the central office of the University of Colorado in Boulder. Again, wholehearted support and cooperation have been established with employers in these divisions and the university administrative officials.

Applicants are required to submit an affidavit of actual financial need, verifying nonsupport or evidence of family income to qualify for the College Work-Study Program. Counseling interviews are held and every effort is made to refer the student to an occupational area relating to his field of academic concentration.

A research study was recently completed, concerning seventy low income students, followed by an additional review, and significant results were derived. Analyses showed that this particular group under study since February 1966, achieved better academically than did the average of the freshman class as a whole. This survey of College Work-Study students indicated that students who worked tended to organize time more efficiently than did the non-employed. This specific survey concerned seventy students who were categorized as being "question marks" in their academic ratings previously established, thus constituting a relatively weak group of achievement. However, with sufficient counseling and direction, these students were motivated to attain a surprisingly good academic level. The Office of Financial Aids is staffed with individuals who have a genuine concern for nurturing the potentialities of the students of the University of Colorado. Further, there is central administration of loans, grants, scholarships, and work, permitting an efficient packaging of financial assistance to meet individual requirements.

The average expense of attending the University of Colorado, including tuition, fees, room, board, and minimum incidental costs, is, for the school year 1966–67, approximately $1,800. The Office of Financial Aids provides an invaluable service in its well-organized program, offering an opportunity for any capable student, regardless of financial status, to attain a university degree. The practicality of such provisions is evident in the number of students in attendance. During the academic year of 1966–67, enrollment in the institution exceeded sixteen thousand at Boulder, with a total registration of nearly twenty-seven thousand including the centers located at Grand Junction, Colorado Springs, and Denver.

The University of Colorado believes most strongly in the intangible, as well as in the tangible benefits of student employment. Part-time work can afford a most valuable supplement to the totality of higher education. Among the best employees are those individuals who have no true financial need but want the experiential gains accruable. The financially needy students are given priority in placement, but there are definite values to be realized by all students in work situations, in terms of maturation, development, and initiative. The qualities of self-sufficiency and resourcefulness are of paramount importance in the totality of the student's education, aiding immeasurably in the education of the individual.

FORT HAYS KANSAS STATE COLLEGE, HAYS, KANSAS

Fort Hays Kansas State College offers a comprehensive financial aid program, including part-time employment, scholarships, grants, and loans, directed by the Office of Student Aids. The total budgetary allocations for the academic year of 1966–67 were approximately $835,000, and officials predict that the program funding will increase during coming school years.

A significant percentage of students are part-time employees, working in assignments under the specific supervision of the university or in college approved off-campus projects. As documented by file records, more than 25 percent of the forty-five hundred students, including residents, nonresidents, and graduate students, are participating in the total program of employment.

All means of financial assistance are centralized in one office, providing applicants with information as to the various avenues of student assistance. Students seeking financial aid are interviewed by the counseling staff of the Office of Student Aid; employment-screening procedures are conducted, and the applicants are evaluated in regard to their interests and abilities. Qualified workers are referred to campus departments and college units, as well as to off-campus programs, supervised by the college. Necessarily, the philosophy of Fort Hays Kansas State College is based upon a genuine concern for the academically capable student of very limited means. Frequent contacts are made with high school faculties throughout the state, and guidance counselors are encouraged to search out needy, worthy students who can achieve in higher education.

The package program of loans, grants, scholarships, and part-time employment has proved most beneficial in administration, and approximately three hundred students are recipients of such multiple aids. The estimated cost of attending Fort Hays Kansas State College in the 1967–68 school year is approximately $1,500, this amount covering tuition, housing, board, and incidental expenses. It is readily observed that a sizeable percentage of high school graduates would find the yearly cost of attending college merely an aspiration, not a reality, if a substantial program of financial assistance were not provided.

The scope of off-campus work opportunities is impressive, including such areas as Civil Defense, the County Agricultural Extension Office, and Chamber of Commerce, the Girl Scout Council, the High Plains Mental Health Division, the Human Development Program, the historic Old Fort Hays Museum, the Office of the Probate Judge, and the Unified District School System. Such employment extending outside the periphery of the college offers invaluable experience to the student workers, as well as efficient service to community agencies.

In addition, many students obtain employment in the area through individual application and there is no established figure as to the number who find work opportunities through their own initiative. In the on-campus program, covering nearly seventy points of placement, more than 1,075 students were employed during the academic year of 1966–67.

Genuine interest in the student as an individual is emphasized by the Office of Student Aid, and academic achievement is not hindered in the interest of employment. Work is a most valuable asset to the totality of the student's college experience, but academic standing must not be sacrificed.

One of the most salient characteristics of the on-campus and off-campus work opportunity programs is the diversity of areas of work, ranging from entry positions to progressively higher levels of assignment, providing experiential value as well as offering a means of acquiring college degrees in the chosen field.

HARVARD UNIVERSITY, CAMBRIDGE, MASSACHUSETTS

The Student Employment Program of Harvard University has been developed as a result of the commitment of college officials to the thesis that no candidate should be denied admission because of a lack of financial resources. The faculty and administration of the university have consistently made every effort to break down jobs into small segments of time, on schedules and at rates of pay attractive to students.

Because the program has received its stimulus from the financial need of the students, effort has been made to meet the requirements and desires of the individual, resulting in a great variety of opportunities. Representatives of the university have designed programs to provide training in skills and have sought intellectually stimulating work. Education of the students in the process of job hunting, in the evaluation of their goals and abilities, and in their responsibilities to employers is provided through interviews, literature, and seminars.

The Student Employment Office of Harvard University is part of the Financial Aid and Admission Programs. As a result, the work plan is utilized fully as an asset to both programs. Some five hundred incoming freshmen each year are granted "assured jobs" as part of the determination of their total awards. These jobs may be offered in conjunction with scholarships and loans, or they may be offered as an alternative. No student is required to accept a job in order to receive a scholarship. Each year, three to four hundred incoming freshmen elect to work during the academic year for an average of ten hours per week.

To provide proper counseling, as well as to secure the widest possible choice of jobs, the office works closely with others within the college, including the Dean's Office, Personnel Office, Placement Office, Bureau of Study Counsel, and many service offices. The underlying purpose is to bring as many faculty and administrative members into contact with the students as is possible.

The Harvard Student Employment Program operates during the regular academic year and during the summer session. During 1966 some two thousand students, or approximately 38 percent of the undergraduates worked during the academic year. Some four thousand students are making use of the summer employment program. Earnings of the students are approximately $800,000 during the academic year and approximately $2.1 million during the summer.

Major sources of employment are work assignments in the dining halls and libraries and on dormitory crews during the academic year. Although smaller in number of students participating, the Harvard Agencies, Inc., and the Faculty Aide Program provide particularly stimulating work for students. Others who prefer to work by accepting one-time-only jobs are assisted in Casual Work through the office. The College Work-Study Program, in which the university is participating is being incorporated to provide "seed money" to encourage departments of the university, as well as nonprofit organizations in the community, to offer intellectually challenging work in the student's field of concentration or related to his career interests. This program is also being used to seek jobs which involve skill development and training wherever possible. It will be used in large part to provide summer jobs, especially to incoming students and to sophomores who most need help.

Studies at Harvard have demonstrated that the majority of students can work, and that with proper guidance they may also participate in extracurricular activities, without jeopardizing academic goals. It is noteworthy that two of the Rhodes Scholars as well as the First Marshall of the class (also the basketball captain), the stroke on the Varsity Crew, and the number one man on the Varsity Golf Team, among others, held major work responsibilities in the program of the Harvard Student Agencies, Inc.

Students are able to carry out heavy academic commitments and also work because considerable effort is made to assist them in planning sensible schedules and in finding work which meets the demands of the individual concerned.

There is a continuous searching to discover talents and hobbies and to provide training in skills which are marketable. As a result of the effort to find a sufficient variety of opportunities to match the needs of the students, the program has developed a careful exploration of students avocations and capabilities and a means of reading the market for such skills. A student who ground his own telescope lens was placed in contact with offices which could use his inventiveness and ability. Musicians, magicians, and puppeteers have been made available to alumni and members of the community seeking entertainers for adults' and children's parties. Photographers find opportunities in the News Office, writers are utilized in the Publicity Office, and athletes are welcomed in boys' clubs and settlement houses.

Frequently, students may be offered a rudimentary learning skill or a skill for which their fields prepare them. Thus, a course in waiting on table was developed to assist resorts, and a course in computer programming was provided to aid computer owners. Other courses in such areas as short-order cooking, small engine repair, bookkeeping, office machine operation, programmed learning, waterfront instruction, sailing, program leadership, personal interviewing, and others have been offered. Most important, the student employment officials capitalize upon the student's invaluable asset—his ability to learn quickly.

The Harvard Student Agencies, Inc. (HSA) evolved from a search in the 1950's for better jobs for students. They sought better jobs in terms of higher rates of return per hour of effort and better results in terms of more flexible hourly, weekly, and seasonal work schedules.

It was not difficult to foresee that sales work provided substantial potential if students could be encouraged to experiment in this merchandising area. Entrepreneurs had historically sold beer mugs, class rings, and magazine subscriptions. The HSA was an organized effort to provide capital, facilities, and encouragement for students to create and to develop small businesses as a source of self-help. Since 1957, it has provided some $850,000 in earnings to students, contains twenty-three small businesses, and involves over three hundred students each year. Currently (1966), sales exceed $1,250,000 per year, and earnings to students range from $120,000 to $130,000 per year, and the returns are expected to continue to grow. Among the more exciting small businesses are the *Student Guide to Europe* and the Information Gathering Service.

The *Student Guide to Europe* is written, published, and distributed on an international basis, with 50,000 copies produced by students each year. It has a staff of ten to twelve editors who travel abroad, collecting European data as the basis on which the book is written. Other members of the twenty-five man staff sell advertising in New York; arrange distribution nationally and overseas, including orders requested from South Africa and Australia; do cartooning and cover designs, and perform layout work. Also, they handle shipping and do their own accounting and billing.

The Information Gathering Service (IGS) provides student researchers in the range of disciplines available in the university, extending from undergraduate economics to advanced physics. Because library detail and other forms of research are of interest to students and because their work is often in their fields of concentration, the most able students in the university are happy to participate. Since most firms cannot maintain personnel possessing the range of experience available to a university, it is not surprising that businesses are willing to pay a high hourly rate for this service. Thus, both undergraduate and graduate students are employed on projects ranging from the state of the art studies in plastics chemistry to legal research, translating, and consumer studies.

The Information Gathering Service was initiated by a group of students in 1962, and it has now grown to a point where some hundred students are involved in projects in 1966. During the fiscal year, the participants will earn more than $20,000.

A major element in the development of the program has been through publicity given to the jobs available to students, and equally, the listing of the abilities and skills of students available to industry. In addition to posting jobs in all appropriate offices, a full page in the student calendar is devoted weekly throughout the year to advertising jobs, announcing seminars and skill courses, and providing general advide.

It is also standard practice to provide pamphlets and even individual resumés to a wide range of potential employers each year to acquaint them with the kinds of skills and talents which they may be able to secure through the office. Basically, the program could be characterized as one which attempts to create and to sell new kinds of employment to students and attempts to promote better understanding of the extensive range of student skills available to employers.

KANSAS STATE UNIVERSITY, MANHATTAN, KANSAS

Totality of financial assistance services is afforded in Kansas State University as provided by the Office of Aids, Awards, and Veterans' Service. The university listed approximately eleven thousand students during the academic year 1966–67, and statistical analyses show that more than 25 percent of the university students were employed in the College Work-Study or in the regular institutional part-time work programs.

Officials of the university anticipated that the total institutional fund expenditure for the student payroll in the 1967–68 fiscal year will involve approximately $1 million, an increase over the previous year's expenditure of $850,000. Included in the overall financial aid services of the university are scholarships, loans, part-time on-campus employment placement funded by the university, the College Work-Study Program, and Veterans' services.

A survey recently conducted by the university staff indicated that 40 percent of the male students and 30 percent of the female students were employed at some period of the academic year. Such a substantial proportion of part-time employees is an endorsement of the philosophy of the institution that meaningful work is not only a financial aid but also a valuable supplement to education in its true sense. Administrators emphasize that education should be not only academic training, but experiential, as well.

A unique feature of the financial assistance office is the provision of all administration of Federal programs available to veterans. Recent legislation offers benefits to all qualified veterans who have served since 1955. Such a program grants the opportunity of higher education to all who can certify and benefit from academic programs. It is the logical approach to include Veterans' Service in the total financial aids program, since the men and women discharged from service will return in great numbers to campuses across the country.

Definitive procedures are performed in determining the true need of a student applicant requesting financial assistance. The College Scholarship Services are utilized for Education Opportunity Grants, followed by the university's individual verification of requirements of need for other programs. The Economic Opportunity Grant recipients are documented as to status and reviewed periodically as to authenticity. In addition, the Office of Aids, Awards, and Veterans' Services verifies students' financial qualifications each year for students participating in the College Work-Study. The minimum payroll rate is $1.00 for entry positions on regular campus employment with no top-wage limit established, except that the College Dean's approval must be obtained to pay in excess of $1.50 per hour. Some student workers can earn as much as $3.50 hourly; such employees may be either undergraduate or graduate students, but they will normally possess meaningful experience or skills. The College Work-Study wage rate, in 1967, is established at $1.25, in conformity with federal regulations.

Although it is necessary that priority be given, especially in the College Work-Study Program, to the needy, capable student, it is the belief of the AAVS staff that the educational value of work can almost take precedence over some need. It is the tenet of the Office of Financial Assistance that no student, insofar as is possible, should be denied the experience of meaningful employment. Further, it is the philosophy of the staff not to state decisively that freshmen should be discouraged from performing part-time work. Rather, it is a philosophy of the staff to encourage working as an occasional change from studies.

A research study, not as yet fully completed, is illustrative of the case in point. A sampling was made of first-year freshmen who received $200, based upon financial need. A check was made to determine how many of them worked during the period from October to January, on regular student work assignments of ten hours or more per week. The object of the survey was the determination of demand on their time during a prescribed period. The group surveyed had comparable American College Test scorings, similar high school standing, and equivalent hours of completed university study. This grouping was matched with students of equated characteristics who received aid but were not employed. The intent of the study is to analyze a grade comparison to determine whether work is a hindrance to academic achievement. The research work involved forty-six matching pairs, and initial results indicate that working has no significant effect upon scholastic performance.

The Office of Aids, Awards, and Veterans' Services has a genuine concern for the needy, capable student and also for those who have no actual requirement for financial assistance but are motivated to work for the experiential values accrued. However, it is the philosophy of the office that differentiation must be defined between basic and acquired needs. Foremost in fund planning and allocation is meeting the true requirements of students at Kansas State University. Such provisions are available under the well-organized and articulated program of financial assistance.

THE UNIVERSITY OF KENTUCKY, LEXINGTON, KENTUCKY

The University of Kentucky and the eight Community Colleges under its direction enroll some twenty-thousand students, with approximately fourteen thousand in Lexington and six thousand-plus in the institutional centers. Nearly 25 percent of the students in Lexington are employed at some time during the academic year and earn approximately $504,000.

The system of university student employment is established on an essentially cooperative basis. Individual colleges and departments are permitted to hire and to set the rates of pay for students but are encouraged to employ only those who have been referred by the Financial Aids Administration Office personnel. Thus far, excellent cooperation is in evidence. Until fairly recently, there was no centralized unit of student employment in the University of Kentucky, and the financial services operation was conducted by the Office of the Dean of Women and the Young Men's Christian Association. In February 1964, coordinated efforts were made to organize disparate departments and to unify the service.

Excellent counseling services are now provided for students seeking part-time employment, and interviews are arranged with office personnel and applicants to determine the extent of financial need. The students are rated in terms of A, great need; B, some help; and C, not a great need, but the applicants wish some work experience. The philosophy of the Financial Aids Administration is that all students can benefit greatly from practical work situations, particularly so when the employment is related to the academic interests of the individuals concerned.

The scholarship program was not well defined until 1961 since prior to that time there was no central office of evaluation. During the 1966–67 school year, however, nearly 350 scholarships are to be awarded upon the recommendation of an advisory committee and an evaluation of applicants by the Financial Aids staff.

There is no actual provision of the cooperative type of work program as a recognized component of the overall program of financial assistance. The length of time required for cooperative work is the actual reason that it is not an active part of the total function. However, engineering students can assist in industry, and science majors can be employed with area firms on a part-time basis during the academic year, or full time in vacation periods. The University of Kentucky, located in a community of some 125,000 residents affords opportunities for such employment which the students can obtain independently. The off-campus worker can also find part-time employment in areas such as the City Recreational Department. Information is kept current concerning vacation resorts, national parks, and other seasonal work opportunities.

The federal College Work-Study Program provided employment for some five hundred students during the academic year 1966–67. In this particular assistance program, there is a rigid adherence to the standards of eligibility for work and to the number of hours which a student can be employed, with the limitation set at fifteen hours per week.

Certification of the eligibility of the student to receive grants and aids is defined by the Financial Aids personnel, but there are exceptions in special grants in such areas as music and arts, where departmental standards are set. The scholarship program receives no funds from the state, and until 1963 funds from alumni, friends of the university, and business supplied the necessary financing for the establishing of scholarships. The Financial Aids Administration enforces the policy that a student should not receive more than one scholarship. Over 1,500 loans are made annually, with more than $2 million in all types of financial aid administered by the Office of the Financial Aids Administration.

Until 1962, scholarships were not distributed from a centralized agency, nor was there a clear-cut definition of those available. More than 300 scholarships are currently listed and allocated by set policies and procedures, with an advisory committee assisting the Financial Aids personnel in determining the recipients of such awards, as well as those receiving grants and aids. The eligibility of the student must be duly authorized before such financial assistance is granted. The significance of the College Work-Study Program in the University of Kentucky is noted in that more students receive assistance in this division of financial aid than they do from grants.

Approximately $825,000 was administered during the 1966–67 academic year by the loan program. The scope of the loan services, however, does not appreciably affect the operation of the student work program. Some loan allocations can extend to $2,500, in instances where the need is urgent and the student is deemed capable of maintaining good scholastic progress.

The Financial Aids Administration staffs six administrators, six part-time employees, and five full-time secretaries to conduct a comprehensive program of assistance. It is anticipated that the Office of Financial Aids Administration will be able to assure any qualified student a definite fund program in terms of employment in specified hours at determined rates of remuneration, as well as in reference to the established program of loans, scholarships, and grants. It is further hopefully predicted that there will be expansion in the area of scholarship and loans, with the assistance of the state legislature, contributing to the overall program operation.

THE UNIVERSITY OF MISSOURI, COLUMBIA, MISSOURI

One of the salient points in the philosophy of the University of Missouri is summarized in the brief statement, "We believe in freedom of truth, not merely in freedom of speech." It follows that rules and regulations are prescribed and adopted by the faculty and students of the university; however, such limitations are not narrow or archaic. Rather, the policies provide a framework for the pursuit of truth, which structures the procedures of the institution.

Emphasizing this basic principle is the provision of equal opportunity for any qualified student who wishes to further his education in the University of Missouri. A very comprehensive program of financial aids and part-time employment is established, offering diversified forms of assistance to the academically capable, needy applicants.

The College Work-Study is an important element in the total program of financial assistance in the University of Missouri, with some 550 students participating in the service. In addition, grants totaled approximately $430,000 for the academic year of 1966–67. It was anticipated that this sum would be increased appreciably during the subsequent year, with nearly $330,000 allocated for the first half of the twelve-month academic period.

The off-campus division of the College Work-Study Program is well developed, with approximately 90 different cooperating units under the supervision of the Office of Student Work. The work projects are established throughout 114 counties of the state, consolidating some of the separate counties into districts for efficient administration. Contact is made with area high schools to determine the number of deserving and financially needy students. Further, it is the intent to deal with true need as such and not to consider merely the listings of students in terms of quotas per county. In some sections of the state, the financially needy student is often in an area where virtually everyone is as lacking in funds as he is. It is possible to arrange summer employment for a high school graduate under the provisions of the university program and enable him to earn hourly wages ranging from $1.25 to $1.50. In such circumstances, it is possible for the employee to enter the university fall session with approximately $300 realized through vacation period savings. Not only does this function reward the needy student in terms of financial assistance, but it adds greatly to his maturity and self-reliance. The program entails much time and genuine work on the part of the Financial Aids personnel, but it has proved to be one of the most successful divisions of the overall service.

On the average, 20 to 25 percent of the student body, 17,500 in the 1967–68 enrollment, are employed on a part-time basis during the school year. In addition to the students on assistantship appointments, the departmental units of the University of Missouri employ some thousand students on the regular departmental hourly rolls. Although these assignments are not directly under the Student Financial Aid Office, there is close cooperation. The Aid office helps the departments to locate good workers, and the departments provide lists of available jobs for worthy students. The Aid Office, with its Work-Study funds, has an additional allotment of approximately $200,000 of university funds to insure its ability to provide work assignments to a thousand needy students, in addition to those hired by the departments. After the students are selected and promised jobs, they are assigned to work where needed throughout the university—in libraries, classrooms, laboratories, cafeterias, offices, clinics, farms, research, and general services.

Included as provisions of the total services of the Office of Student Financial Aids are National Defense Education Act Loans, amounting to nearly $800,000, and Educational Opportunity Grants issued in the sum of approximately $200,000. Guaranteed Loans are also provided, and this service is functioning well regarding collection repayments. Financial Aids officials determine the extent of true financial need of the applicant, whether he requires several or all of the resources available, and individual package programs are designed to conform to actual requirements.

In evaluating the extent of financial requirements of individual students, the services of the College Scholarship Board are utilized initially, in combination with the university's alternate income form, determining the monetary need based upon the family income, size of the family, and the number of actual dependents. Evaluations of the true need of the student are made annually to determine if the financial requirements are at the same level as in the preceding period. If necessary, the student is offered a loan, subject to final approval. If he requires a National Defense Education Act loan, it is approved in the Financial Aids Office and verification is sent to the Purchasing Office.

Monthly records are maintained concerning the National Defense Education Act student loans, on an individual and a cumulative basis. With the indexed system, it is possible to determine the current standing of any student or ex-student of the university. Now, 1967–68, $484,000 is on lending basis, with a first semester balance of repayments of $131,000, and the total of the Note Revolving Fund at approximately $4 million. Accordingly, an accurate picture is available concerning note repayment. During the academic year 1966–67, some forty-eight hundred individual students borrowed amounts, averaging less than $600 per loan.

Permanent records are on file for ready reference in all aspects of the various divisions of the financial assistance program. Every working student is represented on the monthly sheet issued in a code, indicating the location of the work assignment, and a master card system is maintained listing the total hours of employment performed. Student payroll checks are issued monthly at the present time, but it is anticipated that wages will be paid on a bi-weekly payroll in the near future.

The total amount of student employment expenditures was approximately one and one-third million dollars during the academic year 1966–67, the range of wages paid during this period falling between $1.10 and $1.75, to be increased from $1.25, minimum pay, to $1.85 in 1967–68. These figures do not include students on part-time appointments as assistants on the graduate level.

The other campuses of the University of Missouri share equally in the totality of the financial assistance programs, including the campuses in Kansas City, Rolla, and St. Louis. The individualized work programs in these areas operate separate programs, not centralized by the Columbia campus of the University of Missouri. Equally, the loan programs are under the direct control of the individual campuses, with supervision provided by separate chancellors as chief administrative officers.

Although it is difficult to set an arbitrary sum as that which is necessary to attend the University of Missouri, a general figure of $1,600 to $1,800 per year is set as meeting these financial requirements. In summary, fees cost $350; room and board, $850; books and supplies, $125, and personal expenses from $275 to $475, yearly. In review, financial aids offer Curators' waiver-of-fees, the Educational Opportunity Grant, scholarships, part-time employment in College Work-study and student labor, and loans in National Defense, University of Missouri lending, Health Professions Nursing Loans, and Insured Bank Loans.

The University of Missouri proposes to provide the finest educational opportunities possible for all qualified students who can benefit from the facilities of higher education. In the event that a capable student cannot summon resources required to meet university expenses, the financial aids office of the university is most willing to set up means to offset the lack in such funding. A true consideration for the individual and his particular needs is shown in the series of interviews and counseling sessions, and the financial aid that is available from a combination of resources, tailored to specific circumstances.

The Office of Student Financial Aids, Housing, Admissions, and the Cashier's departments are all grouped together in a central building, constituting a cluster of essential services for students of the University of Missouri. The financial assistance provided by the institution serves as a great channel of opportunity to the attaining of higher education. If there were no such well-articulated program of assistance, many capable youths would be denied academic benefits, merely because of limited financial resources. Particularly, the university underscores the worth of work, believing that part-time employment is simultaneously educational, per se, as well as financially beneficial.

THE UNIVERSITY OF NEW MEXICO, ALBUQUERQUE, NEW MEXICO

Centralization of financial services is afforded to students in the University of New Mexico through the auspices of the Student Aids Office of the institution. Scholarships and grants have long been included in the planning of administrative officials, but the student employment division is virtually an emerging service, truly organized in structure only since 1965. The pressing need for such a well-designed program is evident in that one-third to one-fourth of the student body are participants in the total employment program of the school. In addition, there is a preponderance of bilingual students in attendance, constituting an urgent need for counseling and appropriate placement of students in College Work-Study Programs since the great majority of this group come from families of low income.

It is anticipated that in the near future the program provided by the Student Aids Office of the institution will direct all phases of student work, including intake interviewing, referral, and assignment. At present (1967–68), allocations for employment are being made by the central administration to the various departments of the university; however, fund listings are maintained to avoid any possible inequities in disbursement. The individual departments receive a stipulated sum and can individually determine the number of students who can be employed partially under the provisions made.

Of real significance in the overall program of student assistance in the University of New Mexico is the scholarship program, affording some $190,000 awarded by the school and approximately $150,000 in scholarships from additional sources, including private and industrial donors. The total figure for aids and awards exceeds $465,000; in addition, $236,000 is provided by the Economic Opportunity Grant Program.

The emphasis being given to the federal Work-Study Program is readily visible in comparing the initial number of participants, thirty-two, underwritten by a fund of $2,800, with the present figure of six hundred students, supported by $465,000; these are part-time employees in full-time attendance in the university. Such an expansion in program development attests to the efficiency and merit of the national program, as administered by the University of New Mexico.

The National Defense Student Loan has achieved marked success in operation, with a mere 2½ percent deficit in collections. Such a repayment of borrowed funds is most commendable and reflects well upon the integrity of students requiring sizeable loans.

During the academic year of 1966–67, the student enrollment was approximately thirteen thousand, including some three to four hundred foreign registrants. Because of its desirable geographical setting, the University of New Mexico attracts many students from widely dispersed areas of the country. An additional incentive for applicants lies in the fact that Albuquerque is an established center of culture, particularly in the literary and fine arts fields.

In order to acclimate the first year student to university life, officials do not emphasize a great deal of employment for freshmen. Necessarily, many students will urgently require part-time work to meet academic and living expenses; however, university officials feel that there should, ideally, be a brief transitional period, permitting the new student to adjust to a campus milieu.

Student Aid Officials anticipate that in the near future, a time block of working hours can be established for the student, permitting him definite, free time for employment scheduled about his course of studies. The major barrier to setting up such particular sections of working time is the relatively few evening classes provided. Most of the late sessions are community college courses, not applicable to the general university curricula.

The Student Aids Office is concerned with the student as an individual, and it does not restrict services to areas of financial assistance alone. At times, students are advised to complete remedial courses in order to perform successfully on the university level. In many instances, bilingual students are not truly prepared for higher education although they have potentialities for successfully completing a college degree. Of paramount importance in the overall function of the office is consultation and advisement. Frequently, students are requested to report to counselors to determine if part-time work is adversely affecting academic standing. If it appears that the combination of work and study is too great a burden, officials will recommend a temporary removal from the employment program. However, students are not peremptorily taken from the work program; customarily, at least one month's notice is given before dismissal from assignment.

It is the present intention of the university not to expand the College Work-Study beyond the limit of one thousand students. At this level, officials believe that the service can function at peak efficiency, with due consideration for the individuals concerned.

The Student Aids Office maintains time sheets of student work performed and check listings, permitting the university to deposit checks directly in the bank of the student's choice. All payrolls and work sheets are prepared in the Student Aids Office and audited, providing for continuity of program direction. The 1967–68 hourly rate of student wages ranges from $1.25 to $3.00, with $1.25 to $1.75 as the average scale.

The Office of Student Aids is considering the advisability of including a cooperative program as a portion of the total employment picture. However, such a program demands a larger staff than is presently employed by the university. There are real potentialities and advantages in such a project, including the opportunities with the Land Management Section which could offer meaningful work experiences. The summer session of the 1967–68 school year provides for only an eight-week session, and the contemplated cooperative program virtually demands a trimester or four-quarter academic year.

During the period of 1966–67, the total amount of money expended in the overall operation of student employment was approximately $1,500,000, excluding graduate assistants but providing work opportunities for qualified graduate student workers. The urban location of the campus also permits part-time job opportunities, ranging from semiskilled to near-professional levels of proficiencies. Although the staff of the Student Aids Office is limited, its efficiency is evident in the steady growth and expansion of service to deserving and willing students, as well as in its provision of qualified part-time workers who perform valuable assignments in departmental and divisional units of the University of New Mexico.

NORTHERN ARIZONA UNIVERSITY,
FLAGSTAFF, ARIZONA

A salient characteristic of Northern Arizona University in Flagstaff, Arizona, is its dynamic and spiraling enrollment. During the academic year of 1966–67, there are approximately six thousand students enrolled, and institutional officials project that there will be seven thousand-plus freshmen and upperclassmen on campus in September 1967. Statistics show that Northern Arizona University is a rapidly growing school, percentage-wise. It is estimated that the enrollment figure will range between eleven and twelve thousand within the next five years. Judicious planning and wise administration of funds are requisites for such an ever-enlarging student population. Undergirding the academic programming is a supportive platform of monetary assistance, administered by the Office of Student Financial

Aid, providing needy, capable students with the means of acquiring a higher education.

Since approximately 90 percent of the student body comes from the Southwest, particular emphasis is given toward meeting the requirements of the area residents. One of the major concerns if fulfilling the needs of the bilingual students, particularly those of Indian and Spanish-American nationalities. Such a student frequently has considerable difficulty during the first year of university study in becoming acclimated to the institution. At times, these constitute a marginal risk in academic success unless they receive considerable assistance and counseling. Although the students possess good academic potentialities, skills in communication often need to be developed and improved. In recognition of the real problems encountered by many of the students, limited or remedial English courses are provided to help them correct their deficiencies.

In the 1966–67 academic year, Northern Arizona University directs a Student Financial Aid Program of approximately $1.3 million including part-time work, grants, loans, scholarships, and federal Work-Study. This sum does not include graduate assistants, undergraduate assistants, or recipients of music and athletic awards. Also, many students are employed in off-campus positions, and the U.S. Forestry Service, U.S. Geologic Survey, Job Corps, U.S. National Park Service, and State Museum cooperate with the institution in offering employment to qualified applicants. Commercially operated services such as food service and book stores provide job opportunities for on-campus entry positions. Excellent cooperation is maintained with departmental offices of the university, and, whenever feasible, students are placed in positions with instructional divisinos which relate to their major fields of academic interest.

The need for financial assistance looms large, considering that upwards of 75 percent of the student body comes from areas listed and defined as poverty pockets. The overall expense of attending Northern Arizona University is estimated at $1,600-plus, and the housing and board facilities are comparable in cost to that in metropolitan areas. It is evident that if a full package of assistance is not made available to applicants, the lack of resources will force some students from the university for purely economic reasons. One of the primary concerns of the Office of Student Financial Aid is the advisement of the probable financial drop-out, as well as the apparent academic failure. Future plans for the improvement of services include the development of additional educational programs for needy individuals, helping them learn essential, meaningful skills while acquiring a college degree.

A well-constructed program of Student Financial Aid is being built by the administrative staff. In the academic year 1967–68, a profile of students will be designed, including in the analysis the gross family income, the number of siblings, and the source of income, applicable to all student workers, not merely to the participants in the federal Work-Study Program. Data will be processed by computer systems, providing comprehensive records of personal data and work assignments, filed for ready reference.

It is believed that a genuine service can be brought to the offices of financial aids in Arizona's institutions of higher education through the consolidation of functions, the addition of expanded funding, and the extension of work opportunities in institutional works. With the construction of systematized application forms, common application dates, single procedure for establishing need, the universities and colleges can be in general agreement in policy throughout the state.

In the planning stage are a series of seminars for the training of counselors in the area of financial assistance; such would be a most worthwhile adjunct to the overall growth and building principles of higher education. In view of the fact that the junior college development is in its initial stage of growth and virtually certain to expand, a state-wide financial program is essential. Statistics indicate that 10 to 15 percent of the projected enrollment will be registered in junior colleges within the next ten years. At the present time in Arizona, less than 1 percent of the student population attended such two-year colleges.

Many avenues of financial assistance are available in Northern Arizona University, including the federal Work-Study, Economic Opportunity Grants, National Defense Student Loans, United Student Aid Fund sponsored Guaranteed Loans, the institution's student employment program, and off-campus work. The hourly rate of pay ranges from $1.25 to $3.00 for undergraduate students in on-campus positions under the Work-Study, or hourly-pay programs with the average wage approximately $1.35 per hour.

It is the philosophy of the university that work is one of the best means, if indeed not the best, of assisting needy, capable students. Through such employment experience it is contended that the student can gain experientially as well as materially, furthering his maturity and self-reliance. All applicants who use the service of the Office of Student Financial Aid are interviewed, and their needs and deficiencies, as well as their skills and resources, carefully evaluated.

Northern Arizona University is genuinely concerned about the individual student and his particular needs. It is the thinking of the institutional officials that cluster campuses are a promising solution in meeting the educational needs of today's students. Although many universities propose to expand to an enrollment of twenty thousand-plus students in the near future, Northern Arizona University would elect the construction of smaller institutional divisions, centering around the existing campus.

Plans for expansion of academic services and financial assistance in Northern Arizona University include five campus centers of approximately three thousand students in each of the divisions. All of the areas will be allied to the central university, but each will maintain individual faculties and staff. Such a cluster campus approach will obviate the many difficulties inherent in a university of great dimensions and maintain the ready communication between the faculty and the student body. Purposely, the faculty-student ratio is kept low, on an 18 to 1 basis.

Accordingly, there is opportunity for much assistance to the individual student in the classroom. In addition, many extra-class hours are given by the faculty and staff in valuable counseling and help sessions. A university of large enrollment cannot feasibly provide for an emphasis of individual consideration and attention. Concern for the educational and maturative growth of the student is basic to the principles of Northern Arizona University and is reflected in the operation of the Office of Student Financial Aid of the institution.

THE UNIVERSITY OF OKLAHOMA, NORMAN, OKLAHOMA

A diversified program of financial aids is provided by the University of Oklahoma, offering to qualified, capable students the means of furthering educational goals. A combination of scholarships, both on the undergraduate level and in the graduate school, loans, grants, the federally supported Work-Study Program and the University part-time employment comprise a composite means of financial assistance available to any willing and worthy student. In addition, personal budget counseling is given by Financial Aids Program personnel in recognition of the fact that sound foreplanning can make the graduation of a student more assured. The scope of the overall program of student employment is shown in the total amount of funds allocated during 1965–66, in the sum of approximately $2,050,000, including the hourly payrolls of graduate and undergraduate students and the College Work-Study participants, all participating on a part-time basis while enrolled in the University as full-time students. The enrollment during the 1967–68 academic year is more than 15,500 students.

It is estimated by university officials that at least one-third of the students have been granted financial aid while enrolled in the University of Oklahoma. Evaluation of individual need is determined by the Office of Financial Aids, based upon analyses of the family income, the number of dependents within the parental home, and whether there is family support or if the student is self-dependent for meeting educational expenses.

A program of significance is in the College Work-Study, with some 550 students participating in the program. The average rate of wages for such part-time work is $1.31 per hour, with the average maximum earnings of the undergraduate student fixed at $600 annually, and of the graduate student, at $750. However, the maximum pay rate may rise to $3.00 hourly for skilled or semiprofessional student workers.

Considerable information concerning students on the Work-Study Program is coded for computer processing with permanent data recorded for reference. The work applicants are processed through the Student Employment Office and are referred from there to departmental offices or units for selection. The employing department is responsible for controlling the number of hours which a student may be employed. A letter of authorization is directed to the employing departments, certifying the student's eligibility for employment. When the student is employed, a notice is issued to the accounting office, and the specific job assignment and the maximum earnings which are to be enforced are listed.

The regular university student employment program restricts student work to twenty hours per week, Monday through Friday, with an additional eight hours for weekends during the academic year, or forty hours per week, including weekends, during vacation periods or those times when classes are not in session. Careful attention is given to the rates of pay, the hours of employment, and the academic standing of the student. Workers are paid once a month, but it is anticipated that the 1967–68 payrolls will be issued every two weeks.

In addition to university-supervised student work, there are off-campus employment opportunities within the immediate area for part-time positions. Firms and industries are encouraged to call the Student Employment Office to list job openings, and students may personally call upon business personnel for consideration.

The staff of the Financial Aids Program includes a director, two general counselors, a chief clerk, a part-time counselor, and secretarial-receptionist employees. All students requesting a form of financial assistance are interviewed by personnel of the Financial Aids Office. All pertinent data of financial resources, including the College Scholarship Service, are utilized in determining the extent of aid required on an individual basis.

In addition to National Defense Loans, providing a maximum of $1,000 for undergraduates and $1,800 for professional students per year, Guaranteed Loans, Health Professions Loans, and Nursing Student Loans are handled by the Office of Financial Aids. Emergency loans are also available in small amounts for briefer periods of time.

Scholarships are awarded by the University Scholarship Committee on the evaluation of academic achievement and financial requirements on a general basis, with both freshmen and upperclassmen eligible for consideration. Also, special scholarships are provided in the fields of journalism, music, and athletics, as well as other departmental scholarships for students with specific ability in a particular academic area, and the Will Rogers Memorial Scholarships for handicapped students. Also, scholarships and fellowships are established in nearly every area of graduate study. All of the funding provided for the undergraduate scholarships is allocated each year, and the recipients are carefully selected on the basis of academic potentiality and performance, as well as financial need.

Educational Opportunity Grants are provided for students with great financial need and successful scholastic performance, and such grants are available to both freshmen and upperclassmen.

The cost of attending the University of Oklahoma during the 1967–68 school year is $12.00 per credit hour, or $384 annually for residents of the state. Nonresidents pay $30.00 per credit hour. Housing ranges from $350 per semester to $450 for room and board. Room accommodations alone cost approximately $100 per term. Operating on a semester basis, university expenses are estimated at $1,750 ($2,350 for nonresidents) per year, including tuition, fees, housing, and incidental expenses, as a minimum figure. If it were not for a soundly structured program of financial aids, provided by the University of Oklahoma, many truly capable, ambitious young people would be barred from securing higher education. It is the philosophy of the institution that the college-age generation constitutes the true wealth of our country, and the University of Oklahoma is dedicated to searching out and encouraging such talent to help to insure our national future.

THE UNIVERSITY OF SOUTH FLORIDA, TAMPA, FLORIDA

Part-time student employment with the University of South Florida in Tampa is under the direction of the Placement Services of the Institution. Not only does this office provide assistance to students in obtaining part-time work while enrolled in school, but it also is the centralized Placement Services Office serving graduates and alumni of the university.

Underlying the basic functions of the service is the philosophy of offering the greatest possible assistance to insure that part-time or full-time summer or seasonal employment is available for students requiring work. Whenever possible, the students are referred to positions related to individual career or vocational objectives.

There are three specific categories of student employment as defined by the University of South Florida:
1] On-Campus Employment
    a) College Work-Study Program (CWSP)
    b) Regular Student Assistant Employment
2] Work Scholarship Student Assistants
3] Off-campus Employment
    a) Part-Time
    b) Summer or Seasonal

During the 1965–66 academic year, a total of 843 students were placed in on-campus employment. A total of 98 students were provided with Work-Scholarship assignments. During this same period, a total of 666 off-campus positions were listed with Placement Services. A well-articulated program of financial assistance is administered by the central office of the University of South Florida.

Any student wishing on-campus employment must initially make application for work with the director of Financial Aid. Based upon an evaluation of the student's financial status, the director determines whether the applicant is eligible to participate as a student assistant under the College Work-Study Program or as a regular student assistant. When the need has been defined and approval for employment has been granted, the student is referred to the Placement Services Office.

There is a continuity and cooperative planning in the operation of the university's work program. All colleges of the campus list their job requests and requirements for regular students with the Placement Office. All College Work-Study applicants are referred to the colleges and administrative departments at the beginning of the academic year by the Personnel and Placement Offices. When certified for on-campus work, a staff member of the Placement Office conducts personal job interviews with the students. During the counseling period, evaluation is made concerning the type of work desired, type of skills possessed, major field of study, and future occupational and educational plans. Based upon this information, genuine effort is made to refer a student to a job which best fits the objectives of the applicant. Ideally, the student should work with a department of his major interest; however, if he is not referred to an area relating to his major field, he can, nevertheless, acquire valuable employment training.

There is an hourly rate span ranging from $1.25 to $2.00 for undergraduates and from $2.50 to $5.50 per hour for graduate assistants, with the differentiations based upon college study level, skills, and type of work. An incentive is added in that the students, whether regular or College Work-Study employees, can receive merit increases based upon the recommendation of the supervisor. Academic standards are not sacrificed for the sake of employment, however. Regular student assistants are limited to twenty hours of work per week, and the College Work-Study Program students are restricted to no more than fifteen hours of employment weekly.

Many off-campus employers contact the Placement Office, listing position qualifications, hourly rates, and type of worker desired. The students personally contact the employer and are interviewed by the company personnel. Many companies interview graduating students for full-time employment, as well as recruit them for summer work. Students interested in positions with these firms make appointments for interviews with management representatives through the Placement Services Office.

In addition, deserving students may receive Work-Scholarships, as determined by the Director of Financial Aid. Such a scholarship waives tuition fees, but there is a qualification that a student recipient must work forty-eight hours on campus during the quarter in which the award is given. These job assignments are allocated to the various colleges by the Personnel Office and Placement Services Office. All students awarded Work-Scholarships are interviewed in the Placement Services Office before their referral to an appropriate assignment.

The range of work opportunities is extensive, spanning five general levels, including jobs requiring no specific skills, minor skills, skilled assistance, semiprofessional, and beginning professional. Among the specific assignments are Research Assistants—Laboratory Assistants, Helpers, Library Assistants, Student Instructors in Subject Matter, Classroom Assistants (Graduate Teaching Assistant or Tutor Remedial Instruction), Interviewers and Counselors, Athletic and Recreational Assistants, Technicians, Editorial and Printing, Arts, Crafts, and Related Workers. Skilled work is reserved for the junior, senior, or graduate students. Freshmen and sophomores customarily are assigned to employment in departmental offices or the library.

During the academic year of 1967–68, a total of approximately eleven hundred students are employed on campus under the provisions of the Student Assistant Program, including the College Work-Study Program and the regular assistant division. The enrollment in the University of South Florida is over nine thousand students, and the percentage of students employed under university direction ranges between 12 and 13 percent. The ratio of employed students to the total enrollment figure reflects the efficiency and the detailed operation of the on-campus program, supported and endorsed by the administration and faculty of the University of South Florida.

SOUTHERN ILLINOIS UNIVERSITY, CARBONDALE, ILLINOIS

Southern Illinois University is a multi-campus university with an enrollment of approximately thirty-five thousand students. It is a policy of the administration to allocate as much of the work of the school as can practicably be undertaken by full-time students, employed on a part-time basis. The principle stems from the philosophy of the school that academically capable and financially needy high school graduates should have an opportunity to develop their potentialities in institutions of higher learning, in the best interests of the students and also in the enrichment of our democratic society.

In keeping with the university's philosophy and policies, the student work program serves three major purposes. First, it provides work experience, which is educationally worthwhile for any student, contributing to his maturity and to his development into a productive citizen. Such work experience is, whenever possible, related to the academic program of the student. Second, it provides part-time employment on a priority basis for students with great financial need who are academically capable of working and attending college. The on-campus program is so designed that students with extreme financial need can, although they are not advised to do so, finance their entire college education through employment with the university. Third, to be effective as an educational and financial aid program for the participating students, the work program must also operationally serve the university.

The on-campus student work program has grown from six hundred part-time employees in 1955 to a monthly payroll of some five thousand part-time employees in 1969–70, of which number no less than one thousand are students from low-income families. The latter are participants in the federal government's College Work-Study Program and work a maximum assignment of fifteen hours a week, with the opportunity to work full time during one quarter, three months of the four-quarter academic year. Such an arrangement enables the student to maintain the same academic progress as his fellow class members, while affording him the opportunity to earn additional money. The four-quarter system also offers advantages to the cooperative-education students who are usually off campus in full-time work during one of the four terms, thus allowing a full academic year of study.

Student job diversity extends from unskilled entry jobs to those student work assignments requiring advanced college training. Work opportunities exist for students in virtually every academic, administrative, and service division of the university. More than 200 different on-campus student jobs have been described, coded, and classified in the Southern Illinois Work Program. The student hourly rates range from $1.15 to $2.50 per hour, and the total on-campus expenditures for self-help during the 1969–70 fiscal year will exceed $3 million.

Prior to 1965, the Student Work Program was a separate operation on the Carbondale and the Edwardsville campuses of Southern

Illinois University. Financial Assistance (Scholarships and Loans) was also an individual operation. In August 1965, the programs on both campuses were fused in an all-university operation of Student Work and Financial Assistance. The new organization provides a unified service for students in keeping with individual and institutional needs. Administratively, the office makes maximum use of the multiple programs of financial assistance, including work, loans, and grants sponsored by the United States Office of Education.

A professional staff is responsible for carrying out policies, procedures, coordinating supervision, and providing student counseling. The priority given to guidance and counseling as a functional service is possibly unique in college personnel work. The need for such service stems primarily from four sources: the special problems and pressures which arise from financial circumstances in the cases of needy students; the need of youth to develop skills, understanding, and attitudes toward work in our economic society; the possibility that part-time work will enrich the student's experience and contribute to his overall education; the concern that part-time work may jeopardize the student's academic progress, thus defeating his primary purpose in attending college.

In order to provide maximum service in view of these factors, vocational counselors must have a thorough knowledge of academic programs, as well as experience in appraising the academic potential of students. Counselors must ever be aware of the educational goals of the students and be alert to recognize those specific job situations which offer meaningful work experiences, supplementing the classroom learning. The student job classification plan, which lists some 200 job descriptions, is a useful tool in the hands of our vocational counselors.

Staff personnel of the Office of Student Work and Financial Assistance cooperate with the Office of Student Affairs and the Admissions Office in a precollege counseling program which reaches many of the high schools in the state of Illinois. The Office of Student Work and Financial Assistance also sends counselors to area high schools to work directly with secondary school guidance personnel in a special package program of work, loans, and grants for academically qualified high school graduates from low-income families. This special program is financially supported by funds allocated by the United States Office of Education.

The particular duties delegated to the Student Work Office include the following:

The Office sets the standards and reviews the qualifications of students to determine eligibility for any and all forms of financial assistance (work, loans, scholarships, and grants).

It provides personal interviews for all applicants wishing part-time employment.

The office authorizes the hours of employment and determines the rates of pay for all students employed by the university. It maintains permanent employment records, academic records, and work evaluations for each working student, with the work evaluation becoming a part of the student's placement records.

In addition, the office makes research studies for evaluation purposes and for future development, promotion, and growth of the program. It should be noted that Southern Illinois University has made a number of studies concerning working students and their academic achievements. In all studies conducted, it was found that working students, as a group, achieved as well or better than did the non-working students. The important factor for the student is to maintain a proper balance between the academic class load and the part-time employment assignment. To make certain that student work does not interfere with academic progress, counselors study the weight of the work and the academic loads, and, if necessary, the office may restrict either or both.

The office conducts or sponsors student training programs for the various departments as an aid to supervisors in employing new students and as an orientation to work situations for the students.

The major occupational divisions and groups of the Student Work Program follow.

CLASS I: PREPROFESSIONAL JOBS.   Class I has some 75 separate student jobs where from 750 to 1,000 students work in three major occupational groups: Group A, Instructional and Related Jobs; Group B, Supervisory Student Jobs; and Group C, Technical and Related Jobs. A common characteristic of this classification is the requirement of a minimum of one or more years of college education. In general, the jobs demand a high degree of mental activity and judgment. Most of the jobs in this category afford the student worker the maximum educational experience attainable from a work situation.

CLASS II: CLERICAL JOBS. Class II has some 60 different jobs where from 1,800 to 2,000 students work in three occupational groups: Group A, Office Jobs; Group B, Library Clerk and Attendant Jobs; and Group C, General Clerk and Operator Jobs.

A common characteristic of this classification is that the minimum educational training needed is usually available in the high school curriculum. Essentially, the jobs in this class require considerable mental activity, manual dexterity, and clerical skills as measured by performance tests. In general, the jobs of the students of Class II are not as closely related to the university's instructional program as are the Preprofessional Jobs in Class I. However, the opportunity to become a proficient clerical worker, from either a vocational or avocational viewpoint, is afforded to a great number of students.

CLASS III: SERVICE JOBS. Within this classification, from 1,500 to 1,700 students find part-time employment in four occupational groups. The subdivisions include Food Service Jobs, General Events Jobs, Maintenance Jobs, and Protective and Security Jobs.

The common characteristic shared within this class is that few jobs, if any, require previous work experience or educational training beyond the high school. Since work experience is not a requirement, a variety of student training programs is used to help in preparing the student workers for their assignments. The jobs in Class III are a very important portion of the overall student work program. First, they provide an opportunity for the student in need of financial assistance to earn money. Second, they teach the inexperienced worker how to serve with and for others. Third, the large number of students employed in this class gives the high school graduate some assurance that he can be placed. Fourth, work experience in Class III is a basic preparation for promotion to career-oriented jobs.

CLASS IV: PRESKILLED AND SEMISKILLED JOBS. In Class IV, some 300 students are placed in work situations in three occupational groups: Farm and Related, Semiskilled, Printing and Related. Probably the closest approximation to possession of a common trait in Class IV is mechanical aptitude, plus a willingness to exert physical effort.

A preprofessional type of work experience is offered by Southern Illinois University in the Program of Cooperative Education. This division, operating through an arrangement made with numerous companies and Southern Illinois University, permits students to integrate classroom study with practical work experience. Normally, the program will include alternating periods of on-campus study and periods of employment, and it is completed in five calendar years with the awarding of the bachelor's degree.

In essence, the goal of education is the enrichment of the individual and ultimately, the betterment of society. Southern Illinois University seeks to recognize and to emphasize special student capabilities, in addition to providing a sound, basic academic foundation. The student work program is an integral part of the educative process, providing avenues for maturation and self-sufficiency, requisites for the truly well-educated citizen.

The student work program sets as its objectives the following:

1] To develop skills, relating the work experience to the educational program as often as is feasible, that is, to assign the working student to a job which is related to his academic studies.
2] To develop other skills, not necessarily related to the academic program which will enable the student to increase his span of work experience.
3] To encourage the development of good judgment and insight.
4] To promote a desire to be productive, a respect for honest work, and a sense of pride and accomplishment in achieving worthwhile tasks.
5] To develop characteristics of dependability, honesty, and loyalty.
6] To foster the ability to get along well with others and to work cooperatively.
7] To promote a sense of personal responsibility and self-confidence.
8] To encourage the growth of initiative and creativity, and to provide opportunities which may foster leadership.
9] To reward initiative and high-level performance with additional responsibility and remuneration, thus increasing the breadth and the depth of the educational experience for the student.

The foregoing primarily concerns the on-campus job opportunities for students of Southern Illinois University, under the direct control and supervision of the Office of Student Work and Financial

Assistance. We recognize fully the merit of off-campus work also, although such jobs are not directly under the control of the university. However, area employers work closely with the work-office staff in the placement of university students in part-time work. It is significant that some forty-five hundred students are employed outside the university in communities within commuting distance of the school. Also, summer employment in camps, resorts, and cooperative work-study programs with business and industry are important aspects of the student work program.

Although the average earnings of students employed either on or off campus vary considerably, it is not uncommon for upperclass students in technical and skilled jobs to realize between $1,000 and $1,500 annually.

Southern Illinois University believes that the diversity of the student work program swings wide the college doors to those students who are academically capable and willing to exert mind and muscle for the sake of earning a coveted degree.

TUFTS UNIVERSITY, MEDFORD, MASSACHUSETTS

The student employment program at Tufts, a university of some forty-five hundred students in Medford, Massachusetts, performs a well-defined aid service. An integral part of the student financial aid offered to needy students in the 1967–68 school year is composed of guaranteed campus jobs, affording earnings of at least $250 to $450 during the school year. Sums of $150 or $350 taken from the scholarship budget are added to these earnings to form "Work Scholarships," worth $400 or $800 in credit established with the Bursar's Office of the University. Also, various employment services are offered to all students and employers to the extent that they can be provided by the Assistant Director of Financial Aid, a part-time secretary, and a CWSP student.

Until the late 1950's student employment for financial aid purposes at Tufts was not an articulated policy. Each campus employer, the faculty and various office and departmental heads, had individual budgets for student labor. There was no centralized source of referral; rather, student workers frequently assigned their jobs to their friends upon termination of academic work. Wages were low, yielded pin money, and contributed little toward substantial college bills.

To "capture" the departmental student labor funds so that they could be committed in advance to students demonstrating need, the Work Scholarship Program was instituted. The Provost of the University informed all campus employers that vacant student jobs were to be listed with the Financial Aid Office and that preference in selection must be given to those individuals recommended by the office. Needy students who agreed to earn a set sum by working regularly during the school year were promised an additional amount in scholarship funds, which were set aside from the scholarship budget. The combined amount of expected hourly wages plus the scholarship funds was credited in advance to each student's account in the Bursar's Office in anticipation of his earning the required amount.

In accepting a Work Scholarship, each student agrees to work at the time specified by the employer from the Orientation period in September through final examinations in June. Work Scholarship wages are debited monthly to the student's account in the payroll office until he has earned the required amount. If he earns his $250 or $450 before the end of the school year, he is then paid in cash for all subsequent earnings. However, he is expected to continue to work a minimum number of hours each week unless released by his employer. During the academic year 1966–67, a full Work Scholarship of $800, composed of $450 in earnings and $350 in scholarship, required ten to thirteen hours of work per week, depending upon the hourly rate of the individual job.

Both students and departments have endorsed the Work Scholarship Program. In the 1967–68 school year, approximately 250 of 900 undergraduate aid recipients have obtained this form of assistance, usually in combination with a gift scholarship, a loan, or with both forms of aid. A very needy student may receive as much as $3,000 in an academic year; for example, a $1,400 scholarship, an $800 loan, and an $800 Work Scholarship. Turnover of student workers has been radically reduced since the effective wage is over $2.00 an hour and the loss of a job means the loss of both expected earnings and the Work Scholarship itself. Employers are very willing to cooperate in the overall program because they are now provided with well-paid student helpers who have an incentive to work regularly and well throughout the entire school year.

In implementing this Work Scholarship Program, several questions of policy had to be resolved. Should freshmen work? How many hours should students work? Who would supervise the students? Most important, could all, or should all on-campus employment be reserved for financial aid recipients?

Based upon experience with a demanding academic schedule at Tufts, it was decided that most entering freshmen should not contract for regular hours of work every week, at least during the fall semester. Therefore, freshmen are not usually awarded Work Scholarships nor are they recommended for part-time work until advisory grades become available in December. A survey of the claims on student time indicated that most students should not work more than fifteen hours per week while classes are in session. However, there is no absolute prohibition against working more than the necessary number of hours to complete the contract. Of course, students paid under the College Work-Study Program are limited by law to a maximum of fifteen hours weekly while college is in session.

Student supervision of workers is provided in many areas by senior clerical and other hourly personnel. In the food service and the dormitory switchboard areas, students in their junior and senior years schedule and supervise generally the work of almost one hundred undergraduates. Supervision of students by other students has been so successful that additional departmental units have begun to consider the feasibility of student labor management.

The College Work-Study Program (CWSP) proved to be a very large factor in the expansion of student employment at Tufts. Campus employers who were not lured by the Work Scholarship Program now are actively seeking federally subsidized student workers through the Financial Aid Office. CWSP has been integrated without much difficulty with existing employment programs both on and off campus.

For summer employment, local and distant, off-campus agencies have been contacted and contracts written for CWSP jobs. Few off-campus contracts are made during the school year since campus work opportunities are more plentiful. The off-campus agencies require more attention than do other types of campus employment, but the exposure to careers in the social services, together with the impact upon the communities in which these students can be employed, makes the added time and attention worthwhile.

A vital aspect of student employment is the hourly rate of pay designated by a university. The Work Scholarship Program at Tufts in recent years has tended to keep student pay rates from rising since campus employers and University Business Officers considered the scholarship portion as a wage supplement. As the total value of each full Work Scholarship was raised periodically from $500 in 1960 to $800 in 1966, there was no real pressure exerted upon Tufts to increase student wages. Until the spring of 1966, student wages were almost uniformly set in a range from $1.00 to $1.25 per hour.

However, these rates became increasingly out of line with hourly wages in the metropolitan area. The constricted wage span permitted little room to increase the wages of students performing highly skilled work, as compared to those holding unskilled or custodial jobs. Following a thorough study of the situation in Tufts and in nearby institutions, four student-job classifications were established, based upon the degree of skill and experience demanded by the job. The Class A starting wage in 1967 is $1.10 an hour with a maximum rate after raises to $1.25. The job criterion for this classification is that such a position permits the student some time for study after performing required duties.

Class B has a starting rate of $1.25 with a maximum rate after raises of $1.45. In this classification, the student is employed in work which requires little or no previous training or experience. Job tasks are quickly learned and mastered, and most on-campus employment is within this category.

Class C has a starting rate of $1.50 with a maximum rate after raises of $1.75. Students are assigned to an area which requires previous skill and knowledge as well as good work habits. A skilled typist would be assigned a Class C job.

Class D positions start at $1.75, with increments arranged with the Personnel Office up to $3.00 an hour. Such jobs are reserved for those positions demanding semiprofessional or skilled responsibility and may be filled by undergraduate or graduate students. Federal minimum-wage scales will probably push these rates upward within the next five years.

The Work Scholarship, the College Work-Study, and the on-campus part-time jobs are the essential components of the basic aid program of Tufts University. Supplementing this basic core of employment is the off-campus program. During the winter and early spring, many previous employers of Tufts students are contacted to inquire whether openings will be available for the summer period and whether they wish to interview Tufts students for such work. Also, inquiry is made as to the quality of the work performed by the students formerly employed with these firms. The great majority of employers report most favorably concerning the students' past performance.

Students are encouraged to plan for part-time employment during their college careers. Short, non-credit skill courses of two or three weeks' duration are recommended to improve opportunities for employment. Currently being offered at Tufts are typing and shorthand, computer programming, bartending, and waiting on tables. The first three courses are offered by college departments, and the latter two are sponsored by the Financial Aid Office. Ninety percent of the participants in the 1966 course for waiters and waitresses were able to secure good positions in food service industries during the summer. A skill course in salesmanship is under consideration to encourage additional numbers of students to become involved in this remunerative and educational form of employment.

Some educators and business leaders are greatly concerned that the present generation of college students will graduate with little exposure to or knowledge of business activities. Because small businesses can be a good source of student employment, the Tufts Aid Office initiated a Franchise Committee of faculty and students which supervises student-operated campus businesses. These franchises grossed about $80,000 in 1966–67, which included approximately $20,000 in direct student earnings. Included in these twenty businesses were a dry cleaning service, door-to-door sale of sandwiches, stationery, men's clothes, several travel ventures, a student blotter, and a bartending service.

Tufts encourages its students to consider campus and summer employment as more than just a means of assembling funds to pay for an education. At its best, student employment can be an educational experience which is not usually available elsewhere in a university. The campus positions which approach this ideal are usually those of faculty aides and laboratory assistants, franchise operators of small businesses, and student labor managers and their assistants. The goal of Tufts Aid Office is thus to maintain a remunerative employment program which will enable students to enrich their educational experience and assume greater responsibilities during their college careers.

WAYNE STATE UNIVERSITY, DETROIT, MICHIGAN

Wayne State University in Detroit, Michigan, with an enrollment of some twenty thousand full-time students and approximately ten thousand part-time students in the 1965–66 school year, recently conducted a survey which indicated that 75 percent of the student body is employed during the year, either on a part-time or a full-time basis.

There is a continuity of service in the financial assistance programs, with the University Placement Services and the Office of Scholarships and Financial Aid located in the same quarters. The close relationship of the services provides a means of excellent cooperation in combining available financial assistance with part-time employment opportunities. In addition, a favorable rapport has been established with the diversified business firms and industries throughout the metropolitan Detroit area. During the academic year of 1965–66, the University Placement Services Office received requests for part-time help from 2,705 employers. In addition, 1,609 Michigan employers submitted listings for full-time workers.

Students seeking employment are interviewed by a member of the staff of the University Placement Office. Office procedures are explained, and the student is given an opportunity to discuss his needs and career plans. Following the initial interview, he is entitled to return at any time during the school year. He is requested to meet with at least one member of the staff of the Placement Office once a year. However, if he should have no reason for arranging an interview, his registration card is checked for the authenticity of address, class rank, and major field of study concentration.

Permanent files are maintained by the University Personnel Office, recording pertinent information concerning all student employees, including the university personal data card, a withholding tax card, and other measures of certification qualifying students' names to be approved for the school payroll.

Student employment ranges from unskilled jobs to preprofessional and highly skilled on-campus work. The majority of part-time jobs is clerical in nature, but more specialized work in departmental offices and laboratories demanding a degree of skill is also available. The off-campus work opportunities include clerical, sales, tutorial help, as well as listings for specific skills in music, art, accounting, engineering, and science. Because of the urban setting of the university, there is a great demand for factory work, truck driving, and similar nonprofessional jobs, as well as many requests in the odd-jobs categories, such as yard work and house cleaning.

The undergraduate rates of pay with the university range from $1.35 to $2.00 hourly. Graduates may receive wages as high as $3.50 hourly. Necessarily, off-campus rates of pay are approximately the same, with the generally established rate of pay set at a minimum of $1.50 per hour. The University Placement Office recommends that full-time students work no more than twenty hours per week and fewer hours, if possible.

The Director of Scholarships and Financial Aid is charged with the responsibility for the administration of the College Work-Study Program. Following the certification of eligibility to participate in the program, the University Placement Services places accepted applicants and deals with all questions concerning work from either the student or the employer.

In addition to the customary function of the Placement Office, that of aiding graduates and alumni, it actively aids students seeking part-time and full-time work, both on and off campus. The office also serves as a center for summer employment, receiving and providing information in regard to work opportunities, either on a part-time or a full-time basis, during the vacation period.

During the academic year 1965–66, the Placement Office also handled the graduate credential dossiers of approximately three hundred individuals with advanced degrees. Copies of these credentials were issued to the more than 2,500 requests for faculty in collegiate institutions, and to over 100 requests sent in primarily by research organizations.

Although Wayne State University does not emphasize the screening of undergraduate applicants or evaluate on-campus work performance, with the exception of the College Work-Study Program, the significant statistic that three-fourths of the student body is employed during the academic year is noteworthy. There is a wealth of opportunity for self-help in meeting academic expenses, and students are encouraged to supplement their financial resources through employment. Whenever possible, applicants are urged to obtain meaningful work which is related to areas of academic concentration, enriching their overall vocational preparation.

THE UNIVERSITY OF WISCONSIN, MADISON, WISCONSIN

Student employment is an important service in the overall operation of the University of Wisconsin as evidenced by approximately eight hundred students participating in the College Work-Study Program and some forty-four hundred students in regular university part-time work in the 1966–67 academic year. The institution enrolls more than forty thousand students in the university system which consists of two major four-year campuses and nine two-year campuses.

The College Work-Study Program is an integral part of the financial aid program, with the majority of student participants receiving other aid, either in the form of a loan, scholarship, or both. The program is well defined and parallels principles utilized by many large corporations. There is a job classification system, a salary program, and evaluations of the performance of the student workers and their supervisors. Applicants are interviewed in terms of past experience and training, and determination is made of their educational and vocational goals. The Work-Study Office maintains regular payroll records and conducts follow-up surveys and interviews with both students and supervisors. The office also is responsible for approving rate changes for the various jobs.

Administration of the College Work-Study Program is directed centrally by the University Financial Aids Office. Each campus has its own program, but the broad overall policies are applicable in each of the eleven centers.

More than 2,400 individual jobs are listed in the program, and students are employed in nearly every level of occupation, ranging from medical illustrator to laboratory helper. The University of Wisconsin emphasizes the educational relationship of work to areas of academic work and in a number of cases actually changed the major field which the student wished to elect. Initiative is encouraged, and many students have developed independent studies from their Work-Study job. Some students have published papers based upon work performed in their Work-Study assignments.

The majority of Work-Study students is employed on campus for the convenience of the students and the employing departments. However, there are many off-campus work situations which employ students in public and private welfare agencies, such as the YWCA and the Madison Neighborhood Centers, as well as legislative and judicial departments, including the State Legislature and the Madison City Police Department. Many of the employment opportunities afforded by the Work-Study Program have served as steppingstones to full-time positions upon the students' graduation.

Since the summer term of 1966, a cooperate program has evolved which is in force in the University of Wisconsin, the nine state universities, and a number of private colleges within the state. Such a program permits a student who is qualified for a Work-Study job on his own campus to return to his home town and, if a university or college is located there, he may work during the vacation period under the auspices of the local program. He continues to be certified under the Work-Study Program of his own school, but he is under the supervision of the local Work-Study Program during the summer. Each participating school bills the other institution for the amount of money necessary to reimburse its own funds which were paid to the student for summer work. Institutions participate on a unilateral or a reciprocal basis; schools can simply send students to other institutions to be employed or they can accept students from other schools as full-time summer employees. Such an arrangement is most beneficial to the students as greater savings can be realized while living at home with reduced expenses. It is anticipated that this program will be expanded significantly in the future because of its acceptance and success.

The College Work-Study Program is carefully structured and follows prescribed guidelines. The student applicant may request financial aid or he may be considered for only the Work-Study Program. He completes the necessary financial statement and other required forms to provide the counselor with information regarding his work background, interests, and goals. During the interview, the financial aid counselor considers the student for all of the financial aid possibilities. If the applicant qualifies, he will be offered the College Work-Study as a part of his assistance. When the student is certified as being eligible under the financial conditions of the program, careful evaluation of his capabilities is made by the counselor. A determination of the type of work for which the student is best suited is made in terms of his experience, his training, his interests, and ambitions.

When referred for placement, the students frequently have a choice of six or seven jobs. In many instances, above average rates are paid since the work requires skill, initiative, judgment, and responsibility. Because of the careful screening of applicants, the employer usually offers the student the job of his first choice.

Following the student's placement on the job, the Work-Study supervisor watches the work performance of the new employee. Periodic reports are submitted, and the student is invited to come in for an interview during the semester. At this time, a short discussion concerning the job is held. Also, the counselor will review the student's particular financial situation, as to whether the student has sufficient funds, whether a loan may be reduced in size, and if the student's academic progress justifies the awarding of a scholarship in the following semester. Students are given survey questionnaires periodically, requesting them to evaluate their supervisors, their jobs, and the program itself.

The College Work-Study Program is but a small part of the overall student employment program in the University of Wisconsin. However, it is the strongest part of the total program and sets the pace for the rest of the service. Because of the desirability of the jobs, many students who wanted to apply specifically for the College Work-Study Program were most disappointed to learn that they did not qualify for participation on a financial-need basis. Thus, the program has served as a trigger to improve the regular student employment program, being used as a guideline in developing student wages and job classification programs. The regular employment program is not directly assigned to the central Financial Aids Office and departments hire their own students. However, increasing numbers of departments now list jobs with the Office of Student Financial Aids and work closely with the facilities afforded.

A unique feature has been introduced in the area of student work, called a "Guaranteed Job Opportunity" Program. This service was designed and developed to tie in with the Educational Opportunity Grant Program established by the Higher Education Act of 1965. The structure of the program is very similar to that of the College Work-Study, but the jobs are funded by the regular university payroll, with no federal money involved. Departmental acceptance of the new program permitted a listing of job openings to be awarded to incoming freshmen. Although this program demands additional staff time, it is anticipated that an additional five hundred to six hundred students can be assisted by means of a well-supervised, well-organized program.

Students employed with the University of Wisconsin generally can earn $400–$600 during the academic year. Studies conducted in 1967 indicate that the average hourly rate of pay is approximately $1.41 per hour. The beginning rate is $1.25 and the maximum is determined by the level of job complexity.

A survey conducted proved that students who work generally achieve as well, or better, academically than do the non-working students. The study referred to the student who worked ten to twelve hours per week and probably no more than a maximum of fifteen hours. It is the belief of the institution that any excessive hours of work beyond twelve tends to cut into the student's study, social, and recreational time, reducing some other worthwhile experiences which a student should have during his college career.

It is the philosophy of the University of Wisconsin that employment provides one of the best means of financial assistance to students. The student need not burden himself heavily with debts, he gains valuable work experience which can be transferred to future vocations, and in many instances, his time is better organized so that he may better achieve academically.

THE UNIVERSITY OF WISCONSIN-MILWAUKEE, MILWAUKEE, WISCONSIN

In the fall of 1956, the Milwaukee Extension Division of the University of Wisconsin and Wisconsin State College at Milwaukee were merged to establish the University of Wisconsin-Milwaukee. At the time of organization, approximately six thousand students were enrolled. Nine years later, there were nearly thirteen thousand students registered, and the projected enrollment in 1975 is more than twenty-three thousand. In the fall of 1965, approximately 30 percent or four thousand were freshmen.

The history of student employment in the University of Wisconsin-Milwaukee is long established. There have been untold thousands of students who could not attend this institution without the aid of employment. Because of the rapidly increasing educational costs, the University of Wisconsin-Milwaukee recognized the need to increase student employment opportunities to provide financial assistance to a greater number of students.

The philosophy of the Student Employment Program is in harmony with the aims of the university and the objectives of higher education. The program has been designed to assist the financially needy student and to provide work situations which supplement a student's academic study and to parallel his development as a mature, responsible adult. In addition, the program has been planned to provide an employment market for students with varying skills and abilities.

Financially needy students are offered a package of aid, consisting of a combination of a scholarship, grant, loans, or employment opportunity. An aid recipient is not required to hold a job in order to receive other forms of assistance.

Recognizing that the majority of students work part time to supplement limited finances, the Student Employment Program operates as an integral part of the Financial Aids Program. Any student seeking part-time employment is professionally counseled to determine the student's financial need, physical limitations, special problems, skills, interests, and attitudes toward work. In addition, the student is advised of other means of financial assistance which are available to him. The office is well staffed to provide efficient service to students seeking financial aid. The Director of Financial Aids is charged with the administration, organization, and direction of the Student Employment Program. An assistant is responsible for the supervision of the on-campus employment program, the off-campus employment service for area employers, and opportunities for summer work. Another assistant is charged with the supervisory duties of the federal Work-Study Program. The Financial Aids Office, as an administrative unit, is responsible to the Dean of Student Affairs.

The Financial Aids Office depends greatly upon its skilled staff to provide maximum service to job applicants. Any student wishing part-time employment is provided with a personal interview. His qualifications are appraised in respect to the requirements of various job opportunities. The office then serves as a referral agency to direct qualified students to diversified on-campus and off-campus job opportunities.

The Financial Aids Office authorizes only the rates of pay for those students employed under the provisions of the federal Work-Study Program. The wages of all other on-campus employment are regulated by the various departmental supervisors.

Concurrent with making referrals of students to supervisors, counselors canvass the university and area employers to locate job opportunities for certified students. In conference with the campus employer, the counselor may assist in developing a job description for a specific position. From this description, students who have been evaluated and found suitable are referred to the employer for consideration. In an effort to increase the effectiveness of the on-campus Student Employment Program, a close working relationship is established between the Financial Aids Office and the Personnel Office. Through cooperative endeavor, student wages have been made more competitive with Civil Service salaries for comparable work. In addition, hiring standards which parallel Civil Service employment have been developed for part-time student workers.

In the past, students employed on campus were hired without a guarantee of a minimum amount which could be realized in a particular job. However, since the fall of 1966, students employed on campus are guaranteed a minimum amount which can be earned if the student has completed an application for financial assistance, is approved for employment, and has been offered a combination of aid which includes a job opportunity.

A great variety of work opportunities for students is found both on campus and off campus in the university program. The type of work ranges from the relatively unskilled work of laborers to the preprofessional work of instructional assistants and industrial technicians. Some of the unusual areas of off-campus employment include the following: baker's helper, model, school bus driver, undertaker's assistant, key punch operator, computer program assistant, and pizza parlor delivery man. One of the most singular job opportunities to which students were referred was that of a bank messenger, commuting once daily between two local communities. A motorcycle was furnished by the bank, and the messenger was permitted to have the vehicle at his disposal between trips. The fringe benefits included thermal underwear and a crash helmet.

The majority of first-year students are employed on campus in clerical, food service, maintenance, and library jobs. The off-campus job opportunities for freshmen may include clerical duties, general labor, sales, housekeeping, child care, parking attendants, ushers, and delivery clerks. Students possessing special skills and previous experience often have opportunities to secure semiskilled or skilled work.

It is possible for qualified first-year students to find a job with the federal Work-Study Program which is related to their academic majors, but most beginning students do not initially secure work paralleling their area of study concentration. Usually, freshmen are undecided as to their majors, and they lack required skills or previous training. However, freshmen are encouraged to pursue work related to their proposed majors in order to obtain work experience which may qualify them for skilled and semiprofessional work as juniors and seniors.

The pay scales vary according to the type of work and the location of the job. For the freshman student, the on-campus minimum rate is $1.25 per hour and off-campus, $1.00. The rate of wages is determined by the supervisor according to the skills and the previous experience of the student. Satisfactory performance of work entitles a student to minimum increases in hourly rates of pay. Initiative, special skills, and outstanding performance can be rewarded, with the student reaching the maximum rate of pay for his classification within a short period of time.

A first-year student, working a minimum of twelve hours per week, can earn at least $500 during the school year. During the 1965–66 school year, students holding on-campus jobs earned a total of more than $500,000. In December 1966, there were more than 450 students employed on campus and off campus under the federal Work-Study Program.

It is most difficult to determine the total amount of money earned by the students holding off-campus jobs since no payroll records are maintained by the university for such work. In addition, employment is sometimes obtained by the students through direct contact with off-campus employers. However, it is estimated that several million dollars could have been realized by students holding such jobs during the 1965–66 academic year.

The University of Wisconsin-Milwaukee negotiates more than two dozen contracts with off-campus agencies to employ students under the federal Work-Study Program. Among the agencies contacted are the Boy Scouts, Girl Scouts, YWCA, Volunteers of America, Wisconsin State Employment Service, Milwaukee Boys Club, churches, day camps, and community centers.

It is estimated that more than 90 percent of the University of Wisconsin-Milwaukee students will obtain summer work. This includes the students who will continue to hold their present on- and off-campus jobs, as well as those students who will work in new job assignments, and in resorts and summer camps. The university has assisted students to find employment during the summer by inviting industrial representatives to come to the campus to interview students for possible

6 Work Program Research and Experimentation

THE DEGREE of university endorsement of student work programs within institutions varies markedly. There are those institutions in which there is more or less complete endorsement. Some schools simply accept a work program as a part of the total institutional programming with no particular emphasis given to it, while others believe student work programs should be negligible or have no place in the total programming. Obviously, there are variances within and between the three positions stated. As may be assumed, the problems of experimentation and research are fewer in the first category, but still numerous.

The first responsibility of any institution of higher education is to its academic programming. Classes must be taught, and if highly qualified staff members are to be obtained and retained, opportunities for creative work must be afforded. With rapidly increasing student enrollments, particularly in state institutions, there may be little money for other than those imperatives of the staffing of classes and the providing of opportunities for faculty research, regardless of institutional feelings toward the total and/or certain parts of the work program.

Very few, if any, work programs have the staff needed to do the quality and the quantity of experimentation and research which should be performed. The counselor-student-worker ratio is so high that none or little of the counselor's time is available for experimental or research purposes, even if counselors have the ability to do this work. Obviously, it may not be possible because of finances to employ other individuals who could well devote part or all of their time to research or take over counseling duties so that present counselors with research ability could be so assigned on a full-time or a part-time basis. Compounding the problem of staffing, the basic personnel required to maintain adequate student records may not be available because of inadequate financial resources. The latter circumstance seems to be too much of a constant in most universities, as well as within the various other university functions. Another staff problem related to student work lies in providing the supervisory help needed in the various university functions. Not only is more help required in supervising students working part time, because of their increased numbers, but a higher level of supervisory competency is essential. Basically, university understanding of general staffing needs, if experimental and research projects in student work are to be carried on both qualitatively and quantitatively, is at least a first step which may lead to work-program improvement. The next step is to obtain some additional help which may be used for other than routine responsibilities.

It may be appropriate at this time to indicate some of the factors with which employing officials should be concerned as individuals are selected for administrative posts in the student work programs.

Some prior administrative experience on the part of the administrator selected is desirable, but, at the same time, the administrator should be academically oriented. Administration in higher education is not an end in itself, but it is rather a service to the on-going academic programming. Therefore, administrators should have a strong academic background and educational preparation which is respected by members of their academic and nonacademic peer groups. The work program administrator and his assistants should have respect for human dignity and worth. Further, they should have a concern for the welfare of others. They should believe in the dignity of any type of work and that work should be a major part of the lives of adults who are mentally and physically able to participate.

As is true in so many occupations, it is to be hoped that the administrators and other adult participants in a student work program would be willing to work the number of hours necessary to establish and to maintain a good program. On the other hand, the chief administrators should seek additional personnel to the extent needed to make unnecessary the working of employees beyond the "call of duty."

Programs rarely maintain the same quality level; there are tendencies toward either the upgrading or downgrading of standards. The writers believe that if upgrading is to be the program trend, experimentation and evaluation are necessary; therefore, individuals who are experimentally and evaluatively minded, as well as capable in the same areas, should be those considered for employment.

The university must be willing for an experimental approach to be used in student work programming. It must be realized that in student work, as is true in other university endeavors, the starting point for change comes from "educated guesstimates." Errors can and will be made and must be corrected; this studied trial and error approach is an accepted experimental and research approach.

University willingness for experimentation in converting full-time jobs to part-time student jobs, as well as in establishing additional student jobs as the university functions become larger, will be helpful in furnishing an adequate number base for valid research. This willingness to convert full-time help and establish new jobs is sometimes lacking because of the traditional desire, in general, of operating functions to utilize full-time help.

Although considerable research and experimentation was conducted during the National Youth Administration period, 1935–43, in the College Work Program, the ideas, plans, and methods which were under consideration in 1943 seem to have terminated with the program. Also, research productivity in the field of student work since that time is negligible.

Probably a primary reason for the lack of development of more student work opportunities is that greater emphasis is currently being placed upon other forms of financial aid. To illustrate: the National Student Loan Program has given prominence to a form of financial assistance little known twenty years ago. Even more recent is the Guaranteed Loan Program which makes funds available through local banks for qualified students. Another completely new program called the Educational Opportunity makes funds available as outright gifts to students of low-income families. Students in this category must have the academic potential to benefit from higher education. Educational Opportunity Grant Programs are sponsored by the United States Office of Education and become operational in September 1966.

No doubt, the College Work-Study Program, also sponsored by the United States Office of Education, will aid in revitalizing or establishing research and experimentation in the field of student employment.

In this chapter, the authors will give particular emphasis to aspects of student work programming where research and experimentation may be productive. At least we hope that it will stimulate others interested in student welfare and programs of financial assistance to engage actively in projects in their own institutions.

A.

Purposes of Research and Experimentation

1. *To find out more information about the individual in work situations.*

a) TO DETERMINE THE EFFECT OF STUDENT WORK ON ACADEMIC ACHIEVEMENT. In 1940, a nation-wide survey of 64,805 National Youth Administration college and graduate students was conducted concerning their scholastic standing as compared with other students during the 1938–39 academic year. "The study showed that 1] students employed by NYA received, as a group, higher grades than the average of the general student body in 81 percent of the institutions; 2] nearly two-thirds of the NYA students had scholastic averages that placed them in the upper half of the student body; 3] in each of the states and territories, a majority of the NYA college and graduate students had higher scholastic averages than the general student body."[1]

At Southern Illinois University, research studies consistently have shown that students working on campus as an average achieve higher grade point averages than do non-working students.

b) TO DETERMINE OPTIMUM WORK AND ACADEMIC LOADS FOR COLLEGE STUDENTS, i.e., FRESHMEN, SOPHOMORES, JUNIORS, AND SENIORS. It is suggested that institutions carry on studies on their own campuses to determine student work program policy on the minimum and the maximum hours which students can work.

It would benefit both the individual student and groups if there were better answers concerning the number of hours which students can allot to a work program without endangering scholastic achievement. An illustration in point is that often high school and college counselors recommend that incoming college freshmen do not work during their first year in higher education. However, if research does not bear this out as valid, such is poor counseling, especially if the student needs to work to help earn funds to stay in school.

1 Federal Security Agency War Manpower Commission, *Federal Report of the National Youth Administration, Fiscal Years, 1936–43* (Washington, D.C.: Government Printing Office, 1944), p. 75.

c) TO DETERMINE WHAT INFORMATION AND WORK EXPERIENCE BEST RELATES TO THE STUDENT'S ACADEMIC PROGRAM OR CAREER. Too often, students have little or no idea of what they can actually do or want to achieve careerwise in our society. Knowing the general work-experience background and specific work experiences provided in certain areas which helped to enlighten students vocationally, as well as to train them, should be useful in career counseling. Also, there is the need to develop more occupational information and booklets, based at least in part upon research, which show the contributions work experience can make in planning academic careers.

Educators have too long relied almost entirely upon undirected methods as a means for college students to select their careers. Additionally, not only have we provided little or no vocational guidance and counseling for the college student, but we have provided inadequate institutional leadership and training for guidance people who must direct the programs in secondary schools. As documentation of this statement, look at the academic graduate programs for degree candidates as guidance counselors and see how few courses relate to vocational guidance as such.

In higher education in Illinois, the need for vocational guidance and counseling has received some attention in one publication, *Public Higher Education in Illinois*, which states:

> It must be recognized that a large portion of students have vague purposes and naïve concepts of the relationship of college to careers. Self-appraisals by students of their ability to study in such fields as medicine, law, and engineering are frequently unrealistic. This argues for the development of vocational guidance services within the universities.[2]

d) TO KNOW MORE ABOUT HOW STUDENT WORK CONTRIBUTES TO THE MATURITY AND MOTIVATION OF OUR COLLEGE AGE STUDENTS. It has long been recognized in the college classroom that student academic success without motivation is a rarity. It is also known in the academic world that the high rate of college dropouts cannot be attributed in a majority of instances to low academic potential. In other words, many promising students start college, attend perhaps one year or less, and

2   Gilbert Y. Steiner and Romayne Pontleithner, *Public Education in Illinois* (Springfield: Illinois Joint Council on Higher Education, 1961), p. 173.

quit. Why? In checking for reasons, college officials seemingly too often blame insufficient finances for student withdrawal from school.

However, with the present multiple programs of financial assistance now in existence, such an answer calls for more review than was previously required. Actually, it is time to examine more closely our academic programs as well as our students to determine the true causes of college dropouts, and then we must do something constructive about the situation. To illustrate: Dean Herman Schneider of the University of Cincinnati realized more than fifty years ago that the students planning a career in engineering needed far more preparation than was afforded in the classroom. Thus, the concept of cooperative education became a reality. If the classroom and literary resources could not accommodate the learning needs of many young people a half-century ago, think how unrealistic in a parallel situation the academic programs of today must be for a considerable number of our college students.

e) TO DETERMINE THE KINDS OF COUNSELING WHICH WORKING STUDENTS SHOULD HAVE AND WHEN THEY NEED IT. Most of us are aware of the many problems which college students encounter as a result of the pressure of competition in the academic atmosphere. This pressure is especially intense when an improper career is the goal. It does seem that structured counseling methods and techniques could be utilized at least in part in helping the student to solve his individual problems.

For example, abilities and personal characteristics needed for particular jobs, as indicated by employers, could be compared by students with their own abilities and personal characteristics, with the primary aim being that of student selection of careers, according to capabilities.

The degree and intervals of individual counseling also need to be determined.

f) TO DETERMINE HOW MUCH STUDENTS CAN EARN AND HOW IT COMPARES WITH THEIR INDIVIDUAL NEEDS. Obviously, the financial needs of students will vary considerably within and among institutions. For example, if attendance in 300 liberal arts schools of 750 to 1,500 students each costs an average of $2,800 per year for tuition, fees, housing, etc., then how much of this can a given student earn? It seems that an answer to this question would be important to high school counselors in working with the college-bound students who have financial needs.

g) TO DETERMINE THE EFFECTS OF STUDENT WORK EXPERIENCE UPON VOCATIONAL INTERESTS, BOTH BEFORE AND AFTER GRADUATION. If it can be demonstrably shown that student work helps to develop vocational interests and possibly plays an important part in vocational choice, students should have this information when they enroll in an institution. Further, when work experience correlates with the student's academic major, is there a double reinforcement of work and study? Can it be measured?

h) TO DETERMINE THE EFFECTS OF WORK UPON THE STUDENT'S VALUE SYSTEM. An appraisal of the results of employment upon individual philosophies is another purpose of research. When the term "value system" is indicated, it might be general and mean a student's overall value system as an individual in our society, or it could be more specific and refer to the student's attitudes toward employment only. Specifically, how does he feel about working? Does he feel that society is being unkind to him if he has scholarship potential, yet is forced to do unskilled work in order to earn money to finance his education? Does he think that society owes him only an opportunity and that any honest work is a means to his set goal? The preceding questions should be answered even though the authors believe that any worthwhile accomplishment requires dedication, and, at times, deprivation, to reach fruition.

i) TO DETERMINE BETTER WAYS AND MEANS TO EVALUATE WORK SKILLS, ABILITIES, AND ATTITUDES. There is an urgent need to develop additional studies and research, including techniques, determination of better ways and means to evaluate student work skills, abilities, and attitudes. Further work in this area should be beneficial both to the students and to the institution. The readers may find it beneficial to survey what the authors have written in the chapter of this book devoted to student evaluation.

j) TO DETERMINE HOW THE STUDENT EVALUATES HIS WORK EXPERI-
ENCE WHEN A FRESHMAN, SOPHOMORE, JUNIOR, SENIOR, AND AFTER
GRADUATION.   Intensive and widespread studies are needed in the
area of student evaluation to indicate the consistency of evaluation
throughout the course of a student's academic career. As examples:
Does evaluation change or remain somewhat consistent? Is the type
of job a major influencing factor?

2. *To emphasize student work as an institutional operational program.*
a) TO DETERMINE HOW BEST TO USE PART-TIME STUDENT WORKERS
AND FULL-TIME EMPLOYEES IN AN OVERALL EMPLOYMENT OPERATION.
More study and experimentation is needed in decision-making
related to the proportion of the total number of employees to the
number of student employees. Such study and experimentation is required for schools according to size and types of job opportunities. A
review of the present ratios of student workers to supervisors should
be helpful. In addition, according to the type of work performed,
reasoned estimates could be made as to appropriate ratings to be
maintained. The results of experimentation in implementing estimates
could then be used for appropriate upward or downward revisions, if
needed.

b) TO DETERMINE THE EFFECT OF PART-TIME WORK EXPERIENCE UPON
THE STUDENT'S FULL-TIME EMPLOYMENT AFTER GRADUATION.   A
determination of the effect of part-time work experience upon the student's full-time employment after graduation calls for a longitudinal
approach which, in many instances would extend over a considerable
period of time. Follow-up studies of school graduates should be made
in which graduates have been paired by social-economic research and
attitudinal factors, as well as by whether or not they worked while in
school. The results of such research could be most helpful to placement offices as well as to prospective employers.

c) TO DETERMINE WHICH INSTITUTIONAL JOBS SHOULD BE SET ASIDE
FOR STUDENTS.   A decision, related to determining which institutional
jobs should be set aside for students, depends in part on making a
number of studies related to sizes and locations of institutions. Of
course, any determination will depend to a major extent upon the
emphasis to be given to the work program or the proportion of possible

work which a given institution wants to make available to its students. Obviously, institution personnel at the decision-making level must believe in student work if any real progress is to be made in setting aside additional jobs for students.

d) TO APPLY THE PRINCIPLE OF JOB ANALYSES AND WORK ANALYSES TO STUDENTS AND JOBS. Applying the principle of job analyses and work analyses to students and jobs is a continuous operation since job duties and responsibilities are rarely, if ever, constant in any enterprise.

As may be seen, the purpose given is really multiple in nature. Initially, duties and responsibilities invariably change when supervisors are changed. Also, as functions change and grow, duties and responsibilities seem to expand into new areas. It should be pointed out that the initial classification of jobs in an institution with an extensive work program is a long and difficult project.

The latter part of the purpose stated presents another type of analysis. From the individual psychological point of view, a worker analysis is actually a disparate operation. It would appear that a worker analysis could be fruitful since it involves researching the psychological needs and sociological backgrounds of the students, thus increasing our knowledge of human behavior. Since most institutions employ some of their students, it is surprising that their own psychology and sociology departments particularly have not availed themselves of the opportunity to study students at work.

e) TO DETERMINE THE RANGE OF RESPONSIBILITY WHICH CAN BE ASSUMED BY STUDENTS. To determine the range of responsibility which can be assumed by students is difficult because it will vary at least by age group and job. But some guidelines should be developed through experimentation and study which will actually help the institution and the student alike. No doubt, many institutions, through experience and records, have ideas as to the amount and the degree of responsibility which students can reasonably be expected to assume. However, in regard to actual research reports or studies to guide other schools, there appears to be a void, at least to the knowledge of the authors. Our experience has been that college students can assume far more job responsibilities than are usually delegated. Also, they seem to want more responsibility, possibly because this places them in an adult, rather than a student role. Further, our experience has demonstrated that students placed in supervisory roles over their fellow students use the experience as a means of showing their leadership abilities.

f) TO DETERMINE IF PART-TIME STUDENT HELP, FROM AN ACCOUNTING POINT OF VIEW, CONSTITUTES AN INSTITUTIONAL ASSET OR A LIABILITY. It would seem that the question in determining if part-time student help, from an accounting point of view, constitutes an institutional asset or a liability is not related to whether we should or should not have students working. Even if research should show that it might be more expensive to employ such workers, it might yet be better to maintain a student work program from the standpoint of the educational value and financial assistance to the students. In reality, the actual concern or that which needs to be determined is the efficiency and effectiveness of part-time help based on institutional costs for such workers. Can we provide valid answers as to how much more expensive it is, if it is more costly, to utilize student help in a work program operation than to use full-time personnel? If it costs more for full-time people than it does for part-time student help in certain university operations, this information might be useful to other institutions who are either expanding their operations or who want to initiate a comprehensive program. In either instance, research and experimentation should be employed, using cost accounting insofar as the work program operation is concerned for answers concerning expense. (*Note:* The writers believe that a great many schools would be interested in research in this particular area.)

g) TO DEVELOP TRAINING PROGRAMS FOR SUPERVISION OF STUDENT WORKERS. In any operation of large scope which has jobs of various levels of difficulty and purports to place an educational emphasis on the work experience, it would seem necessary to have staff supervisors who have considerable understanding of the personal characteristics of adolescence, basic supervisory principles, and knowledge of work operations. If this be true, then it would seem that training programs and accompanying manuals should be developed to help guide the supervisors of working students, since past experience of supervisors does not often include these desirable understandings.

Too often, the working student is thought to need the same supervision as a full-time employee, which is actually not true in most instances because of a lack of general work experience or specific work experience in the type of job assigned and also because the employee is a student with different goals than those of a full-time worker. Basically, a part-time student whose principal goal is academic achievement is unlike the part-time worker with no such standard.

h) TO DEVELOP TRAINING PROGRAMS FOR STUDENT WORKERS. If students are to be used to a major degree for work in a large university, it would seem that programs are needed to train and prepare them for the different types of jobs which are to be performed. In fact, the writers believe that it is quite important that institutions develop training programs under such circumstances. The size of the institution and the scope of the work program will help to determine the kinds and number of training programs to be incorporated. More specifically, possibly a comprehensive training program for clerical workers would not be necessary in a school of five hundred students because supervisory help would be more or less concentrated. However, a school of some fifteen thousand students, using one thousand student clerical workers, should have orientation and training programs for such employees if the needed degree of parallelism is to be maintained between jobs.

Studies are needed which show the skills and the abilities required for student part-time work and the vocational courses which the secondary schools could offer, e.g., typing and shorthand, which would aid students in a part-time college job. An analysis of skills needed by students in such work, followed by a grouping of these skills analyzed as part of the high school curriculums, with the results evaluated as to worth, could be a most interesting research project. Additionally, the results would help in determining the extent and type of training programs needed.

i) TO DETERMINE THE RELATIONSHIP OF STUDENT WORK TO OTHER FORMS OF FINANCIAL ASSISTANCE. Studies in determining the relationship of student work to other forms of financial assistance would center about the need of the student, varying the numbers of working hours in conjunction with scholarships and loans of differing amounts. The package type of program is especially designed for students from low-income families. The institution which can offer such a combination of work, scholarships, and loans can definitely provide for more individual needs of these students than can the institution which does not have such program provisions. It should be remembered, however, that any one form of financial assistance, work, scholarships, or loans, may be all that certain students require to underwrite their college education. Further, many students will need no financial assistance when based upon actual money requirements, but if a total education is considered to include practical employment experience, work may constitute an important part of their educational needs. Studies and research are necessary to guide the various institutions in the directions which they should take for their particular situations.

j) TO DETERMINE AN APPROPRIATE RATIO OF STUDENT EMPLOYEES TO STUDENT WORK OFFICE COUNSELING PERSONNEL. Institutions truly concerned with the problems of working students recognize that the ratio of the number of students to the number of student work office personnel must be relatively low in order to deal with the difficulties of working students. Obviously, interviewing and placing students is a time consuming task. In addition, the counselor often is called upon to advise concerning problems relating to the work operation or personal matters.

In the secondary school, it is frequently recommended that there be 350 to 400 students to one full-time guidance counselor. In regard to work programs in higher education, one counselor to every 500 working students may be a good ratio with which to experiment. Ultimately, the ratio will depend upon the emphasis which an institution places on the student work operation. Accordingly, a definitive, static ratio cannot be set; continuing evaluations should be made of available counseling time in comparison with needed counseling time.

k) TO DETERMINE THE TRAINING AND EXPERIENCE WHICH BEST EQUIP ADMINISTRATIVE PERSONNEL TO DIRECT ORGANIZED PROGRAMS OF STUDENT EMPLOYMENT. Considering the federal underwriting of student work programs, as well as the present on-going organized programs and their expansion, it is necessary to determine the staff members to administer and to serve as counselors in the program, including the training and experience which they should have to carry on these responsibilities. Furthermore, when it is decided what, if any, additional training the staff should have, how and where can this schooling be obtained? Studies should be initiated to determine the relative effectiveness of guidance counselors, former school administrators, and others who are presently engaged in work programs, and the characteristics, qualities, and abilities of these people which have led to effective programs.

Also, since college personnel graduate programs are giving more time and consideration to the ever-increasing need for trained financial aids administrators, after their employment the personal characteristics, qualities, and abilities which have led to the effectiveness of these graduates should be studied.

l) TO DETERMINE WAYS AND MEANS TO EVALUATE A STUDENT WORK PROGRAM. It appears that additional consideration may have to be given in the future to evaluating overall work operations in addition to the individual parts which have composed the program. This may be especially true since there are funds available from the federal grant for the College Work-Study Program. It should be remembered, however, that continuing evaluations of each function are needed. Comparisons should be made of student work accomplishment with accomplishment expectations from full-time personnel performing the same type of work. The comprehensive treatment of evaluation is contained in another chapter of this text.

B.
Problems of Research and Experimentation

On the surface, it may seem that the problems of research and experimentation are too numerous in institutions of higher education to be resolved satisfactorily. However, within almost any institution, there are many individuals, both academic and nonacademic, vitally interested in the welfare of students. Furthermore, many of these same persons realize that if this nation is to achieve its potential, opportunities for education beyond the high school must be made available to those individuals who can benefit personally, as well as make maximum contributions to the society of which they are a part, from such educational opportunities. These people will help to resolve problems, making time available before or after working schedules if necessary.

In many of the purposes and methods previously indicated, related specific problems were given or inferred; however, there is a genuine need for the consideration of research over and beyond the definite projects suggested. This section will indicate some of the problems with the thought that when the problems are apparent, answers can be determined, at least in part.

Controlling the many variables, such as hours, rates, academic programs, etc., seems virtually impossible at times. For example, the hours worked by students may vary considerably from month to month, making continued study of students grouped within hourly limits difficult. The problem of wage rates is seldom settled satisfactorily, as may be assumed from the differentiations which exist among various institutions, even those with parallel purposes. Academic achievement is not consistent with academic potential in many instances. This factor, including motivation and attitudes, tends to cloud predictions. Further, there is the element of change in supervisory personnel which may interfere with regular practice and procedures.

1. *Qualified Personnel.* One of the urgent necessities of work programs is the obtaining of personnel with the training and the experience for research projects. One of the problems encountered, it appears, would be to find personnel with adequate training and experience to perform the research which is necessary. There has to be an evidenced concern for an operation which has not had a great deal of attention or emphasis for some twenty to twenty-five years.

A lack of interest on the part of the university may pose a genuine problem. One of the difficulties which is found in many institutions is that people in academic fields do not appear to be as interested in research dealing with student work as in a project specifically related to their particularized field. This is unfortunate in many ways because it no doubt has held back information which could be useful to parts of our educational community.

The existing situation probably will not change until the administrations of top level universities give recognition and encouragement and reward to those academicians who through experimentation and research help to resolve the problems.

2. *Insufficient Funds.* Frequently, there has been a lack of funds to finance research projects, constituting a major problem in this area. However, in the past decade, the federal government has allocated millions of dollars to conduct research projects in higher educational institutions. Granted that the fields of science have been the recipients of the greater portions of federal allocations in the past, nevertheless the pressures of social problems in our society require and are receiving increasing consideration for federal funds. Especially the Economic Opportunity Act of 1964 and the Higher Education Act of

1965 are making operational and research funds available for experimentation and research.

The United States Office of Education is also a primary source for properly designed research projects. Thus, the outlook for additional federal funds to support work-study program experimentation is brighter than it has been in the history of higher education. Also, institutions are becoming increasingly aware of work program problems and student worker problems as increasing numbers of students become participants in both on-campus and off-campus work-study programs.

3. *Operational Change and Work Program Experimentation.* It is usually difficult to orient personnel to operational and administrative changes by means of written directions, alone. However, when such directives are supplemented by personal contact, either on an individual or a group basis, and the employees affected have opportunities to ask questions concerning the effect of administrative change regarding particular operations, orientation can take place to a substantial degree. Actually, the open discussion provides an opportunity for the administrative personnel, on the level where the concepts and ideas emerged as policy and procedure, to explain these concepts and ideas to the supervisory personnel who will implement the changes.

In the instance of a decision to expand a student work program, the point of personal contact must not be overlooked. Work program directors and vocational counselors should utilize the personal contact method to clarify the changes both to the supervisors of students and to the students concerned. As a result of their effort, the transition from old methods to new may be achieved with a minimal amount of personnel resistance, thus assuring a high degree of uniformity in work program operations. Even after programs are implemented, an effort should be made by the administration of the work program to provide personal contact to new faculty and staff members who supervise student employees.

4. *Employment Problems.* One of the recognized weaknesses in attempting to utilize student help is the irregularity of work schedules in an institutional employment operation. Supervisors responsible for a flow of work find difficulty in student part-time operation because of the irregularity of those hours available for student work.

Further, any kind of part-time work adds to the operational

problems, but student help usually contributes problems unique to employment per se. The fact that they are students should immediately place their academic programs, and rightly so, at the top of any priority list of college activities. This may be contrasted with the full-time employee who for the sake of livelihood may set his work above all other matters.

Another problem for the institutional supervisor of student help relates to the institution's purpose for maintaining a self-help program. If the program exists solely as the means of providing financially needy students with assistance, the real values attainable in a work situation may receive little or negligible attention from either the supervisor or the financial aids office. In such instances, the students are quick to learn that little in the way of actual work may be expected of them. The results, of course, are that the seeds of poor working habits and attitudes have been embedded in fertile soil for further development. Unhappily, such mind-sets may be reinforced in the most unlikely place imaginable, in an institution of higher learning.

Another instance worth noting is found in the institutional purpose which is designed and best served by employing students to work in operations which lend themselves to part-time employment, but with the institution giving little consideration to the development of other areas in which the student may work and advance, experientially. In such situations, continued employment is contingent on productivity; accordingly, the student is expected to perform on a level comparable with that of full-time employees. The authors take no issue with the work performance of students, but we do take strong exception to a narrow scope of student work opportunities and to the attitude of the institution which virtually states that the student employment program should serve only the institution.

Another problem frequently associated with students, one used to curtail the student employment operation, is the lack of employment skills of many college students. Supervisors will point out that students seeking jobs will rarely have had sufficient work experience or training to qualify for anything of a skilled or semiskilled nature of employment. Any attempt to use students on a large scale would be costly economically and an operational hazard from the standpoint of efficient operation. However, institutions which desire to expand their student work operations should explore the possibilities of training programs for student employees.

5. *Student Work and Unions.* Difficulties may occasionally arise with unions in some work areas. No doubt in some institutions the unions will pose difficulties insofar as developing and/or expanding the student work program operation to the extent necessary to provide groups of sufficient size to secure valid research. However, studies should be made, and the unions should be solicited for help in making studies to determine where the students can best be used and where the least conflict should arise.

It must be kept foremost in mind that without the students there would be no institutional labor jobs. Further, it behooves the unions to cooperate by reason of the fact that the sons and daughters of union employees also need work experience for the educational values as well as for the remuneration. It has been the authors' experience that when union leaders understand what the institution is undertaking in the name of work experience, cooperation will result. In fact, union supervisors, like many other nonacademic personnel, seem to take more interest in their workers than do some of the teaching-research faculty in their students. Partially, this may be explained in the formal relationship of teacher-student as contrasted with the more informal association of student work supervisor to the student worker.

It is also to be noted that a work supervisor may see his student worker two or three hours a day over an extended period of time, whereas the teacher in his classes is seldom in contact with any one student oftener than five hours per week during a term or semester. Further, the teacher may have seventy-five students or more in each day while the supervisor may have only five to ten student workers, with rarely over twenty-five in his working unit for a time block involving two or more hours.

Institutions of higher education which have relied almost entirely upon full-time personnel to perform most, if not all, of the work of their institutions should not displace full-time employees with students in a plan to expand student work opportunities. They may wish to consider some of the following matters of concern.

1] Enrollment increases create additional positions both on the academic and nonacademic level. In nonacademic areas, if students have the qualifications they are entitled to a share of the work.

2] Normally, academic units can justify additional clerical help since college professors have a definite need for student aides to assist in para-professional duties. Such part-time work experience can be most beneficial to the students' overall education. 3] If an institution identifies certain work experiences as a part of the students' educational program, be it for academic credit or non-credit, then full-time, nonacademic employees, whether union or non-union, have no authority to interfere with the academic programming of such a college or university. One needs but to visit Berea College at Berea, Kentucky, or Blackburn College at Carlinville, Illinois, to note the educational values manifested in student employment.

7 Evaluating Student Work Experience

IN ALL likelihood, most authorities would agree in theory that the personal characteristics, traits, and abilities of student employees should be evaluated. The criteria for individual worker evaluation and of the best possible use of the results depend to a great extent upon institutional philosophy, including the emphasis which is placed on student work as a contributing factor in the total education of the student and the degree to which the philosophy is implemented.

As an illustration, Blackburn College, Carlinville, Illinois, requires as a part of its total educational program that all students participate in work experiences supervised by the college. Such experiences may range from baking bread to building dormitories. Berea College, Berea, Kentucky, blends work and study into a total educational experience for its students. Antioch College, Yellow Springs, Ohio, requires its students to participate in a cooperative education program which places its students alternately in full-time academic study and full-time work. Needless to say, such definite emphasis upon work must be evaluated in regard to the educational values received. However, at the other end of our institutional work evaluation scale, one can find institutions whose philosophies lead to educational efforts which are directed, totally or almost totally, toward academic studies. Work for students, other than academic work, is not looked upon with favor in those latter institutions.

Because the authors believe that work experiences are good educationally for students and furthermore that such work experiences must be evaluated, this chapter, concerned with the purposes, methods, and problems of student work evaluation, has been included. Within this chapter, also, several designs for worker and work experience evaluation are given.

A.
Purposes of Evaluation

As was stated previously, the purposes of work evaluation will vary greatly among institutions. Although the variances are great, the writers believe that most of the major purposes can be categorized and placed in two evaluative divisions for study. This has been done as follows: First, consideration is given as to how such evaluation can benefit the student employees; and second, how the institutions can profit from such an appraisal.

1. *The Benefits Accruing to Student Employees (Workers).* It seems reasonable that one of the purposes of evaluating the personal characteristics, traits, skills, and abilities of a student in a work situation is to help the student to understand his strengths and weaknesses, relative to the performance expected in the job to which he is assigned. Again, it is to be anticipated that a standard of performance will vary in accordance with institutional and supervisory expectations. In a sense, this situation is parallel to that which is expected of the academic studies of the student. There is a standard of performance established, but standards vary among teachers.

To illustrate, three professors may be teaching the same academic course but the level of performance expected from students may differ considerably. Also, the academic preparation may vary from one to three hours, depending upon the amount of study time required of students. This is not a criticism, but it is rather a calling of attention to individuality which is inevitably involved. Somewhat parallel to the above, in a work situation, a supervisor in evaluating the work performed by the student may be comparing the student's accomplishments with that expected from a full-time employee performing the same work. In another instance, the supervisor may have his standard of performance keyed to the past performances of student employees. Thus, in both the academic and work experiences of the student, evaluations may vary greatly unless cooperative efforts reduce differences.

If the evaluation is to benefit the student, he must be informed as to his progress in a working situation in order to obtain maximum benefits from his job. In many instances, it is only as the student is informed of his strengths and weaknesses that he improves. Evaluations by the supervisor also have a tendency to make students more capable of self-evaluation. Most students want to be held in high esteem by their employers, and if workers know that both verbal and written evaluations are to be made, they have a marked tendency toward making self-appraisals, with resultant behavioral and work changes that will lead to recognized improvement with respect to evaluation. The student on the job, as in the classroom, is dependent to a certain degree upon the faculty and the staff to guide his learning accomplishments.

The good supervisor who provides for transfer of training for students in jobs, which leads to appropriate transfer, does much to coordinate academic and work experiences. Also, in all jobs, supervisors can set up situations which will lead to changes of attitudes in positive directions for students. For example, students can learn to appreciate the dignity of work, as well as the worth of the individual. Also, they can be taught to have a concern for the welfare of other members of their peer groups and supervisors.

Evaluation can serve to assist in determining which students should be given merit increases within a given unit, and who is worthy of promotion. It is rather obvious that good evaluative procedures will be of benefit to the able student workers. Merit pay increments and promotions will accrue to the deserving students. The work supervisor who determines the merit increases and promotion of students in his employ, parallels the academic instructor who determines the grades to be received by students enrolled in class.

For clarification, a merit increase should be interpreted to mean an increase in pay because of a high level of performance in a particular position. A promotion should be seen as an elevation from a position requiring one level of skills or training to a position necessitating a higher plateau of training and performance.

Probably one of the most important uses of student worker evaluation is the inclusion of the results as a part of the student's permanent record in the placement office of the institution. Of course, it is understood that the record is a reflection of the student's performance, and a student with poor work habits, irregular attendance, and irresponsible traits will hardly find that his record is an asset to help him in obtaining full-time employment. Students should know that their work records will become a portion of their permanent placement file.

Accordingly, it behooves the students to work in harmony with the expectations of their employers; this, in itself, is an all-important lesson to learn.

It is readily seen that seniors with outstanding work experience records in their placement files, coupled with a good transcript of academic performance, have a decided advantage when recruiting officers are selecting graduates for full-time employment. Just how great an advantage would accrue could be both an interesting and informative piece of research.

Analysis of student worker evaluation may evidence a relationship between employment strengths and occupational interests. In such instances, a vocational counselor would utilize these evaluation reports to the benefit of the student in a counseling situation. Student work interests, attitudes, skills, and accomplishments, as reflected in an employment situation, may be considered as a practicum in career guidance for the college student. In brief, if a student has a career in mind, and if his part-time student job requires some of the skills and job characteristics which are needed in full-time work in his vocational field, a positive degree of job satisfaction should appear in his job performance.

If a student has not selected a career, however, his supervisors' evaluations may help him discover employment aptitudes of which he was previously unaware. It is understood that a record of the student's employment should be treated with the same care and confidence as is his grade transcript.

2. *For the Benefit of the University or College.* The responsibility of the work supervisor to rate the student's performance, potentialities, judgment, and maturity requires that the supervisor be aware of the significant role which he performs in the employment training of the student. Such a responsibility should help to create and to sustain a better and a higher level of institutional supervision.

Unless supervisors and students mutually strive to attain a common goal of effective and efficient operation, the student work functions can be a detriment to the institution, as well as contributing to poor training and the development of careless work habits on the part of the students. Such consequences would defeat the philosophy and purpose of student work, as the writers interpret student employment. On the other hand, if the students receive good training and develop good work habits the net result assuredly is a benefit to the university.

Student work evaluation may also serve the university in that it provides a basis for determining Work-Study planning and direction. Planning may be continuous under such conditions, but, in addition, educational blueprints can be made which will lead to overcoming weaknesses and increasing strengths, as perceived through evaluative processes. Of special concern and importance are those aspects of the work program in which the work experience of students can be related to their academic programs. The institution, from a financial point of view, must defend its expenditure of funds relative to program allocations. This is understandable because relatively good evaluations can be obtained in a minimum of time. In the instance of a student work program in which the institution can justify the expenditure of funds for students participating in a program which is both educational and affords financial assistance, the dimensions of the program inevitably change. This leads to a program which is better educationally, since there is more student job diversity, more student counseling, more institutional training programs, and more faculty participation in such an expanded program. In regard to this latter point and as more programs are improved, the university with graduates who are increasingly better qualified for taking their places in the world of work add to the stature of the school in the eyes of the people who support it.

Although increasing enrollments, crowded universities, and anonymity of macro-campuses are making education a somewhat impersonal experience, students working part-time for the institutional staff may develop a strong personal attachment to the institution through their jobs and association with work supervisors. Thus, the writers theorize that students who work for their college or university as student employees are less inclined to feel alienated from the institution than are the non-working students.

B.
Methods of Evaluation

There are institutions which consider student employment as existing beyond the sphere and influence of the institution's educational program. In such instances, the accomplishments of student workers, either in on- or off-campus jobs, generally receive neither acclaim nor blame; thus, the result is little or no evaluation.

However, the most common type of evaluation is that obtained through the use of rating scales and/or checklists. This is an accepted practice because relatively valid evaluations can be obtained in a minimum of time. Some institutions, however, tend to use the personal interviews with supervisors as the sole basis of student work evaluation. Such a practice, although good, can result in a long and involved process. If many students are working, it necessitates the interviewing of large numbers of supervisory personnel. Nevertheless, this is one method which can be utilized. More often, representative samples of interviews are incorporated with other evaluative means.

Still another method may be that in which the students evaluate themselves. This may be accomplished by means of questionnaires, rating scales, or by interviews. Yet another means employed by some institutions is an objective statement written by the supervisor.

Since rating scales and checklists are most commonly used, as was previously pointed out, they deserve particular consideration as evaluative instruments. Inevitably, there would be differences of opinion as to the content of the measurement. The concern of one group might be directed only toward accomplishment, another group would include work attitudes, and still another would build a case for the inclusion of personality traits. Also, there would most certainly be a differentiation in the point scale which is accepted. Some might prefer a system similar to that used in the recording of academic grading. To illustrate:

POINTS	WORK EVALUATION
5	*Superior*
4	*Good*
3	*Average*
2	*Poor*
1	*Failed*

A variation frequently used is exemplified by the form designed by Southern Illinois University for the evaluation of part-time student workers (see Appendix A). It may readily be seen that a combination of a rating scale and checklist is used. Quite a number of the characteristics are to be checked for each student, but, at the same time, the checks are to be made in terms of a comparative A, B, C, D or N scale.

Again, some might prefer to show more individual differentiation than the five-point scale will provide by employing a scale as illustrated below:

0| | | | | | | | |10| | | | | | | | |20| | | | | | | | |30| | | | | | | | |40| | | | | | | | |50

unsatisfactory probationary   satisfactory   good   superior

Still others may prefer to use only a four or a three-point scale. Regardless, when properly designed and administered, rating scales and checklists can be useful instruments in evaluating the part-time employment experience of students.

In conclusion, it should be noted that an institution may employ a combination of methods to evaluate students' working experiences to meet the individual requirements of the university.

C.
Problems

Among the more difficult problems associated with evaluation are the following: First, there is the practical problem of time required of supervisors to appraise the abilities, skills, attitudes, and personalities of the students under their supervision. Second, some supervisors may have difficulty in being objective, whether this be in terms of written statements, rating scales, checklists, or a combination of the preceding methods. Third, there is the problem of inexperience or immaturity of some supervisors which makes the validity of their ratings questionable.

In respect to the third problem, a training program for the supervisors of students employed in college jobs would provide a means of improving supervisory evaluative techniques. The individual conference between a student work office counselor and the supervisor of students is another corrective procedure which may be used.

Fourth, some students do not remain on one particular job a sufficient length of time for a supervisor to render a fair work-evaluation. Fifth, the frequency of the evaluation of students may pose a problem. For example, a university employing some two thousand students may well find a semiannual evaluation to be a time-consuming undertaking.

Sixth, there is the problem concerning the advisability of the supervisor's discussing the work evaluation with the student. The writers take the view that evaluation of a student's performance on the job should be handled in the same way as the evaluation of a student's performance in class—discuss the evaluation with him.

D.

Evaluation and the Coordinative Duties
of the Office of Student Work and Financial Assistance

We have previously discussed some of the benefits of work evaluation as it concerns both the student and the university. There is a coordinating office whose functions and services relating to evaluation can mutually benefit the institution and the student. In colleges and universities this office may have different titles, such as Student Personnel Office, Financial Aids Office, Financial Assistance, Student Employment, or Student Work.

The degree of responsibility which the institution delegates to this office will determine to a marked degree the extent of its functions and services. For instance, if the Financial Aids Office is understaffed, the need to evaluate the student worker, important as the function appears to be, may not be included in the agenda of work because the interviewing of students, the referral and placement of students in campus jobs, and the counseling functions may all have received higher priority than the evaluation of students in work situations.

The writers recognize that there is inadequate funding and staffing of many student work offices, and that the kind of office we believe is urgently needed in work evaluation may be a goal some two to five years hence in many institutions. It must be recognized, however, that the role of the federal government in the area of financial assistance (loans, work-study, and grants) is all but phenomenal in its development. In less than a decade, the budget of the United States Office of Education has gone from a zero appropriation to approximately $500 million in student financial aid, with the College Work-Study figure well over $100 million.[1]

Evaluations of programs in schools receiving substantial amounts of the available money seems imperative if a continuation of such programs is to be justified. Also, it does not appear unreasonable to assume that institutions must give more emphasis to both their financial aids program and the number and quality of personnel who administer such programs. To illustrate: the possibilities of developing a diversity of student on-campus work opportunities which will benefit the student both financially and educationally are most propitious.

---

1 Edward Sanders, *Remarks*. Financial Assistance Workshop, University of Indiana (Bloomington, Ind., June 20, 1966), p. 4.

However, as is true in the academic community, as it should rightly be, more research and evidence as well as continuous evaluations are needed as programs are activated and further developed.

It should be noted that the methods and procedures for the determination of financial needs of college students to assure that they qualify for the various aspects of financial aids have been refined and substantiated during the past few years. The college scholarship service, to name one program, has provided the leadership in this area. However, a similar effort toward even identifying some of the educational values attainable in multiple programs of financial assistance has not as yet been fully realized and appears to await future development. Perhaps the American Council on Education will recognize this void and give due consideration to the problem, or perhaps the United States Office of Education will channel more funds to research the projects which will provide enlightenment.

For practitioners in the field of financial assistance, the academic community might turn more of its research attention toward this problem since it appears, at least to the writers, that educational values inherent in work and financial assistance programs are the concern of the entire educational community.

In the area of student work in Southern Illinois University, effort is being directed toward work-experience evaluation. The major part of the remainder of this chapter will be concerned with illustrating the role of the student work office in coordinating the methods and procedures for student work evaluation.

E.
Evaluating the Student Worker

It would seem reasonable that the objectives of work experience and the evaluation of the worker are directly related. With this point in mind, we list the objectives of work experience as set forth in the Southern Illinois University publication, *Supervisors' Handbook.*

Since the supervisor is directly in charge of the student worker, he is a key person in making the student's work a valuable educational experience. The following are the basic educational objectives of work experience concerning student employees in the university's student work program:

1] To develop skills by relating the work experience with the educational program as often as this is possible. (That is, to assign deliberately the working student to a job which is related to his academic studies, e.g., the chemistry major to a job in the chemistry laboratory, the future teacher to a job as an instructional aide, the business major to an office, the agriculture major to a job on the University Farms, the mathematics major to the Computing Center, etc.)

2] To develop other skills (not necessarily related to the academic program) that will enable the student to increase the breadth of the work experience. These skills may be used in later life to supplement his vocation or to enrich his avocation. Students often realize this objective during the first two years of college while qualifying themselves to move into a major-related field during the final two years.

3] To encourage the development of good judgment and common sense.

4] To promote a desire to be productive, a respect for honest work, and a sense of pride and accomplishment in achieving something worthwhile.

5] To develop characteristics of dependability, honesty, and loyalty.

6] To develop the ability to get along well with others and to work cooperatively.

7] To develop a sense of personal responsibility and self-confidence.

8] To encourage the development of initiative and creativity, and to provide opportunities which may foster leadership.

9] To reward initiative and high level performance with additional responsibility (and remuneration), thus increasing the breadth and the depth of the educational experience for the student.

The responsibilities of the supervisor of student workers, including the routine and mechanical details of carrying out these responsibilities insofar as they apply to all supervision, can be considered to fall into five main categories.

1] Listing the job
2] Interviewing and employing the student
3] Supervising and training the student
4] Evaluating the student
5] Terminating the student's employment.

In the following discussion, we are primarily concerned with procedures in evaluating the student, although indications of some values which justify procedures are also included.

At Southern Illinois University, in order to emphasize the educational values of a student's work experience on the campus, evaluation ratings of the job performances of each student employee are made at least annually. These ratings are of value for the student worker's permanent file, insomuch as they may be used for the purpose of counseling the student, making referrals to job openings, and making recommendations when requested by future employers. Also, they are of value to the Student Work Program in the overall evaluation of the worth of the program.

The evaluation ratings become a part of each senior's file in the University Placement Office, where they become available to prospective employers of the graduates of the institution. Ratings of a student's work experience can, therefore, become most important to him in securing permanent employment after graduation.

The Student Work Office sends the forms entitled, "Evaluation of Part-Time Student Workers," to each supervisor. The forms for rating seniors are sent so that the rating can be completed in November of the school year in which the student is to graduate. Supervisors receive the forms for all other students so that the ratings can be made in January of each year.

Each supervisor is encouraged to keep a supply of the evaluation rating forms in order that temporary workers and students terminating their employment can be rated. These forms are available in the Student Work Office of the University and may be obtained on request. An evaluation of the student who quits his job, who is asked to change jobs, or withdraws from employment for any reason is forwarded to the Student Work Office with the notification of the termination of employment.

The ratings shown in Appendix A can be completed simply by checking each of the twelve evaluation criteria listed on the form used prior to the Spring of 1967. A revised form is now employed in student work appraisal, and a copy of the current evaluation sheet is included in the Appendixes (see B). An evaluation criterion can be rated as follows:

    A *Superior*
    B *Above Average*
    C *Average*
    D *Below Average*
 and E *Poor*

If the criterion does not apply, or if the supervisor does not have sufficient information, no evaluation is given, and the supervisor checks

"N," indicating None. Additional space is provided on the form for explanatory comments, recommendations, or special information.

The twelve criteria which appear on the evaluation rating form are listed below:

1] SKILLS AND ABILITIES: Does the student worker have the knowledge and ability essential for the work and a good background in the field of work he does?

2] DEPENDABILITY: Is he trustworthy, punctual, reliable? Does he fulfill his responsibilities? Is he good in attendance?

3] QUALITY OF WORK: Is the student employee's work accurate, thorough, and acceptable? Does he use materials and time economically? Does he take care of materials? Is he eager for improvement?

4] INITIATIVE: Does the student worker have the ability to think along original lines; to find new and better ways of performance; to look for useful work and to organize new operations and perform new functions with exceptional skill?

5] LEADERSHIP: Is he able to influence and inspire others to do better work? Is he able to organize and direct the work of others?

6] PERSONAL APPEARANCE: Is he neat, clean, suitably dressed? Does he have poise and balance? Does he have good posture?

7] JUDGMENT: Does the student worker have good self-control? Does he have the ability to make sound decisions? Does he use common sense in the performance of his duties? Is he tactful in his relations with others?

8] COOPERATION: Does the student worker have the ability to work well with fellow workers, supervisors, and others? Is he deeply conscious of his responsibility to the working group?

9] ATTITUDE TOWARD WORK: Is the student worker courteous, cheerful, and interested; willing to work at difficult and disagreeable tasks; able to take instructions cheerfully?

10] PHYSICAL VIGOR: Is he enthusiastic about work, active and energetic; does he keep himself in a state of good health, and is he emotionally stable?

11] QUANTITY OF WORK: Does the student employee have the ability to do a comparatively large amount of work of above average quality? Can he work under pressure as well as under normal conditions?

12] POTENTIALITIES: Does the student worker have a high degree of potentiality for future improvement and development as he matures?

In evaluating student workers, it is recommended that the supervisor compare a student worker with other student employees of similar age and experience. Student workers should not be compared with full-time employees unless they are equal to these employees in age, training, and experience. Age and lack of experience should receive due consideration when the supervisor rates freshmen student workers. At times, there is a tendency to expect the same performance from a new freshman employee that is anticipated from a more mature senior —an unfair comparison.

The supervisor is encouraged to use the annual evaluation rating as an opportunity for an individual conference with the student worker in helping the student to develop his potentialities and skills. The evaluation is much like a grade or mark which he may receive in an academic class. It is likely, also, that the evaluation form ratings will be used in many instances by Student Work Office personnel in counseling the student concerning his work and his development as a useful, productive citizen.

Two evaluation forms (Appendixes B and C) used by Southern Illinois University are included to illustrate the types of ratings of student workers which may be utilized. The second evaluation sheet is a revised edition of the form previously issued.

OTHER EVALUATIONS

Southern Illinois University, through the efforts of individuals and groups, has made a considerable number of evaluations of its program and parts of the program. The results of some of these evaluations are shown in the chapter concerned with research.

Additionally, the writers have been recently concerned with devising questionnaires which could be used for assessing the value of student work experiences, as seen both by supervisors and students, as well as for the purpose of obtaining vital information about the two groups. Although these questionnaires have not been distributed and results have not as yet been compiled, the writers have included them to stimulate thinking on the part of the readers, particularly those who will be concerned with work program evaluation.

8 Preparation for a College Part-Time Job

THE COLLEGE WORK-STUDY PROGRAM OF THE United States Office of Education is a major contributory influence in making institutions aware of the importance of student work. Thus, it is not surprising that institutional financial aids officers are exerting considerable effort to expand and to diversify student work experience. One of the methods employed is that of encouraging students to prepare for jobs which require more skills and training than is usually associated with campus student jobs. When the student has the skills, abilities, and work knowledge to qualify for certain kinds and levels of work, he may receive consideration for such employment. However, until such time as the student can adequately perform the duties and accept responsibilities which the job demands; the institution can ill afford to employ him for such work. For example, most institutions have more clerical positions than can be filled by both full-time and part-time clerical workers who qualify for such positions. It should be noted that the skills primarily needed for those clerical jobs are attainable in the high school curriculum.

It is the thinking of the authors that preparation for a student job should have its beginning in the secondary schools. With this aim in mind, Chapter 8 will concentrate on three areas: academic preparation, work experience, and applying for and obtaining the job, as a means of preparing students for more college work-study employment opportunities. For the benefit of high school students who will be seeking employment on a full-time or a part-time basis following graduation, the authors have set down the details in explaining the employment process, the job application, preparing for a job interview, the actual interview, the job referral, employment, and work orientation.

A.

Academic Preparation (High School)

Whether for financial reasons, educational requirements, or both, teen-agers should initiate their preparation for working their way through college while still in high school. It is to be understood, of course, that this necessitates planning as well as preparation.

First and foremost in the planning stage is a decision on the part of the student to continue his education beyond high school, be it a junior college, a four-year college, or a university. It is quite necessary that the student discuss his plans with his parents, teachers, and guidance counselors. If the student has a college education in his planning, his academic preparation for both school and future employment on a college level constitutes a goal. If for some reason the student does not immediately enroll in college following high school graduation, it is the writers' opinion that the previously indicated planning and preparation will place him in a favorable position for immediate full-time employment, the military service, or whatever else he has in mind.

Let us examine some of the subject areas in the high school curriculum which can make a direct contribution to equipping the student with that which is commonly termed in the employment market as salable skills. It is, of course, understood that any and all subjects in the high school curriculum should serve as a contribution to the student's education. Also, it is agreed that any and all students should take the required general education courses. In addition to the basic courses there is that large group of subjects called electives, from which each student may select those studies which will best complete his academic experience in his high school program.

1. *Vocational Business Training.* If one were to examine the high school course offerings of a number of schools of varying size, it is probable that typing would be listed by virtually all schools but required by very few. Yet, the high school student going on to college has need of typing skills, to be utilized both in academic courses and employment. A student with proficiency in typing, either a boy or a girl, is almost certain to find employers both on or off campus who will pay for such ability. In addition, the student who will take sufficient shorthand training to become proficient in dictation and transcription is in much greater demand than is the typist. Not only do such students have a definite advantage in job placement, but such

training is of great benefit in the classroom. The lecture method of teaching on a college level necessitates note-taking by students. It is readily seen that students who possess the ability to take shorthand accurately are thus able to set down lecture notes precisely, assuming that the proficiency level is such that the notes can be rapidly transcribed as needed. Also, college courses which do not require typewritten reports or term papers are indeed rare. As has been indicated, the typing skills will serve as benefits, both in terms of time and money.

Those students whose career plans are in the field of business, journalism, or teaching are greatly advantaged by the possession of good clerical skills developed in high school. Imagine the benefit accruing to a newspaper reporter who has shorthand skills, as compared with the writer who sets down material in longhand, or the reporter who has good typing skills, as contrasted with a hunt-and-peck typist. The teacher in almost every subject area who can type has more time to prepare his lesson plans and supplementary materials, and he is still making use of the skill which may have helped him work his way through college.

The future teacher who elects a major in business courses can be graduated from college with a background of both theory and practice. The executive secretary can receive a bachelor's degree, plus a business speciality, a liberal arts education, and a proficiency demonstrated by a fine work-experience record.

The young lady with skills in shorthand and typing, plus work experience, who marries before her college graduation rarely encounters difficulty in obtaining employment. Also, after marriage, she may find her clerical employment skills extremely useful, ranging from preparing household budgets to filing income tax returns.

Assuming that the writers' views regarding business subjects (shorthand, typing, general business, office practice, etc.) are accurate, then why do not more students avail themselves of such work-study opportunities? There are a number of reasons, and we shall present some of the most significant.

First, there are varying opinions as to how a high school student should best prepare for college. There are those authorities who affirm that four years of science, four years of mathematics, four years of English, and at least two years of foreign language are requisites for all college bound students. Such a view may be referred to as the traditional approach. The high school student who follows such an academic preparation finds that few elective courses may be taken in completing work for his high school diploma. Thus, the possibilities of developing vocational skills to any degree are remote.

One might, however, question the need of four years of mathematics, science, English, as well as two years of foreign language study as an established standard for college preparation. The first question directed to the student, his parents, and guidance counselors might be, "A college education—for what?"

Do the student's career plans call for a thorough background in four academic disciplines? Fulfilling the requirements for a major in any one of these fields in college is often difficult. It appears that a careful consideration of the question, "Education—for what?," deserves considerable attention on the part of the prospective college student. Necessarily is this true since the diversity of academic fields is so great and the number and the variety of courses within a given field are so extensive that one could spend a lifetime in a major university and never repeat the same course of study. The writers do not wish to give the impression that the college student cannot change his career plans; many can and should make such decisions. However, exploration should be accomplished as early as possible, at least in high school or during the first two years of college. In fact, many junior high school authorities indicate that exploratory activities should start in early adolescence, during grades seven through nine.

Another reason that one should look with some skepticism at the rigidity of a high school program consisting of four years of science, mathematics, and English, as well as two years of a foreign language, is the possible negative effect upon some students. For example, a young lady may have both the creative ability and the motivation to achieve on a high level in the language arts, but be all but a failure in the fields of science and mathematics. By the time that she graduates from high school, if compelled to study four years of mathematics and science, she may rank so low in her graduating class that few colleges will accept her as a student. Even worse, she may think of herself as an academic failure and find even the language arts uninteresting.

The point which the writers are emphasizing is that good guidance in such an instance would have provided a minimum of courses in science and mathematics and a maximum of language arts and related subjects. Again, in college, such a student should be allowed to take only the required number of courses in her weaker academic areas and permitted to concentrate in the areas of her strengths.

One might consider the example of a young lady who demonstrates particular ability in the areas of mathematics, science, and English, but has no time for the business or vocational courses. However, in her sophomore year of college, she marries and drops out of school to obtain a job to aid in financing her husband's education. It is not unusual for girls to marry and drop college, regardless of scholastic ability. Employmentwise, her skills in English would seem to be most helpful. However, a knowledge of typing, coupled with skill in English usage, would be much more of an employment asset. At the same time, her science and mathematics skills have not as yet reached a level of professional efficiency to constitute proficiency. Accordingly, for all practical purposes, an employer would probably classify her as unskilled, and her employment might well be in an entry job area.

One might consider the same young lady with the circumstances changed somewhat. Instead of completing four years of mathematics in high school, she has studied this subject for only two years (still quite adequate for entrance in most colleges) and has spent two years in study of business courses. She graduates from high school with skills in both shorthand and typing. During her first year in college, she works fifteen hours a week as a part-time student secretary in one of the business offices of the university. At the end of her freshman year, she has fulfilled her academic program requirements, and has a year's work experience. Also, before leaving college for marriage, she checks with the personnel office of the university and may find that she is eligible for full-time employment as a university civil service secretary. Further, she may learn that while working in a full-time job, she is eligible to take a college course or two during each term. In such circumstances, she can still make some progress in her own academic career while working forty hours per week.

A significant reason offered, although it is not a valid argument, as to why more students are not enrolled in high school shorthand and typing courses is the attitude of boys toward participating in such studies. There is, somehow, a stigma attached to shorthand classes which causes high school boys to avoid this subject as if it were the plague. Such a bias is most unfortunate since a larger percentage of boys than girls usually work part time to help finance their college education. A boy with good shorthand and typing skills may not only find campus work, but his high school training can be an asset in the business world. The male avoidance of such training is a problem for parents and school personnel. Convincing the high school boy that a shorthand class is not merely a female province is a task to be mastered.

Still another factor to be considered in connection with enrollment in high school business courses is the national pressure upon secondary schools for academic excellence, with particular emphasis upon the physical sciences, chemistry, physics, and mathematics. It is interesting to note that the insistence upon scientific academic excellence became of national concern following Russia's successful launching of "Sputnik." However, excellence in any and all subject fields has always been a goal of educators.

Nevertheless, the influence of the space age has placed the high school science and mathematics programs in the academic spotlight, setting humanities, social studies, and vocational programs somewhat in the background. Fortunately, now, there is an increasing emphasis on the humanities and social studies. Citizens of this country will have to learn to understand and to work with their countrymen and the people of other nations.

One need not defend the necessity of vocational programs such as agriculture, industrial arts, crafts, home economics, distributive education, and diversified occupations in the secondary schools. It is common knowledge that only a little more than 50 percent of the students who enroll for a high school education at the present time pursue education beyond the secondary level.

However, the number and the percentages of high school graduates who continue their educational training beyond high school are increasing, and we may further add that this group appears to enjoy more recognition and social prestige than do those terminating education at the high school level. Nevertheless, in the name of democracy and practicality, equal attention must also be given to the vocational preparation of individuals and groups who plan to complete their formal education during, or at the conclusion of, the high school years. It is the thinking of the authors that vocational education should be diversified and comprehensive to the extent that these students who plan college careers in similar vocational fields will find in their high school vocational subjects, theory and practice which are prerequisites for their college courses.

It should also be kept in mind that the terminal programs in the junior college and the vocational technical institutes will be demanding far more high school preparation in vocational fields in the future than is now available. It may be necessary in some rural areas for several high schools to pool their financial resources and centralize certain fields in order to have the technical equipment and the level of instruction required to educate and to train students for immediate employment or post-secondary education of a vocational nature. It is quite understandable that in an age of space, automation, and technological change that all institutions (high schools through universities) must be alert to the need for refresher courses, workshops, new courses, seminars, and retraining in general as means of keeping the practitioner and his art, craft, trade, or profession in pace with the times.

For the college bound student who must rely on part-time employment to assist in financing his college education, high school vocational courses can be an asset. High school home economics majors, agriculture majors, and industrial arts majors who attend large universities which offer advanced studies in these same fields have an excellent opportunity for part-time employment. In brief, the high school agriculture major who plans to obtain a college degree in general agriculture or a related field will usually find part-time on-campus employment opportunities in the school of agriculture. It has been the experience of the authors that girls majoring in the field of home economics on the college level have limited part-time employment opportunities in the department of their major. However, home economics students with good typing skills fare much better since they can be of clerical assistance to the faculty in the various departments of their school.

Industrial arts majors and applied science and engineering students rarely have sufficient job choice in their particular fields during the first two years of college study. In fact, many work in other jobs on campus. However, by the time that they reach their junior year, students will usually find that departmental employment opportunities will increase. Also, engineering students find additional summer employment opportunities open to them rather than to most other college students.

Since the demand for graduates of the school of engineering is usually in excess of the supply, the young engineer has little difficulty in finding employment after graduation. In fact, most seniors majoring in this field have secured jobs before they receive their diplomas.

2. *General Education* (*High School*).   In referring to general education, the authors mean primarily the high school subjects (usually nonvocational), a definite number of which must be successfully completed in fulfilling the requirements for high school graduation. Briefly, the subjects referred to are a required part of a high school

curriculum in keeping with the educational policies of the state in which the school is located. It is understood, of course, that variation in subject requirements will exist among all of the states of the nation, as well as among high schools in any one state as long as minimal state requirements are met.

The most standard requirement of subject matter in any and all high schools is an emphasis upon English. Most, if not all, high schools require at least three units (years) of English study. However, the individual subjects which are classified as English vary greatly from school to school.

The basic requirements in a majority of high schools list a minimum of sixteen units of study for graduation, with a minimum of three units of English, one unit of social studies, one unit of mathematics, one unit of science, and one unit of physical education, which may or may not include certain state health requirements. The remaining nine units needed for graduation are selected by the student, usually with the advice of a counselor.

The authors emphasize that the one single subject area which can probably best prepare a student for higher education is English. Students, parents, and teachers must underscore the importance of the English language as essential in reading, comprehending, speaking, knowing, writing, and communicating, as basic to career preparation on a college level, and as quite necessary for employment following high school graduation.

A typist will have difficulty in holding either a part-time or full-time position unless she has a good knowledge of spelling and grammar, regardless of her typing skills. The engineer must communicate through the language of words as well as by numbers and symbols. The vocabulary of the scientist may be specialized within his profession and difficult for the nonscientific mind to comprehend fully, but his oral and written communications still rely upon a good command of English. The interpretation of art in all its forms, including music, painting, sculpture, design, drama, inevitably are subject to language for valid appraisal and evaluation.

English may be the most important subject of general education courses taught in the high school in regard to college preparation, but other subjects are essential in contributing to the students' overall schooling preparatory to taking definite places in our democratic society. The privilege of the freedom which we enjoy, our culture, and our way of life primarily are all transmitted from one generation to the following generation through the efforts of our schools. Therefore, a knowledge of the history and the development of these United States is an imperative for all of its citizens. Actually, a citizen must not only know of the historical past of our nation, but he must equally be a part of democracy in action.

Health and physical fitness training for youth is mandatory if our nation is to remain strong, viable, and dynamic. An appreciation of the fine arts is a part of our heritage from the past and must be sustained. The unrest in the world and the technological revolution demand increasing numbers of highly trained personnel in all branches of the social sciences, humanities, and natural sciences. We must provide the academic environment which will nurture, encourage, and inspire young people so that they develop many avenues of interest to develop their potentialities.

The business and industrial development of our nation is necessary to sustain the high standard of living which we enjoy. Management and labor must be constantly supplied with young employees who have initiative, resourcefulness, imagination, skills, abilities, and values. However, we must not overlook the prime ingredient which has made this nation truly great, work!

Our belief in the dignity and the worth of the individual and the work which he performs must be taught anew to each generation. All honest work, by its nature, has genuine dignity; different kinds and levels of work may require special skills and talents, and those who possess the talents and skills may receive more in the way of remuneration. But work, no matter how menial it may be, if well done, is commendable. We can ill afford to educate youth who do not believe in work.

Students who take additional courses in their general education programs in high school, considerably beyond the usual requirements, as previously indicated, may have little time for vocational subjects. This does not indicate that such students will not find some part-time work opportunities available on the college campus of their enrollment, but rather that the work opportunities will probably exist in student employment areas classified as unskilled labor. The authors find nothing wrong or unfair about students, regardless of academic potential, being employed in such sections as food service and plant maintenance. The point which the authors stress is that students lacking special training or skills should not expect employment in institutional student jobs requiring particular vocational abilities.

B.

The High School Student and Work Experience

College bound students can greatly improve their opportunities for part-time employment in college if they have had some previous work experience. However, an increasing number of high school graduates arrive on campuses of colleges with little or no significant work experience. This is not a criticism, as such, but it is rather a statement of fact.

There are a number of reasons for the high school students having negligible job experience. First, the high school student's school day allows little time for work other than in the evening hours. Second, weekend work in most communities finds more applicants than there are job opportunities. Third, many parents provide such generous allowances that their children are not motivated to work for their own spending money. Fourth, the social and academic activities for this age-group can be very demanding. Fifth, not enough parents can provide sufficient work responsibilities around the home for their teen-agers. Sixth, few teen-agers have salable skills. Seventh, Child Labor Laws eliminate or regulate employment in a number of occupations. Yet, farm work, one of the areas considered by many authorities to be hazardous work, is still acceptable for youth under the Child Labor Laws.

1. *Camping and Resort Work.* Most high school youth through necessity or inclination seek employment during the summer months. The availability of vacation period employment for these young people is often quite limited. However, communities, regions, and businesses depending upon the tourist trade for their livelihood usually provide some work opportunities for teen-agers. Summer camps offer a number of jobs both for the high school and the college-age youth. Such work experience usually is classified in three categories: camp counselors, food service workers, and water safety personnel. Customarily, the younger worker begins in food service areas, and the college youth usually in counseling and safety jobs. Regardless, the high school student who can find such summer employment will not only have a worthwhile work experience, but will gain financially since most camp jobs include some salary in addition to room and board. The high school student who performs well in a summer camp job may have his summer work assured for several years.

Motels, hotels, restaurants, stores, and gasoline stations located in major vacation areas, especially near national and state parks, usually provide vacation employment for more youth than those who reside in the immediate vicinity. Yellowstone National Park, the Rocky Mountain National Park, and the Great Smoky Mountains National Park, to list but a few resort spots, attract thousands of visitors in the summer months. To accommodate the visitors, tourists, and campers necessitates a number of business and service enterprises in the resort area which, in turn, provide many seasonal employment opportunities.

Also, communities located on or near the major interstate highways often rely upon automobile and truck transportation traffic, tourist or otherwise, as a means of bringing business to their areas. Again, the summer months are the periods of heaviest highway usage for vacationers and sightseers. In such communities, motels, restaurants, and service stations usually require additional help to man their businesses, and the high school student can often be employed to fill the temporary seasonal jobs.

Such work experiences are valuable for high school students for a number of reasons. First, the opportunity to earn one's own money and have the responsibility for budgeting and spending a salary are all worthwhile experiences. Second, the opportunity to carry out duties and to assume responsibilities through assigned work tasks exposes the student to the atmosphere of the adult world, a world of which he will soon become a continuing part. Third, the opportunity to participate in a cooperative activity enables the student to meet and to know better the characteristics of people from various parts of the country. Fourth, the opportunity to initiate a good work record will be useful in future employment. Fifth, the opportunity to develop self-reliance, display initiative, accept both criticism and praise for one's work are all important in the progression from childhood to adulthood.

Occasionally, a high school student will find a summer job with a local factory, but, more frequently, factory and industrial work are reserved primarily for full-time personnel. There are exceptions such as the canning industry which uses thousands of additional people during the peak seasons of harvest and canning months. It should be kept in mind that during the summer months, an estimated four million college students seek summer employment on a full-time or a part-time basis. It is understandable that in the competitive labor market the high school student frequently ranks second-best. Although this situation may be somewhat discouraging for the high school student, it is a realistic matter in our competitive society. Filling out application forms and being interviewed for summer work are actually sound educational experiences for the high school youth, even if he does not immediately find work.

2. *Farm Work*. The need for additional farm labor in the summer months still assists boys in rural regions to earn money. In spite of phenomenal changes in farming methods during the past fifty years, such as the transition from animal power to mechanical power, there is still work to be performed which is not automated. Frequently, the nature of farm work is such that it offers one of the best physical fitness programs possible for high school athletes. For example, long days of stacking hay bales on wagons makes men of boys physically. Contrary to the thinking of some adults and even some parents, the high school boy, particularly the athlete, is not looking for an easy summer job. In fact, the opposite is probably nearer to his liking.

Also, sixteen and seventeen-year old boys usually prefer working outdoors in a man's occupation. There is something about an experience which combines hard manual labor, a summer day, country air, and a cooperative effort which is truly rewarding and lasting to a boy. Even though the situation has changed today, the authors recall with pleasure and pride their youthful experiences pitching wheat bundles for a threshing machine. Of course, the harvesting and threshing of wheat in southern Illinois, at that time, was also a social occasion. Wheat harvesting and threshing was a neighborhood effort. When the threshing rig was set up at a farm, the neighbors, men and women for several miles around, would gather to work. The womenfolk vied to outdo each other in the culinary arts which, to say the least, resulted in daily feasts. Perhaps it was the cuisine which the authors remember most vividly about those days and not the physical effort involved. The menfolk, aside from labor, found time to talk of farm problems, politics, and to exchange tall stories.

3. *Nurses' Aides*. An excellent work experience for the high school girl can now be found in many private and community hospitals. The work experience begins with simple, unskilled tasks, but it can build up to a semi-professional level, one of prestige. Since nursing is one of the major professional occupations for women, it can readily be seen that if a high school girl selects nursing as her career choice, she can

gain both skill and knowledge in this profession by serving as a nurses' aide. If she is not certain of her career choice, her experience as a nurses' aide will provide practical experience upon which to base a decision. Again, discounting the professional career possibilities, the practical nursing experience is desirable employment for a young lady, regardless of her future vocation, because of its practical application when she assumes the role of a homemaker in the future.

From the standpoint of the professional nurse, she welcomes assistance with many of her routine duties, allowing her to be free to perform more highly skilled tasks. Hospital personnel directors are well aware of the shortage of nursing personnel. Also, nursing homes and the provisions which Medicare allots have placed a tremendous demand upon the entire medical profession and its facilities. So, the hospital or nursing home, by sheer necessity, must utilize more semi-trained and semiskilled personnel in their services.

4. *Market Employment.* Another area of part-time and summer-time work for high school students is in the supermarkets. Stock clerks, check-out cashiers, and vegetable counter attendants all acquire employment training transferable to similar jobs in markets near college campuses. In other words, a boy or girl who becomes proficient as a check-out clerk in a large market has an employment record with the company. When the student leaves his home town, the manager will often write a letter of recommendation to the manager of the chain store supermarket in the college town. The student may have a part-time job assured before he enrolls in the college or the university. Such clerking experience is always good student employment training, even if the skills do not specifically carry over to another job. The constant contact with the general public provides a repertory of experience useful in almost any type of future employment.

5. *Odd-Jobs.* Not infrequently, high school students become initiated into the world of work by means of the odd-jobs route. Girls will often begin their employment as baby sitters, and boys usually start by doing yard work. Parents should encourage their children to assume such tasks and emphasize the importance of performing any duties efficiently and conscientiously.

C.
Applying for and Getting the Campus Jobs

Frequently, well-qualified personnel miss good employment opportunities because of unfavorable impressions which they leave with the personnel interviewers. Applicants have difficulty selling their most precious asset, themselves. Some "freeze" during the interviewing sessions and are all but uncommunicative. Some fail to supply important facts about themselves, such as their past employment records, previous job earnings, promotions, special training programs completed, and general qualifications for the job which they are seeking.

Others may discount entirely the importance of appropriate clothing and general appearance, even though this usually is of great significance to the employer in filling a specific job. Some applicants may rely too heavily upon whom they know than what they know. Others may consider the interview as of only minor importance, and their casualness may well cost them a job opportunity.

Having interviewed hundreds of students for employment purposes, the authors would like to list those items which they consider to be important and which the student should consider prior to his employment interview. Such "homework preparation" should aid the student applicant in almost any eventuality.

1. *The Employment Application.* Customarily, one initiates the job seeking process by filling out an application for employment. The employment papers should be answered with care and completeness; failure to follow simple instructions may give the job interviewer the impression that the applicant is careless. Above all, in filling out an application, be truthful in answering the questions. Employers have a way of checking statements made by potential employees. Although employment application forms vary with the employers, general information required of the applicant is approximately the same, but specific job information will differ. The application used in student employment with Southern Illinois University is illustrative of the kind of data required of student applicants (see Appendix D).

2. *The Student Employment Interview.* An employment interview is essentially a conversation in which the interviewer is both seeking and giving information. It is customary for the interviewer to be business-like, but friendly. The professional interviewer has a number of

personal techniques which he uses to put the applicant at ease. Regardless, an interviewee has much at stake and it is expected that he will be nervous, but it is a sign of poise when he does not show it.

In discussing the student employment interview, the authors will present both the role of the interviewee (applicant) and the position of the employment interviewer or counselor as he is frequently called. First, we shall list information which we consider as useful in preparing the student for his job interview.

1] BE PROMPT. If possible, arrive five or ten minutes before the time set for the employment interview. If one is entering a building for the first time on an unfamiliar campus, look for unique features in or around the building to identify it since several trips to the employment office will probably be required.

2] BE WELL GROOMED. Cleanliness is most necessary. Wear fresh, appropriate clothing and be careful to avoid overdress or wearing something extreme or faddish. Simple, business-type clothing is always in good taste. If you are a young lady, leave your glittering earrings, patterned hosiery, and exotic bracelets at home. A very brief skirt may be long enough for dancing, but it is too short for an employment interview. Makeup for a young lady should call attention to her natural attractiveness, not to obviously accentuated cosmetic application. Theatrical eye shadow, layers of pancake powder, and pallid lips could well be a detriment, not an asset to the applicant. Most student employment interviewers do not encounter would-be stage stars, nor do they have jobs for them. A girl's hair should be her crowning glory and not a traffic-stopper. Continuing the subject, long hair is appropriate, apparently, for some musical groups, but in respect to student employment and future campus jobs for boys, it is not desirable. What is wrong with wearing a clean shirt, tie, socks, polished shoes, and a well-pressed suit or sports coat-slacks combination? Nothing! Remember, if you are employed on a campus job, you are a representative of the university, not only as a student but as an employee. Your attitude toward your job is often reflected in what you wear, and this attitude greatly influences job performance and efficiency.

3] BE FRIENDLY AND SINCERE.   There is little need to elaborate further since the importance of these qualities are obvious.

4] SIT ERECTLY IN YOUR CHAIR AND LOOK AT THE INTERVIEWER. Remember, if you are a young man, and you drape yourself in a chair and set your gaze languidly upon the traffic beyond the window, the interviewer may refer you to Health Service, not as an employee but as a patient. Look alive! If you are a young lady, sit properly and show a smile; such an attitude may be your referral card to a student receptionist's job. Do not wring your hands or tie knots in your gloves; do not take this opportunity to freshen your makeup. You may be nervous, but learn not to show it. If you feel that you must smoke, be certain to ask permission of the interviewer.

5] ANSWER QUESTIONS HONESTLY AND QUICKLY.   Remember, the smallest white lie may emerge later as a great embarrassment. The interviewer is on your side, but he must know certain things about you in order to find suitable employment for you. Do not take offense at what may appear to be a number of personal questions. Answer questions intelligently and briefly. Try to avoid slang; in fact, use your best grammar without being stilted. Also, in a student employment interview, the counselor will assess or review your financial need and will want to know if you have a scholarship or a loan. He will probably inquire as to your academic goals, your previous work experience, and the employment of your parents. He will probably want to know about your high school record and ask you to list your hobbies. He will usually inquire as to your job interests and future career plans. Be prepared to answer or discuss such items intelligently.

6] ASK QUESTIONS AND SHOW AN INTEREST.   It would seem that you would want the interviewer to tell you of the kind of work for which you qualify, the number of hours of work, and the beginning pay rate. You should inquire as to the possible effect work might have on your academic grades. You may use the interview time to find out about other forms of financial assistance such as scholarship awards, National Defense Education Act loans, the Guaranteed Loan Program, and the Educational Opportunity

Grants. Even if your interviewer does not have this information, he can direct you to the appropriate office where you can find answers to your questions.

7] GET YOUR GOOD POINTS ACROSS. Be tactful at all times, but have no reluctance about expressing your job interests and career goals. If you are a young lady who has had two years of high school typing and shorthand training, do not hesitate to make this fact known. If you have had several summers of office experience, this should definitely interest the interviewer. If you ranked in the upper 10 percent of your high school graduating class, do not be so modest as to allow this fact to escape the interviewer. If you have no work experience or special skills, do not try to cover up this lack, but tell the interviewer that you are willing to learn. If you must work in order to enroll or remain in college, emphasize this fact since most colleges and universities give financially needy students a job placement priority, assuming that the applicant is academically capable. This does not mean that you will be able to select a specific job, but rather that an all-out effort will be made to place you in work which you can perform and earn necessary funds. If you want a part-time job primarily for the experiences and educational values which can be obtained, be sure that your interviewer knows this. The needy student may have priority, but when such applicants are accommodated with jobs, the student employment office will try to locate work for any and all students who sincerely want to work.

8] DO NOT GIVE UP EASILY. If you are not placed in a student job within a few days, you may feel that your services are not needed by your college or university. In all probability such is not the situation, but you can aid your cause by returning to your job interviewer, if need be, every day for a week or more. When your interviewer sees how persistent you are, he will be more inclined to give your situation additional attention. Interviewers know that a sizable number of college students who seek jobs are not faced with a financial crisis at the time but want the security of work since their money may disappear before the semester ends. The student who is persistent in requesting a job immediately, usually will obtain results.

9] EMPLOYMENT PROBLEMS ON THE JOB. Once you are placed in an on-campus job, your immediate supervisor is your boss, and you should feel free to discuss problems with him. However, the student employment interviewer (counselor) has special training in personnel work, plus a record of your employment, so you should have no hesitancy about contacting him. Also, the student employment office has a responsibility to serve both the working students and the university. Therefore, it is an important part of the work of the personnel in this office to be interested in your problems. Some colleges and universities have staff members in their financial aids offices who specialize in the guidance and vocational counseling so vital to a successful work-study program.

The authors attach a maximum importance to the student employment interview which is the beginning of the student's work experience education. Since the significance of the interview in the employment process for full-time employees is an accepted fact, a thorough and appropriate interview for students who apply for an institution's part-time employment would hardly need to be defended. Nevertheless, institutions which recognize the importance of the interview are aware of the time and money which the institution can save in the prevention of problems and misunderstandings by means of good initial interviewing for part-time jobs.

Although the authors favor the central approach to student work program administration, the discussion and outline which follow, concerning employment interviews, should be adaptable to institutional differences in organization.

The student employment interview should be so structured that the interviewer can obtain information, impart information, and make evaluations. The interviewer accomplishes these purposes through the processes of observing, questioning, listening, and making objective judgments based upon the information obtained as indicated.

1. TO OBTAIN INFORMATION. This, we may call the interviewer's overview since he is interested in an overall picture of the student as the applicant might fit into the employment situation.

a) Observing the student with respect to such factors as
1) physical attributes such as neatness, attractiveness, appropriate

dress, voice quality, and personal size;   2) personality traits such as friendliness, warmth of personality, confidence, emotional control, control of tension or nervousness.

b) Questioning the student in regard to   1) high school background and training;   2) work experience, quality of experience, abilities, skills, interests and hobbies;   3) the extent of financial need and other forms of financial assistance for which application has been made;   4) career plans, course of study, and what the student hopes to accomplish by working;   5) awareness of purpose for a college education and the priorities of work and study over social activities;   6) willingness to make personal sacrifices, such as working during vacation periods or weekends.

c) Listening to the student   1) analyzing how he feels about his past successes and failures; how he has met new or changing situations (maturity); how he expects to rely upon his own resources (degree of responsibility);   2) deciding how he feels about his parents, personal relationships with others, his background, his schooling (necessary in order to obtain insight into the student's sense of values, attitudes, motivation, and personality pattern).

2. TO IMPART IMFORMATION CONCERNING   a) duties and responsibilities involved in the job;   b) skills and quality of work required; c) definition of what is expected in regard to cooperation and work relationships with peers and supervisors in the job situation;   d) policies of the student work program which are directly related to the situation;   e) rates of pay and possibilities of merit increases and promotions on the job;   f) potentialities for self-development on the job;   g) the importance of the work to be done;   h) the privileges and the responsibilities which accompany employment with the institution.

3. TO MAKE EVALUATIONS   a) as to how the student's skills, abilities, and personality traits correlate with those required in the job;   b) as to the probability that the student will be able to perform well in both work and study;   c) as to the possibility that the student will need financial assistance in addition to the funds he can earn working.

4. TO INTERVIEW PERSONNEL APPLICANTS   *a*) make careful plans in advance of the interview and know what he, the interviewer, hopes to accomplish;   *b*) be objective and direct the interview;   *c*) note carefully the facts which are given;   *d*) be at ease, comfortable, friendly, and make the student feel as relaxed as is possible;   *e*) display an attitude of acceptance, but neither approval nor disapproval of the student, as a person;   *f*) initiate the interview with general questions but later lead into specific questions;   *g*) exercise skill in asking leading questions;   *h*) pace the interview so that not too much time is spent on one or two items;   *i*) recognize the differences in cultural backgrounds and customs in students;   *j*) avoid prejudice;   *k*) be aware of possible misunderstandings which arise because of semantics;   *l*) give the student adequate time both to ask and to answer questions;   *m*) have a clear conception of the qualifications which are necessary for success in various possible jobs;   *n*) adapt the interviewing process to the particular student and his needs.

3. *Referring a Student to a Job.*   Referring a student to either an on-campus or an off-campus job is the last step in the process of student interviewing. When the interview is not terminated with a job referral, usually the student employment interviewer arranges another period for the student to return in order to complete the referral process. The job referral is a most important part of the student employment procedure since it indicates certain conditions have been met, as listed below.

1] THE EMPLOYMENT INTERVIEWER'S FAVORABLE EVALUATION OF THE APPLICANT MEANS THAT THE STUDENT HAS THE NECESSARY QUALIFICATIONS TO PARTICIPATE IN THE WORK PROGRAM OF THE INSTITUTION.   It should be noted, of course, that the United States Office of Education College Work-Study Program has its own specific qualifications for student employment. The interviewer should note whether the student meets the College Work-Study Program requirements, as well as the institutional standards.

2] THE STUDENT, IN ACCORDANCE WITH HIS SIGNATURE ON HIS APPLICATION AND THROUGH THE OPPORTUNITY AFFORDED HIM IN THE INTERVIEW, AGREES TO WORK UNDER THE CONDITIONS SET FORTH IN WORK POLICIES FOR STUDENT EMPLOYMENT, AND THE STUDENT

MUST MEET THE INSTITUTION'S ACADEMIC REQUIREMENTS FOR WORK PROGRAM PARTICIPATION.

3] IF FINANCIAL NEED IS A FACTOR IN THE STUDENT'S QUALIFICATION FOR WORK, EVIDENCE TO SUBSTANTIATE HIS NEED IS RECORDED IN HIS PERSONNEL FILE.

4] THE INTERVIEWER'S JOB LISTING BOOK DETAILS EMPLOYMENT OPPORTUNITIES WHICH REQUIRE SKILLS AND TRAINING APPROPRIATE TO THOSE OF THE STUDENT'S AGE AND EXPERIENCE. Therefore, to refer the student to one of those jobs so listed would indicate that both the university and the student should benefit from the student's employment. In order to perform his job well, the employment interviewer must have a thorough knowledge of the institution's currently available student jobs. Institutions which employ several thousand students in a wide variety of jobs may use interviewers assigned to specific student job groups. To illustrate: A student employment counselor may spend virtually all of his time interviewing and referring only clerical workers; however, his associate may interview and refer only applicants for service jobs. The student's actual potentiality can be better realized through consultation with one who is well versed in a particular area of employment.

5] THE STUDENT SHOULD EVIDENCE A TRUE WILLINGNESS TO WORK. The interviewer's experience has taught him that some students, just as some staff people, have a much greater interest in the money to be received, than in the task to be performed. A gold-bricking student worker can damage a work program considerably.

6] THE EMPLOYMENT COUNSELOR MAY USE SEVERAL MEANS, SUCH AS LETTER, TELEPHONE, OR CARD, TO REFER THE STUDENT TO THE SUPERVISOR (EMPLOYER). The most commonly employed method is the use of a referral card, which usually serves such purposes as *a*) to introduce the student to a prospective employer; *b*) is evidence that the student meets work program regulations; *c*) is evidence that the student qualifies for the job as listed by the supervisor; *d*) is a record both for the employment interviewer and the supervisor; *e*) can be signed by the supervisor and returned to the interviewer as an indication that the student was employed.

The referral process may be considered as complete when the student is employed. This does not indicate that a student is always employed with a single referral because the supervisor may wish to interview several qualified students. In addition, the student may have referral cards to several different supervisors, giving him a selection of jobs.

The authors call attention again to the interviewing and the referral process described as one designed primarily for institutions having central administration of the student work program. In institutions with decentralized employment procedures where each department has the authority to employ students without the approval of a central office, it is unlikely that one would find a standard procedure for student employment interviewing and referral. In fact, the opposite situation can be anticipated with some students employed in institutions without the benefit of an interview, preceding employment. The authors find that the trend today is definitely inclined toward central administration in the interests of efficiency.

Institutions which utilize the United States Office of Education College Work-Study Program rely upon the financial aids office of the school to determine the eligibility of students to participate in the program. This means that the College Work-Study Program has a central administration; what remains for many institutions is to place all of the student employment under the control of one central office. The authors favor central administration for student employment programs, with decentralized operation for the employing units or departments. This means that departments will have the authority to employ students, but the students selected for such employment must be referred by the central employment office.

Such a procedure may not be of great importance in colleges which employ fifty to two hundred students; however, colleges and universities employing students in numbers from five hundred to five thousand should consider central administration for reasons of economy and efficiency.

4. *Employing the Student.* As indicated in the foregoing discussion, the student employment interviewer has a definite responsibility for the interview and the referral of the student to a job. However, the actual hiring of the student in an on-campus job is performed by a supervisor in one of the various organizational units or departments of the college or university. The authors use the term "supervisor" to include any institutional staff employee, academic or otherwise, who employs, trains, supervises, and terminates the services of student employees.

It is understandable since the supervisor is charged with the responsibility of student workers under his direction that he would also wish to interview each student applicant referred by the student work office. In all probability, the supervisor will discuss some of the points covered in the employment interview. If so, the emphasis is usually beneficial to the applicant because of reinforcement factors.

Although the supervisor has the authority to hire student employees for his operation, the final approval must have the endorsement of the student work office regarding hourly rate and total hours of work factors of control. The student work applicant, as previously indicated, becomes acquainted with a potential employer (supervisor) by means of the referral card, issued by the student employment office interviewer. It must be recognized by the supervisor that the student whom he employs may be experiencing regular employment for the first time. The supervisor should be aware also that as an employer he may be the determining force as to whether the student is to become a well-adjusted, reliable worker or a careless employee. The first day on the job for the student may constitute a nearly traumatic experience. The supervisor should keep this fact in mind and take certain steps to aid his new employee. The following listing is similar to the one recommended by Southern Illinois University's Student Work Office for the supervisors of student workers. The outline will be illustrative of one approach to new student employee orientation.

WELCOMING

1] INTRODUCTION. The new employee should be introduced to everyone in his immediate office and, if possible, to at least one major executive. Everyone needs recognition, and making the acquaintance of a top official can bolster a student's uncertain ego.

2] SPONSOR PLAN.   Many large companies have found that assigning a sponsor to the new employee will help his becoming a member of the group more readily. Select a satisfactory worker, one who likes people, and request him to invite the new employee to a coffee break, help him with the problems which need not be taken to the supervisor, and generally look after him during the first week or two. The new employee needs to participate, and he needs security. Help him to reach these goals.

DEPARTMENT ORIENTATION

1] THE NEW EMPLOYEE SHOULD QUICKLY COME TO KNOW THE MAIN RESPONSIBILITIES OF THE DEPARTMENT AS A WHOLE AND THE INDIVIDUAL RESPONSIBILITIES OF THE MEMBERS.

2] IN A LARGE DEPARTMENT, IT IS MOST HELPFUL TO DRAW AN ORGANIZATIONAL CHART AND LIST BRIEFLY THE MAIN FUNCTIONS OF EACH MEMBER.   Include this schematic explanation in an orientation manual for all new employees.

RULES AND REGULATIONS

1] ALL STUDENTS ON-CAMPUS ARE EXPECTED TO ABIDE BY THE RULES OF THE STUDENT WORK OFFICE, AS DESCRIBED IN THE *SUPERVISOR'S HANDBOOK.*   The regulations should be reviewed with the new employee very early in his work experience for two principal reasons, *a*) early impressions are of great importance; *b*) discussing these general rules with the new employee demonstrates the supervisor's support of the student work program on the campus, thus providing general continuity throughout the institution, as related to the expectations of students.

2] EACH OFFICE WILL GENERALLY HAVE ADDITIONAL OPERATIONAL RULES, OR AT LEAST MOST UNITS HAVE SUCH REGULATIONS EVEN THOUGH THEY HAVE NOT SET THEM IN WRITTEN FORM.   Employees learn about unwritten rules when such regulations are broken. Therefore, procedures should be set down in writing to save possible conflict. The supervisor should explain the rules and the purposes of and the needs for them. Most persons accept without question those rules and regulations which are understood.

WORK ORIENTATION

This phase is particularly important, requiring time and patience to attain. However, new workers frequently arrive at a busy time when they cannot be given sufficient instructions. For this reason, an orientation manual as described in the following pages is invaluable. A good pattern for job orientation is detailed here, to be presented in small dosages.

1] EXPLAIN THE JOB THOROUGHLY, STEP BY STEP, AND ESTABLISH QUANTITY AND QUALITY STANDARDS WHERE POSSIBLE.

2] TELL WHY CERTAIN PROCEDURES ARE FOLLOWED AND WHAT THE FORM MEANS.

3] REQUIRE A LITTLE ROUTINE WORK, EVEN DURING THE FIRST DAY.

4] ALLOW A LITTLE TIME FOR STUDY OF OFFICE MANUALS.

5] PROVIDE MACHINE ORIENTATION TIME IF APPROPRIATE AND GIVE HELP AS NEEDED.

6] EXPLAIN THE USE AND STORAGE OF SUPPLIES.

7] GIVE TIME TO STUDY AND TO BECOME FAMILIAR WITH THE FILES.

HOW TO DEVELOP A WORK ORIENTATION MANUAL

1] MAKE A JOB ANALYSIS. (See APPENDIX E.)

a) Purpose: *1*) To know what each job entails; *2*) to know what skills, knowledge, experience, and training are required; *3*) to know how the positions in the organization relate to each other.

b) Procedure: *1*) Questionnaire to present to employee; *2*) interview by qualified person; *3*) supervisor's report; *4*) observation by trained personnel; *5*) a combination of the above.

2] WRITE JOB SPECIFICATIONS. (See APPENDIX F.)

3] DEVELOP THE WORK ORIENTATION MANUAL FROM THE JOB SPECIFICATIONS, REQUESTING THE SUGGESTIONS AND ASSISTANCE OF OTHER EMPLOYEES. The following items should be included, *a*) rules and regulations of the office; *b*) departmental organization chart; *c*) job specifications; *d*) samples of forms properly completed with an explanation of their purposes; *e*) samples of other supplies with an explanation of their use; *f*) filing index; *g*) machine instructions, with emphasis on intricacies of operation; *h*) list of ledgers or record books with must be explained but cannot be included in the manual; *i*) drills for developing special skills.

POINTS WORTH REMEMBERING WHEN
SUPERVISING STUDENT WORKERS

The following suggestions may be helpful to the supervisor in his role of supervising student employees.

1] BE ENTHUSIASTIC YOURSELF—DO NOT STIFLE ENTHUSIASM IN OTHERS. Even misguided enthusiasm may become an asset to your operation. Learn to direct it.

2] DEMONSTRATE AN ATTITUDE OF SERVICE—AND INSTILL THIS ATTITUDE IN YOUR EMPLOYEES.

3] BE HONEST AND SINCERE—THERE ARE NO SUBSTITUTES, NO MIDDLE GROUND. Expect honesty from your employees.

4] BE AN INFORMED SUPERVISOR. Make it your business to understand the significance of your work. Keep your employees informed. Individuals are happier when they know the demands of their work.

5] BE A TOLERANT SUPERVISOR—CONSIDER THE VIEWS OF YOUR EMPLOYEES, EVEN THOUGH THEY ARE YOUNGER AND LESS EXPERIENCED. You are not tolerant when you feel superior to others, when you know all of the answers, when you are unreceptive to suggestions and ideas of others, especially those of subordinates.

6] TRY TO WIN RESPECT—RESPECT YOUR STUDENT WORKERS. To earn respect, you must be fair, firm, frank, and friendly. On the other hand, you cannot be "one of the gang."

7] BE A DEMOCRATIC LEADER—NOT A POPULARITY CONTESTANT OR AN AUTOCRAT. Democratic leaders are the ones who share deliberations, consult freely, but accept responsibility for making and standing by decisions. Employees usually develop well under such guidance.

8] BE A TEACHER—ESTABLISH A CLIMATE FOR GROWTH OF YOUR EMPLOYEES AND TAKE PRIDE IN THEIR ACCOMPLISHMENTS, BE THEY ACADEMIC, WORK, OR SOCIAL.

9] MANAGE YOUR WORK—DO NOT LET IT MANAGE YOU. Concentrate on the important jobs for yourself. Do not waste your time and energy on unnecessary details. Build a work schedule—daily, weekly, quarterly, and annually. Manage your time well; have a quiet period each day in which to plan.

10] FACE PROBLEMS—DO NOT TRY TO EVADE THEM. Many little molehills grow massively while you procrastinate. Before you can handle a problem, you must thoroughly understand it, from the employees' point of view as well as your own. Analyze it, seek the best advice available, think about it, then act.

11] TAKE MEASURES TO AVOID PEAKS AND VALLEYS IN THE WORK LOAD. Employee morale will be better as a result. Build lists of jobs which can be done at any time. Plan for the larger tasks well in advance.

Student Financial Aids

9 *Program Analysis and Recommendations*

IN THE CONTENT of this chapter, attention is given to the phenomenal changes which are continuously emerging in student financial assistance. It might be said that the innovations which appear are philosophically oriented in that they are outgrowths of the democratic principle involving equal opportunity for all individuals, regardless of race, color, or national origin.

It was indicated in an earlier chapter of this book that the private colleges of the colonial period of our history supported the belief that the lack of financial resources should not constitute a barrier to higher education. However, for more than three hundred years, colleges and universities, although supporting the tenet of equal educational opportunity, have never had adequate financial resources to convert this basic philosophy into a universal reality for American youth seeking higher education.

It is our thinking that the federal government in providing funds for multiple programs of student financial aid, coupled with the role of the various states in providing public higher education at minimal costs in both junior and senior colleges, are the two major factors which contribute to true equality of educational opportunity.

In this chapter, much of our study is devoted to the factors cited above and concluding recommendations, with the remainder concerned with a proposal for the establishing of a graduate degree in financial aids counseling and administration, presented for the reader's consideration. It is recognized by the writers that we may take an avant-garde position in recommending a professional degree for financial aid officers, but it is felt that the documentation presented justifies the proposal.

A.
Federal Financial Aid Problems and Recommendations

The present role of the federal government as the financial sponsor of multiple programs of student financial assistance in some 2,000 American colleges and universities is forceful and unprecedented. Few of us in higher education a decade ago anticipated seeing in such a brief period the wealth of educational opportunity in higher education available for such numbers of our economically disadvantaged youth, brought about by federally financed programs. At present, American sons and daughters from rural and urban poverty families can aspire for education beyond high school and have some assurance that if they have the academic potential, financial aid in the form of work, loans, grants, and scholarships is available in most of our colleges and universities. It does not follow that each and every student can attend the college of his specific choice but rather that higher education in a senior or junior college is economically feasible for most of our high school graduates.

However, three very significant facts must be recognized. First, a constantly increasing higher percentage of high school graduates has college in their career planning. Second, educational costs continue to rise. Third, to accommodate the higher education enrollment increases will require far more federal funds than the approximate 1.5 billion dollars now allocated per year.[1]

1. *Federal Financial Assistance Particularly for Graduate Students.*
The need for more federal support for higher education is recognized in a recent publication of the Association of American Universities. Of the seven principal recommendations, the following are concerned with financial assistance for undergraduate and graduate students:

> Expand student aid programs to encourage and enable the needy and disadvantaged to obtain higher education, and expanded loan programs to give students wide choice of where and what they will study.

> Recognition that there is a special Federal interest in sustaining, extending, and strengthening graduate and professional education.

---

1 John I. Kirkpatrick, Study Director, College Entrance Examination Board, *Notes and Working Papers Concerning the Administration of Programs* (Washington, D.C.: Government Printing Office, 1968), pp. 5–8.

Such recognition must include additional graduate fellowships and increased cost-of-education supplements to Federal fellowships more closely approximating the real educational cost to the institution.[2]

Neither of the above recommendations stresses the importance of more work opportunities for both undergraduate and graduate students. However, it is well known that institutions with graduate programs rely heavily on graduate students to assist with undergraduate teaching as well as research. Further, graduate teaching assistants, research assistants, and graduate interns are reimbursed for their services primarily from institutional funds, which generally are available in insufficient amounts to meet needs. Because the needs just described are imperative, the writers feel it desirable to make the following suggestions.

a) RECOMMENDATIONS. An expanded federal Work-Study Program with a special allocation of federal funds for graduate students. Such an expanded program for graduate students would serve three purposes:

1) Provide a high level of work experience for graduate and professional students at a fair wage, $3.00 to $5.00 per hour, for a 20-hour week

2) Provide financial relief for institutions since, in effect, federal College Work-Study funds at the present matching rate of 80 percent federal and 20 percent institutional would free institutional funds and other educational funds for different educational purposes

3) Provide financial assistance for more graduate students who are usually married and in great need of financial help

Additional graduate fellowships and additional National Student Loan Funds also are recommended as a supplement to the proposed Graduate Work-Study Program.

2 The Association of American Universities, *The Federal Financing of Higher Education* (Washington, D.C.: Association of American Universities, April 1968), pp. 2–3.

2. *Financial Aid and the Undergraduate at Senior Colleges and Universities.* The benefits to undergraduate students from low-income families who participate in federal financial aid programs such as work-study, loans, and grants, require some analyses and discussion. First, let us take a look at the National Defense Student Loan Program, remembering that this program is having a significant impact upon higher education. The National Defense Student Loan Program has been in existence since 1959, and between this date and 1967, $1,039,058,000 was lent to some 2,033,455 students according to a recent study conducted by the College Entrance Examination Board for the Office of Education.

The report states, "that the National Defense Student Loan Program has been a success is evident from all sources of information consulted for this study. Of respondents to the questionnaires sent to institutions of higher education, only 2 percent indicated that the program was unsuccessful in providing for the needs of students at their institutions. This same conclusion was reached by the study staff after analysis of printed reports, congressional testimony, and discussion with representatives of educational institutions and the Office of Education. Many of those involved, however, have pointed out some aspects of the program that could be modified to increase its effectiveness." [3]

a) NATIONAL DEFENSE STUDENT LOAN SHORTCOMINGS. The glaring weakness in the National Defense Student Loan Program lies in the collection of funds when the loan is in the repayment stage after the student leaves college. Institutional officials responsible for collecting N.D.S.L. funds have found that their principal problem is the locating of the student. One cannot collect from former students unless their residences are known. No doubt, the Guaranteed Loan Program will present the same difficulties to the bankers which the N.D.S.L. has created for college and university officials.

It must be remembered, in the instance of both loan programs indicated above, that a principle of banking has been breached in order to provide financial assistance to college youth. It is a policy of banking to lend funds to individuals who have sufficient collateral or backing to cover such loans. However, in the instance of both the

3 Kirkpatrick, *Notes and Working Papers,* pp. 20–21.

N.D.S.L. and the G.L.P., the loans are frequently made to students whose only collateral is their future earning power. It is obvious that college dropouts will appear to be poor risks since their earning potential without a college degree is, generally, substantially decreased. The result, of course, is a high rate of delinquent collections on the loans.[4]

There is still another factor to be considered concerning collection costs and delinquency rates which are increasing at an alarming rate. This relates to a selection process for loan recipients. Originally, the N.D.S.L. was designed for the academically capable, financially needy students. Admission officers and finacial aid officers were capable of selecting needy recipients who had an excellent chance of completing four years of college. However, since 1965 there has been a heavy emphasis placed upon the financial need with less consideration given to academic potential. The reason for this stress stems mainly from the attempt of the United States Office of Education to provide more financial assistance for the very low-income-family students, often referred to as disadvantaged in terms of culture, education, and economics.

b) EDUCATIONAL OPPORTUNITY GRANT PROGRAM AND GUIDELINE INTERPRETATION. The Educational Opportunity Grant Program, by design, is established primarily for the students who come from families with an income below $6,000 annually. The guidelines for the Educational Opportunity Grant Program are as follows:

"An institution shall not award an Educational Opportunity Grant unless it determines that— *1*) He has been accepted for enrollment as a full-time student at such institution, is in good standing and in full-time attendance there as an undergraduate student; *2*) He shows evidence of academic or creative promise and capability of maintaining good standing in his course of study; *3*) He is of exceptional financial need; and *4*) He would not, but for an Educational Opportunity Grant, be financially able to pursue a course of study at such institution of higher education." [5]

---

4 "Toward a Long-Range Plan for Federal Support for Higher Education," *A Report to the President.* U.S. Department of Health, Education, and Welfare, Office of the Assistance Secretary for Planning and Education (Washington, D.C., January 1969), p. 11.
5 Higher Education Act of 1965, P.L. 89–329, *Legislation Establishing and Amending: The National Defense Student Loan Program, The College Work-Study Program, The Educational Opportunity Grant Program, The Guaranteed Student Loan Program* (Washington, D.C.: Reprinted by the U.S. Department

At this point it would be wise to call particular attention to the U.S.O.E. guideline above that presents a major problem to financial aids officers, admissions officers, and the institution in general, "He shows evidence of academic or creative promise and capability of maintaining good standing in his course of study." The intent of this guideline is probably too often ignored.

It should be noted that the recipient of an Educational Opportunity Grant receives from $200 to $1,000, depending upon his financial need as it relates to the educational cost budget of the particular institution in which he is enrolled. Also, the institution must match the grant of the recipient in other forms of financial aid such as student employment, N.D.S.L., scholarships, etc. However, the amount of the grant may not exceed 50 percent of the institution's student financial aid budget. Thus, an institution with an $1,800 student financial aid budget could not award an Educational Opportunity Grant larger than $900.

c) ACADEMIC STANDARDS AND THE DISADVANTAGED. If one gives a literal interpretation to the guidelines cited, then one would adhere to academic standards normally employed by most institutions in selecting their freshman class members, that is, high academic achievement and/or high college entrance test scores. However, in actual practice, it is becoming increasingly evident that colleges and universities are lowering their admissions standards to accommodate large numbers of disadvantaged high school graduates, regardless of academic potential or achievement but having great financial need. The next step can be anticipated. Most of the disadvantaged students will encounter academic competition which they are frequently ill-prepared to meet.

Thus, the institution may feel it desirable for teachers to lower their academic standards in the classroom or aid the students' plight by affording a variety of costly tutorial projects which will attempt to accomplish in a few months that which has not been achieved in twelve or more years. As previously indicated, the disadvantaged group for which the admissions standards were lowered are generally a group without financial resources. Accordingly, the federal financial aid package, grant, loan, and work, is frequently provided to lower the financial barriers. The problem now may be compounded because if the financial aid officer, who also can interpret entrance test scores and

of Health, Education, and Welfare, Office of Education, Bureau of Higher Education, February 1969), p. 3.

academic achievement records, questions the advisability of admission, as related to the U.S.O.E. Guideline 2, "He shows evidence of academic or creative promise," he is usually advised that admission is an academic matter. Thus, there is the interpretation that the economically, culturally, and academically "disadvantaged" students have just as much academic or creative promise as a higher education institution determines.

d) THE FINANCIAL AID PACKAGE. However, the possible leniency in admission policies as indicated previously, does not solve the problem for the financial aid officer who normally works out a financial aid package for the needy student which includes ten to fifteen hours of work per week, a National Defense Loan, and an Educational Opportunity Grant. At this point, our disadvantaged student has an equality of educational opportunity paralleling the status of the affluent middle class and in a majority of instances has more financial resources than students from the lower middle class. In fact, many financial aid officers are deeply concerned about students from families with income in the $7,000 to $10,000 bracket. This salary group earns too much to qualify for most of the federal aid programs but too little to make a major contribution toward the cost of higher education for their children.

Although the financial aid officer can solve the disadvantaged student's financial problem, he cannot remedy the student's academic problems. Institutions which enroll large numbers of the disadvantaged need a variety of projects such as teaching machines, group counseling, non-credit courses, and special tutors to re-school the disadvantaged students. Frequently, a student with a financial aid package will wish to resign a student job when facing academic problems. It does not appear to occur to such a student that a time budget is in order, taking some social hours and applying them to study needs of various types. Also, if a student leaves his job, additional funds may be necessary from other sources if the student is to remain in school. Additional funds available are usually in the form of loans, either the N.D.S.L. or a Guaranteed Loan. Inevitably the supplementary loans soon burden the student considerably beyond his capacity to repay and too often result in high collection costs and loan delinquency.

It may now be seen that the federal financial aid tripod—work, loans, and grants—for disadvantaged students presents a genuine problem. If the disadvantaged for academic reasons cannot work, and they are poor risks for loans, this leaves only a grant. In the name of disadvantaged students and poverty, one could construct a case for a huge federal grant program which would provide a "free ride" in institutions of higher learning for all disadvantaged youth, culturally, educationally, and economically. Should not these young people be afforded the equality of educational opportunity? Should these young people not see that dream of a college diploma become a reality? Is society not obligated to take care of its disadvantaged since the strong can take care of themselves?

However, one can take another position. Has not society provided free public education for at least twelve years for all of its youth? What did these students do with their time and opportunities? How did they become so educationally disadvantaged? Should society consider poverty as a talent, mediocrity of achievement as academic excellence, and ignorance as creative promise?

e) RECOMMENDATIONS. The writers believe that federal financial aid packaging for needy undergraduate college students will achieve more success and receive less criticism if programs follow guidelines which fall between the extremes previously cited. Therefore, the following recommendations are made:

1] That colleges and universities with four-year degree programs and/or professional and graduate programs refrain from lowering academic standards leading to graduation for any group of students, disadvantaged or otherwise. Obviously, the classroom teacher who is not in an experimental program should retain his classroom standards and hold firm against suggestions and/or coercion from either students or the administration. An experimental program was mentioned in the above discussion. The writers would not take issue with such a program if it were designed for a small percentage of disadvantaged students who would be expected to enter a regular course of study after a period of time, not to exceed two years, and complete successfully the remainder of the program of studies leading to a degree. Hopefully, the findings of the experimental program would be such that they could be used by secondary schools and community colleges in bringing disadvantaged students to the desired academic proficiency level. In general, the writers feel that both the individual and society will benefit more in the course of events if high school students who plan to attend college are brought up to college standards before leaving the secondary school rather than expecting colleges to lower established standards to accommodate ill-prepared high school graduates. If colleges and universities will take such a stand, high school students who include college in their career planning would be more highly motivated to excel in their high school academic studies. However, if students merely coast through high school for four years, then hope to be admitted to college, they should not be disappointed if they are rejected, regardless of their economic circumstances.

2] That, except for those in the experimental program previously described, the federal financial aid package should be reserved for academically capable students who are motivated to obtain a college education but lack the financial resources to continue their academic work. It is a principle of financial assistance that a needy student accept whatever financial aid is available. Accordingly, student work should be a significant part of the student's financial aid package because work experience meets both an educational and a financial need. A student who is unwilling to work for the opportunity to attend a college or university does not deserve such a chance to obtain a degree. Among the better indicators of a student's maturity is the willingness of the student to match his desires for independence with overt manifestations of responsibility. A student who really wants an education will be motivated to expend the additional effort demanded for a job well done in both his studies and his employment.

It is generally recognized that college students will waste fifteen to twenty hours per week unless they have a job or some social activity to consume their non-school time. Next to their studies, we recommend work as the most important activity since its rewards are multiple—educational, social, and financial. There is nothing that removes most college students from the dependent class and places them in the independent class more rapidly than earning their own money. In general, the working student is a contributor and an asset to society—not a liability! Thus, a student who applies for federal financial assistance to attend college should not be too disadvantaged to work.

3] That colleges and universities provide more diversity of student jobs on their own campuses and develop a variety of academically related jobs for upperclassmen with a level of job difficulty which will challenge the college student. Students who attain academic excellence and a rating of excellence in job performance should be recognized by a "Certificate of Merit," and, whenever possible, this recognition should be accompanied by a nominal monetary award. Higher education can ill afford to ignore its scholars and high achievers because to do so would eventually weaken the very fabric of our great democratic nation. Students who prefer to "Pay as you go" rather than "Pay for it later" should be given priority for full-time employment at the college or university during the summer months. Also, low-income-family students should be counseled, and they should clearly understand that a loan must be repaid. Too frequently, youth from low-income families are under the impression that being disadvantaged means that the college or university owes them a grant, job, or a loan. Financial aids counselors must explain to these young people that a job means work! A loan is an obligation which must be repaid; the grant is the only gift, and it must be matched with work or other forms of financial aid. All of the above means of assistance add up to an opportunity—not a just due.

Our youth in this great nation should be reminded that they have been afforded more opportunities for higher education than is offered to youth in any other nation in the world. This does not mean that equality of educational opportunity has been afforded each and every young person in the United States but rather that that few, if any, students endowed with ability, motivation, and a willingness to help themselves will be denied an opportunity to continue their education.

4] That the federal government place more emphasis and money on student work programs for both the undergraduate and the graduate. The College Work-Study Program has been subjected to little or no criticism from the taxpayers. It is a popular program among financial aids officers. It is an established educational program as well as a source of funds for needy students and yet, in spite of all the above, less than 10 percent of the total federal funds for student financial aid goes to the College Work-Study Program.[6] Why? We recommend that no less than one-third of all federal financial aid for students should be channeled into self-help programs.

3. *Financial Aid and the Junior College.* It is generally accepted that the most rapidly growing division of higher education in America is the junior college, often called the community college. The junior college as an institution of higher education is just emerging into its own, and it may be several years before the full impact of the junior college movement is felt by higher education and by the general public, as well.

The objectives of the junior college, general education, vocational education, and adult education, constitute an attempt to meet a need which neither the secondary schools nor the four-year colleges have been able or willing to accommodate. If properly administered and programmed, vocational education of a trade and technical nature, long neglected in the secondary schools, may attain the heights which it so well deserves. It must be remembered that only approximately 50 percent of high school graduates continue their education beyond high school. Hopefully, the junior college with its multiple programs will attract many students who otherwise would not pursue additional education. In an age of technology such as ours, it is imperative that the junior colleges give priority to the vocational curriculum. Such an emphasis does not call for lowering the standards of general education. Rather, it means that vocational education has been overlooked for so long that it will require a major effort on the part of teachers and administrators to build programs which will attract both our youth and adults.

a) EQUAL EDUCATIONAL OPPORTUNITY. It is not the purpose of this chapter to explore in depth the junior college, either to extol its strengths or to point out its weaknesses. It is rather to accept the

6   In 1967, of the estimated $1,581 million federally funded student aid programs, only $150 million was allocated to student employment (9 percent).— Kirkpatrick, College Entrance Examination Board, *Notes and Working Papers*, p. 5.

greatly increased number of junior colleges as another historical landmark which provides American youth with equality of educational opportunity. However, the junior college is still out of the financial grasp of too many American youths, in spite of the fact that educational costs, tuition and fees, are minimal and permit most students to live at home and commute to college. Thus, there is a definite need to establish financial aid programs to provide financial assistance for academically capable, needy students who enroll in junior colleges.

Harold Reents, in his study of junior colleges, 20 in Illinois and 15 out-of-state, enrolling 102,756 students, was concerned in his research with student financial needs and financial aid programs. He found early in his investigation that a significant ratio, 36 percent, of junior college students indicated that a junior college was selected because of their personal limited financial resources. The findings showed that financial aid programs are needed in junior colleges, regardless of how the financial aid programs are fitted into the administrative structure. This great need for financial aid programs for junior college students who live at home should not be surprising. It is to be remembered that many students from low-income families drop out of high school for financial reasons. Also, the hidden costs in obtaining a secondary education have long been the theme of many writers. Reents found that the cost to the students who attended junior colleges in Illinois ranged from $800 to $1,150 per student, depending upon the community. Even allowing for inflation since 1966, these costs are very low when compared to four-year colleges and universities. However, even such costs can set higher education beyond the reach of students from low-income families. From his study Reents concludes:

> The financial aids program, then, should be complete and carefully planned, structured by a philosophy for college and organized for students whose needs have been determined by a need-analysis system. This program should be administered by one person in the student personnel area and should include scholarships, loans, grants, on- and off-campus programs, the College Work-Study Program, and Cooperative Work-Study Programs. All Federal programs should be included in the financial aids program. With financial aids programs incorporating these ideas, the "Open Door College" will become more of a reality to those who have financial barriers to higher education.[7]

7   Harold Reents, "A Proposed Financial Aids Program for Public Junior Colleges in Illinois" (Ph.D. diss., Southern Illinois University, Carbondale, 1966), p. 117.

b) FEDERAL FUNDS FOR ADMINISTRATIVE EXPENSES. Although junior colleges are eligible to participate in federal programs of financial assistance, a well-structured and highly organized financial aid program is rare. There are several reasons why little emphasis has been given to financial aid programs for the junior college. First, with the rapid expansion of junior colleges, priority, rightfully so, must be given to curriculum programming, including the obtaining of personnel to do such programming. Second, there is an acute shortage of trained personnel who are qualified personnel officers in four-year colleges and universities, so one would scarcely expect the financial aid operation in a junior college to be well staffed. Third, the enrollment size of many junior colleges is too small to justify the cost of even one full-time financial aid officer. In such colleges, one can often find a personnel officer who is admissions officer, counselor, and financial aid officer. A three-way split makes it extremely difficult to maintain efficiency in all of the tri-areas. Fourth, the plight of the needy student has not received the attention and concern it deserves.

A recent amendment in federal legislation concerning the administration of federal student financial aid programs, Work-Study, Educational Opportunity Grants, and National Defense Student Loans, will be of great importance in providing funds to employ personnel to assist with the administration of financial aid programs in higher education. In general, the amendment allows 3 percent of the federal funds spent for the Work-Study, N.D.S.L., and Educational Opportunity Grants, to be used for administering these programs. For the benefit of the reader, the Amendment is quoted:

SEC. 463 (*a*) An Institution which has entered into an agreement with the commissions under Part A or C of this title shall be entitled for each fiscal year for which it receives an allotment under either such part to a payment in lieu of reimbursement for its expenses during such fiscal year in administering programs assisted under such part. The payment for fiscal year (*1*) shall be payable from each allotment in accordance with regulations of the commissioner, and (*2*) shall (except as provided in subsection (*b*)) be an amount equal to 3 percentum of (*A*) the institution's expenditures during the fiscal year from its allotment under part (*A*) plus (*B*) its expenditures during such fiscal year under Part (*C*) for compensation of students.

(*b*) The aggregate amount paid to an institution for a fiscal year under this section plus the amount withdrawn from its student loan fund under Section 204 (b) of the National Defense Education Act of 1958 may not exceed $125,000. Enacted October 16, 1968, P.L. 90–575, Title I, Sec. 152, 82 Stat. 1033.[8]

c) THE OUTLOOK FOR FINANCIAL AID IN THE JUNIOR COLLEGE. For several years, individual financial aid officers and their professional associations have worked with the United States Office of Education officials for the enactment of the above amendment. The additional funding for financial aid administration should not only supply the much needed personnel for operational purposes, but it should make a significant impression on college and university administrations as to the importance of financial aid programs. The junior college is in an ideal position to take advantage of the amendment since many such institutions are just beginning to structure their aid programs.

The writers foresee some outstanding financial aid operations being established in junior colleges within a few years. Further, it is believed that the junior colleges in many states will soon take over the leadership in providing good, low-cost education for a two-year period to high school graduates. Because of the community location, junior colleges are in a fortuitous position to implement curriculum innovations to assist the disadvantaged. Additionally, the writers believe that a variety of work-study programs including cooperative education is not only needed on the junior college level but that the community will support such programs. A community with a junior college which has a well-planned and implemented student financial aid program is a community which can truly say, "We have reached the goal; equal educational opportunity is afforded to all of our youth."

B.

Academic Courses and the Training of Financial Aid Officers

Is there a need for specific academic preparation in financial aid counseling and programming for financial aid officers, high school

8   *Expenses of Administration, Sec. 463, Legislation Establishing and Amending: The National Defense Student Loan Program, The College Work-Study Program, The Educational Opportunity Grant Program, and The Guaranteed Student Loan Program* (Washington, D.C.: U.S. Department of Health, Education, and Welfare, February 1969), p. 54.

guidance counselors, and junior college personnel counselors? Yes, the writers think that the time has arrived when the graduate schools in colleges and universities should concern themselves with the academic preparation of professionals for student personnel work, financial aid counseling, and program administration. The above is not an isolated thought or a new idea, because financial aid directors, U.S.O.E. officials, and college administrators who have attempted to employ financial aid officers with professional background and experience have long recognized this need. Probably, the most universal concern has been shown by the United States Office of Education when it states in one of its recent publications:

> Need for more staffing and training of financial aid officers: So rapid has been the acceptance and use of various loan programs that colleges and universities have been hard pressed to provide the administrative machinery to implement them, much less consider the implication of an increasing reliance on credit. Furthermore, of the 1,671 college and university respondents to this study questionnaire to institutions of higher education, only 20 percent worked exclusively on the administration of aid programs while 29 percent spent less than 30 percent of the week administering these programs. In the face of a staggering total of student financial aid esimated at $2.3 billion last year:
>
> 6. It is recommended that the U.S. Office of Education urge institutions to provide adequate staffs to administer student financial aid programs and offer to sponsor training programs to provide the institutions with better trained staff.[9]

1. *The Magnitude of Financial Aid Programs.* From the above, the most convincing evidence that higher educational institutions should allot additional time and support to the formal education and training of financial aid personnel appears in the magnitude of the programs of financial assistance. It should be noted that of the $2.3 billion total in student aid in 1967, some $1.5 billion was from the federal government, and this figure represented an increase of four times that allocated in 1961. Of the estimated funding of $2,242 million in student aid, including all sources in 1967, about 70 percent of the amount came from the federal government. At present, the higher education enrollment of some 7.6 million students lists approximately one of four

9   John I. Kirkpatrick, Study Director, *A Study of the Federal Student Loan Program,* conducted by the College Entrance Examination Board (Washington, D.C.: Government Printing Office, 1968), pp. 5–8.

students as a participant in one of the financial aid programs sponsored by the federal government.[10] It should be remembered that there are a number of agencies besides the federal government which provide financial aid for students, i.e., the institution, the state, and private donors. Financial aid officers, therefore, must be concerned with all agencies which contribute funds for the various financial aid programs.

2. *The Financial Aid Officer; His Duties and Responsibilities.* Prior to 1960, the number of financial aid officers in higher education would probably number little more than the total number of higher education institutions. Most colleges and universities had one person who administered scholarships and institutional loans. Usually, an academic committee reviewed scholarship applications, made the decisions, and turned the paper work over to the financial aid officer. Not infrequently, the financial aid officer had some kind of faculty status or rank, but too often his position was low in salary and high in prestige. Also, it was considered more of a steppingstone position than a career position. In most institutions, student employment was not a part of financial aids; in fact, it was usually administered either by the placement office or the institution's personnel office.

Today, in the emerging profession of financial aids, it is a small college indeed which employs no more than one financial aid officer, and, as most financial aid officers know, their operations are understaffed. No longer is the major responsibility of a financial aid officer that of administering scholarships, unless he is in a large university where the financial aid staff has a number of specialists.

Today, the individual who heads a financial aid operation, be his title coordinator, aid officer, or director, would be knowledgeable concerning no less than three kinds of federal aid programs, namely, work-study, grants, and loans. In the larger colleges and universities, the financial aid administrator usually has assistants to help administer multiple financial aid programs; thus, his role must also include personnel supervision and management. Besides a knowledge of federal financial aid programs which are complicated, state and institutional programs add to the complexity. Not only are the programs complex, but detailed records must be maintained for audit purposes on all expenditures of federal, state, and institutional funds. Need-analysis forms are required on students as well as achievement records

10 Kirkpatrick, *A Study of the Federal Student Loan Program,* p. 5.

and personal counseling files. Capable, needy students must be identified, counseled, and awarded a financial aid package. All of the above procedures require special skills.

Financial aid officers must work with students, faculty. staff, parents, and secondary school officials. In short, financial aids must be service-oriented, and those who perform as financial aid counselors must be student-centered. However, when their duties overlap in administrative responsibility, the counselors must also be program oriented. Thus, in the smaller colleges, a financial aid counselor must wear at least "two hats"—counselor and administrator. In large universities with enrollments of fifteen to forty thousand students, frequently from 25 to 50 percent of the students will have some form of financial assistance. A staff of ten to twenty full-time employees consisting of administrators, counselors, and clerks may be required to administer properly such a program which may have a dollar value in excess of $10 million, whereas a decade ago the dollar value was probably less than $1 million. It is obvious from the above that there is a great need for trained personnel; however, the demand far exceeds the supply.

3. *How Are Financial Aid Officers Trained?*   At present, on-the-job training is still the primary method for learning a financial aid operation. However, a number of institutions and agencies have conducted worthwhile workshops. For example, the College Scholarship Service has sponsored a number of regional workshops for financial aid personnel. This service has done pioneering work with need analyses, and often the workshops center around the theme of financial need. Documentation of financial need is basic to the allocation of funds in the form of grants, loans, or work to student applicants.

For the past five years, Indiana University has offered an annual summer workshop (one week) for financial aid officers in the Midwest region. The workshop is especially designed to help the beginning financial aid officer. This program, under the direction of Donovan J. Allen, Assistant Dean of Students at Indiana University, has been very successful.

The U.S. Office of Education in conjunction with each of its regional offices usually conducts annual workshops to make financial aid officers aware of new policies and procedures affecting federal programs. Also, the workshops serve as a means of getting acquainted, affording the participants an opportunity to discuss problems which often are nearly parallel in institutions of higher education.

All of the above-mentioned workshops are valuable as in-service training for financial aid officers. However, they do not constitute academic preparation to the extent that would enable graduate students interested in a career in financial aids counseling and administration to obtain a Master's degree in Higher Education with a major or minor in Financial Aids, or a Master's degree in Guidance and Counseling with sufficient academic exposure in finacial aids to have the skills and knowledge to assume the duties and responsibilities of financial aid officers.

4. *Additional Factors to Consider for Academic Preparation of Financial Aid Officers. a*) SKILLS AND INFORMATION. Among the factors a college department on the graduate level should consider in designing an academic program including one or more courses in financial assistance is: what skills are to be taught, and how much information is available. The information may be in the form of books, magazines, pamphlets, reports, theses, dissertations, and audio-visual materials. Special skills may be taught in the classroom and learned by means of practicums. The information should be accessible to the students either directly through library facilities, the classroom, or both. There is sufficient knowledge available about the subject of financial aid to defend the establishment of one or more courses in the academic program.

b) INSTRUCTION. The instructor should have adequate teaching skills and sufficient knowledge of the subject to teach and direct the learning of the graduate students. Resource personnel should be available to supplement the instructional staff. It is generally accepted that a doctorate is almost the minimum requirement for the instructional staff on the graduate level. Also, specific training and practical experience are highly desirable.

c) IS THERE SUFFICIENT INFORMATION IN THE FIELD OF FINANCIAL AIDS? It is the writers' professional evaluation that there is adequate information in the field of financial aids to justify academic courses; however, five years ago, such a statement could not have been made. In the past five years, the U.S. Office of Education has made major contributions to the field and deserves the credit for this breakthrough of financial aid information. The writers think that the reference bibliography in this book supports the view. At the same time, there is an awareness of the shortcomings in the financial aid field. More research is necessary. This was indicated in another chapter of this book, but academic programming could do more to provide additional research than anything else. A national journal in the field can be a means of bringing the results of research to the practitioners, financial aid counselors, and administrators. Thus, academic courses in financial aids should serve as a moving force to bring about the above developments.

d) IS THERE A SUFFICIENT NUMBER OF INTERESTED STUDENTS? Probably the most important factor centers on the number of students who have the interest and desire a career in this new, challenging profession. The great shortage of financial aid personnel administrators to manage multiple programs of financial aids, and, especially, counselors to work with capable, financially needy youth has already been pointed out. The writers have documented the need and also presented the U.S. Office of Education Amendment to provide the funds to employ additional professional employees in the field of financial aids. Additionally, other individuals could benefit from the program. There are at present in a number of colleges and universities, graduate students who are majoring in College Personnel Work, and no doubt most of them could gain from one or more courses since financial aids is now a major division in the student services divisions of most of our larger colleges and universities.

Also, there is a great need for high school counselors not only to identify capable, needy students but to have sufficient financial aid information to counsel and advise these students. Obviously, it is believed that academic courses in the field of financial aid would strengthen student personnel services in secondary and higher education.

5. *A Proposed Curriculum for Student Financial Aid Majors.* In designing the academic preparation for student financial aid officers, it is thought that an expansion of the present college student personnel program is necessary to accommodate the specific courses in financial aids that are desired. The writers propose a possible concentration of study that will provide the graduate student with the necessary skills

and experience to be competent in exercising his duties and responsibilities as a financial aid officer. It is within the realm of reason that following his graduation, an initial position could be open to him as director of student financial aid in a medium-size college.

The possible Master's degree program proposed in student financial aids requires a minimum of 60 quarter hours (40 semester hours) of study and is designed to be completed in a calendar year (four quarters—fall, winter, spring, and summer). The program brings together theory and practice while the student is still in an academic environment. The reader will note that of the 60 quarter credit hours, 38 to 44 hours are from required courses with the difference in the requirement depending upon which internship, the six hour or twelve hour, the student elects. A good selection of courses (38 quarter credit hours) are provided as electives so that the student may reinforce his speciality or broaden his preparation by taking advantage of the diversity in course offerings. The program has been designed so that a graduate majoring in financial aids would have adequate training for other college personnel positions in student services such as those in placement, housing, counseling, and admissions.

The writers sincerely believe that the universities which have the facilities and staff to adopt the program shown in Appendix G, or a similar program, will find sufficient numbers of students willing and able to fill the classrooms. It should be realized that the structure of the program is indicative rather than all-inclusive. It is the writers' belief, however, that only when academic preparation for financial aid officers becomes a reality can one say that financial aids is a profession.

Appendixes / Glossary / Bibliography / Index

Appendixes

To: Supervisors of Student Employees

From: Student Work Office

In order to enhance the educational values of a student's work experiences on the campus, the traits to be evaluated should be discussed with each student worker before sending the completed form to the Student Work Office. These ratings are of value for the student worker's permanent file and are used for the purpose of counseling the student, in referral to job openings, and in making recommendations as requested by future employers. They are also of value to the Student Work Program in the over-all evaluation of the Program.

PLEASE OBSERVE THE FOLLOWING PROCEDURES IN SENDING THE EVALUATIONS OF YOUR STUDENT EMPLOYEES TO THE STUDENT WORK OFFICE FOR—

1. SENIORS: Evaluations become a part of the student's file in the Placement Service. These should be made at the end of the student's *junior year* in order to become a part of his credentials.

2. ALL OTHER STUDENT EMPLOYEES: Evaluations should be made in *January* of each year. It is advisable that employers counsel with the student concerning his ratings if the student is to receive maximum benefits from his work experience and appropriate helps in improving his work habits.

3. STUDENTS LEAVING YOUR EMPLOY: Please send along with the termination form an evaluation of the student who quits the job, who is asked to change jobs, or who withdraws from your employ for any reason.

4. TEMPORARY WORKERS: Evaluations should be made for a student who works only one term or at extra work or on a temporary basis, upon termination of his employment.

NOTE: Retain a carbon copy for the departmental files.

Name of Student (Last name first)   Fr. ___ Soph. ___ Jr. ___ Sr. ___ Grad. ___ Uncl. ___
Classification of Student (check one)

College, Department, Service, or Enterprise   Name of Supervisor   Date

Please describe briefly the duties of the student or the type of work performed by the student.

Please evaluate each student employee for each criterion shown below. If the criterion does not apply or if you do not have sufficient information, please check the column marked "N" for no evaluation. Check each characteristic as follows:

A—Superior;   B—Above Average;   C—Average;   D—Below Average;   E—Poor

	A	B	C	D	E	N
1. Skills and Abilities: Has knowledge and ability essential for work and good background in the field of work.						
2. Dependability: Is trustworthy, punctual, reliable, fulfilling responsibilities, good in attendance.						
3. Quality of Work: Work is accurate, thorough, acceptable; uses materials and time economically, takes care of materials; eager for improvement.						
4. Initiative: Has ability to think along original lines; to find new and better ways of performance; to look for useful work and to organize new operations and perform new functions with exceptional skill.						
5. Leadership: Is able to influence and inspire others to do better work; is able to organize and direct work of others.						
6. Personal Appearance: Is neat, clean, suitably dressed; poised; good posture.						
7. Judgment: Has self control; ability to make sound decisions; uses common sense in performance of duties; is tactful in relations with others.						
8. Co-operation: Has ability to work with fellow workers, supervisors, and others; is deeply conscious of responsibility to working group.						
9. Attitude Toward Work: Is courteous, cheerful, and interested; willing to work at difficult or disagreeable tasks; able to take instructions cheerfully.						
10. Physical Vigor: Is enthusiastic about work; active and energetic, keeps self in good state of health; emotionally stable.						
11. Quantity of Work: Has ability to do a comparatively large amount of work of above average quality; has ability to work under pressure as under normal conditions.						
12. Potentialities: Has high degree of potentialities for future improvement and development as he matures.						

Comments: (May use other, side for additional comments.)

Signature of Supervisor   Signature of Dean, Chairman, or Director

Evaluation Rating Form of Student Worker;

EVALUATION OF PART-TIME STUDENT WORKER
(Instructions on back)

Soc. Sec. No. _____

Name _____ Classification ____ ____ ____ ____ ____
      Last   First   Middle   Fr. Soph. Jr.   Sr. Grad.

Department _____

Duties _____

_____

Please evaluate each student employee (as compared with peer group) according to the traits listed below, rating them as follows:

    A—Superior   B—Good   C—Average   D—Poor   N—No Evaluation

Note: All traits may not apply to each student because of the great diversity in the opportunities for employment and because of other variables affecting the work record and financial and personal needs of students. If a trait does not apply, please check No Evaluation.

	A	B	C	D	N
Integrity: *Trustworthiness, honesty and loyalty*					
Dependability: *Promptness and reliability in attendance*					
Responsibility: *Willingness with which work is accepted and performed*					
Initiative: *Ability to plan and direct one's own work*					
Judgment: *Ability to make sound decisions*					
Cooperation: *Ability to work with others in harmony*					
Leadership: *Qualities of understanding people and directing work of others*					
Quality of Work: *Degree of success in applying one's abilities to his work*					
Attitudes toward Work: *Degree of enthusiasm with which one performs his work*					
Emotional Stability: *Poise and self-control*					
Courtesy and Friendliness: *Skills in expressing consideration and kindness toward others*					
Personal Appearance: *Neatness, cleanliness, appropriate dress and grooming*					
Potentialities: *Ability to meet and to apply one's self to new situations*					

FURTHER INFORMATION OR COMMENTS AS APPLICABLE:

Date _____ Supervisor's Signature _____

6690-2.021-7

227

QUESTIONNAIRE   **B**
(Student Employees)

For the Evaluation of Student Experience in Jobs Available
on the Carbondale Campus, Southern Illinois University

Pilot Study

The purpose of this questionnaire is to obtain information from student
workers about their work experience in a job or jobs while enrolled as full-
time students. The results of the data should assist in evaluating better
the Southern Illinois University Student Work Program.

Instructions and Information

Please place a check mark in the parentheses opposite the best answer to
the question asked. Information in regard to individual replies will be kept
strictly confidential.

Part I
Financial Assistance, General

Please indicate your Class

         Freshman   ( )
         Sophomore   ( )
         Junior   ( )
         Senior   ( )
         Graduate   ( )

Sex

         Male   ( )
         Female   ( )

1.   What do you estimate your college expenses will be for this year?

     a. $ 800 - $ 999   ( )
     b. $1,000 - $1,199   ( )
     c. $1,200 - $1,399   ( )
     d. $1,400 - $1,599   ( )
     e.   More than $1,600 ( )

2.   What portion of your college expenses for three quarters can be met
     by your on-campus job?

     a.   0.0 - 19.9%   ( )
     b.   20.0 - 39.9%   ( )
     c.   40.0 - 59.9%   ( )
     d.   60.0 - 79.9%   ( )
     e.   80.0 - 100.0%   ( )

3. In addition to your campus job, do you have any other form of financial assistance?

Yes   ( )
No   ( )

If "Yes," please list type or types of form (loan, grant, scholarship) and the amount involved.

Loan_____ Amount_____

Grant_____ Amount_____

Scholarship
or Award_____ Amount_____

4. Could you continue your college schooling without working?

a.   Yes   ( )
b.   No   ( )
c.   Undecided ( )

Part II
Work, General Information

5. How many different student jobs have you held on campus?

1 - 2   ( )
3 - 4   ( )
5 - 6   ( )
7 - 8   ( )
9 - 10   ( )

6. How many hours do you work on an average on your job per week?

5 - 10   ( )
11 - 15   ( )
16 - 20   ( )
20 +   ( )

7. To what extent do you feel that your job interferes with your academic program?

No   ( )
Some   ( )
Considerable ( )
Great   ( )

8. To what extent do you feel that employment interferes with your social life at college?

No   ( )
Some   ( )
Considerable ( )
Great   ( )

9. What, approximately, is your overall academic average in college?

Below C   ( )
    C+   ( )
    B   ( )
    B+   ( )
    A   ( )

10. If your parents could finance your entire education, would you still want to work part-time?

Yes   ( )
No   ( )
Undecided   ( )

Part III
Special Skills in Work Experience

11. To what extent have you developed clerical skills (office work, library, postal, etc.) from your job or jobs in college?

No   ( )
Some   ( )
Considerable   ( )
Great   ( )

12. To what extent have you developed mechanical skills from your job or jobs in college? (Printer, bus driver, maintenance of machinery, etc.)

No   ( )
Some   ( )
Considerable   ( )
Great   ( )

13. To what extent have you developed numerical skills from your job or jobs in college? (Accounting, Bookkeeping, Data Processing, Recordkeeping, etc.)

No   ( )
Some   ( )
Considerable   ( )
Great   ( )

14. To what extent have you developed verbal fluency, either oral or written, as a result of your job or jobs? (Answering telephone, receptionist, correspondent, reporter, television or radio announcer, etc.)

No   ( )
Some   ( )
Considerable   ( )
Great   ( )

15. To what extent have you developed social skills as a result of your job or jobs in college?

No   ( )
Some   ( )
Considerable   ( )
Great   ( )

16. To what extent have you developed the ability to work with others in your job or jobs in college? (Peers, supervisors, visitors, etc.)

No   ( )
Some   ( )
Considerable   ( )
Great   ( )

17. To what extent have you developed logical reasoning as a result of your job or jobs in college?

No   ( )
Some   ( )
Considerable   ( )
Great   ( )

Part IV
Attitudes toward Responsibility

18. To what extent do you believe that your campus employment has improved your leadership ability?

No   ( )
Some   ( )
Considerable   ( )
Great   ( )

19. To what extent has campus employment provided you with a sense of accomplishment?

No   ( )
Some   ( )
Considerable   ( )
Great   ( )

20. To what extent has your job or jobs on campus helped you to understand better the importance of cooperation?

No   ( )
Some   ( )
Considerable   ( )
Great   ( )

21. To what extent has working in college and earning your own money contributed to your maturity?

No   ( )
Some   ( )
Considerable   ( )
Great   ( )

22. To what extent has working with a university department, business unit, or group developed your sense of loyalty to them?

No   ( )
Some   ( )
Considerable   ( )
Great   ( )

23. To what extent has campus employment in college developed your appreciation for the dignity of all honest work?

No   ( )
Some   ( )
Considerable   ( )
Great   ( )

24. To what extent has work in college been rewarding to you other than in terms of the money which you have earned in your job or jobs?

No   ( )
Some   ( )
Considerable   ( )
Great   ( )

25. To what extent has your student employment helped you to understand university or school business, policies, and procedures?

No   ( )
Some   ( )
Considerable   ( )
Great   ( )

Part V
Values Derived from Work Situations

26. To what extent has your college employment related to your academic studies?

No   ( )
Some   ( )
Considerable   ( )
Great   ( )

27. To what extent do you think that your college employment experience will help you in full-time employment after graduation?

No   ( )
Some   ( )
Considerable   ( )
Great   ( )

232

28. To what extent has your college work experience influenced your career choice?

No   ( )
Some   ( )
Considerable   ( )
Great   ( )

29. To what extent has college work experience given more meaning and purpose to your overall education?

No   ( )
Some   ( )
Considerable   ( )
Great   ( )

30. Do you think that your college work experience has been of sufficient educational value to you that it deserves college credit?

Yes   ( )
No   ( )

(If your answer is "Yes," how many hours of credit? _____

31. Do you think that college part-time employment with the institution should be a part of a student's general education and that during some time of his first two years in college he should, regardless of need, be required to work?

Yes   ( )
No   ( )

(If you answered "Yes," please indicate the quarters (a quarter equals three months) of work in college which you would require, the kinds of work, and the number of hours.)

Quarters   _____

Kinds of Work   _____

Total hours of Work   _____

5 - 10 per week   ( )
11 - 15 per week   ( )
16 - 20 per week   ( )
20 +   ( )

General Comments, if any:

Name   _____
Present Employment:
    College, School, Department   _____

                                         _____

QUESTIONNAIRE
(For Student Employee Supervisors)

For the Evaluation of Student Work Experience
Available on the Carbondale Campus, Southern Illinois University

Pilot Study

The purpose of this questionnaire is to obtain information from supervisors, both academic and nonacademic, concerning the work experience (Student Jobs) available under their supervision in order to evaluate better the Southern Illinois University Student Work Program.

Instructions and Information

Please check the parentheses provided at the right of the question which indicates your answer. Information in regard to individual replies will be kept strictly confidential.

Part I

Information Concerning Supervision

1. How long have you supervised student workers in Southern Illinois University?

   a.   Less than one year   ( )
   b.   1 - 5 years   ( )
   c.   6 - 10 years   ( )
   d.   11 - 15 years   ( )
   e.   16 - 20 years   ( )
   f.   More than 20 years   ( )

2. Please indicate your university employment status.

   a.   Faculty Administration   ( )
   b.   Faculty   ( )
   c.   Administration Staff   ( )
   d.   Civil Service   ( )
   e.   Graduate Assistant   ( )

3. Please check.

   Male   ( )
   Female   ( )

4. Please indicate the number of students directly responsible to you.

   a.   1 - 5   ( )
   b.   6 - 10   ( )
   c.   11 - 15   ( )
   d.   16 - 20   ( )
   e.   More than 20   ( )

5. Please indicate the number of students indirectly responsible to you.

    a. 1 - 10   ( )
    b. 11 - 25   ( )
    c. 26 - 50   ( )
    d. More than 50   ( )

Part II

6. To what extent do student jobs under your supervision provide a valuable experience for the students, regardless of their academic programs or career plans?

    No   ( )
    Some   ( )
    Considerable   ( )
    Great   ( )

7. To what extent do student jobs under your supervision show a close relationship to the institution's academic program?

    No   ( )
    Some   ( )
    Considerable   ( )
    Great   ( )

8. To what extent do you think that part-time work experience influences the vocational choice of college students?

    No   ( )
    Some   ( )
    Considerable   ( )
    Great   ( )

9. To what extent do you think that work experience interferes with the academic achievement of the students under your supervision?

    No   ( )
    Some   ( )
    Considerable   ( )
    Great   ( )

10. To what extent do you think that jobs under your supervision develop clerical skills?

    No   ( )
    Some   ( )
    Considerable   ( )
    Great   ( )

11. To what extent do you think that work experience may motivate students to higher achievement in their academic fields?

No   ( )
Some   ( )
Considerable   ( )
Great   ( )

12. To what extent do jobs under your supervision develop verbal fluency, either oral or written?

No   ( )
Some   ( )
Considerable   ( )
Great   ( )

13. To what extent do jobs under your supervision develop mechanical or numerical skills?

No   ( )
Some   ( )
Considerable   ( )
Great   ( )

14. To what extent do jobs under your supervision provide the student with opportunities to develop social skills?

No   ( )
Some   ( )
Considerable   ( )
Great   ( )

15. To what extent do jobs under your supervision provide leadership opportunities?

No   ( )
Some   ( )
Considerable   ( )
Great   ( )

16. To what extent do jobs under your supervision provide students with opportunities to learn the importance of cooperation?

No   ( )
Some   ( )
Considerable   ( )
Great   ( )

17. To what extent do you take a personal interest in students under your supervision and their problems?

No   ( )
Some   ( )
Considerable   ( )
Great   ( )

18. To what extent are the working students in your opinion more mature in manners and attitudes than are the non-working students?

No   ( )
Some   ( )
Considerable   ( )
Great   ( )

19. To what extent do you think that work experience has helped students under your supervision to develop an appreciation for the dignity of all honest work?

No   ( )
Some   ( )
Considerable   ( )
Great   ( )

20. To what extent do you think that our youth feel that a college education will place them above work?

No   ( )
Some   ( )
Considerable   ( )
Great   ( )

21. To what extent do you think that a student's earning his own money contributes to his maturity?

No   ( )
Some   ( )
Considerable   ( )
Great   ( )

22. To what extent has the supervising of students been a rewarding experience for you?

No   ( )
Some   ( )
Considerable   ( )
Great   ( )

23. To what extent is Southern Illinois University giving too much emphasis to student work?

No   ( )
Some   ( )
Considerable   ( )
Great   ( )

24. To what extent does work experience on campus give more meaning and purpose to the students' overall education?

No   ( )
Some   ( )
Considerable   ( )
Great   ( )

25. Do you think that work experience has sufficient educational value to warrant the granting of college credit?

Yes   ( )
No   ( )

(If your answer is "Yes," how many quarter hours of credit should be given per term?) _____

26. Do you think that work experience on campus should be a part of a student's general education and that some time during his first two years in school he should, regardless of need, be required to work?

Yes   ( )
No   ( )

(If your answer is "Yes," how much work on an average, should be performed, and for how many terms?) _____

_____

27. To what extent do you think that the university should enlarge upon the job diversity for students especially in jobs related to academic programs?

No   ( )
Some   ( )
Considerable   ( )
Great   ( )

General Comments, if any:

Name   _____
Division of Assignment:
    College, School, Department _____

Date   _____

SOUTHERN ILLINOIS UNIVERSITY
Carbondale, Illinois 62901

D

Office of Student Work and
Financial Assistance

Application For Student Employment

PHONE: (618) 453–2388

NAME Mr. Mrs. Miss _____ *Last* _____ *First* _____ *Middle* _____

(NOTE: Must be full name)

Term you want employment to begin: _____ 19 __

Record Number: _____

Local Address: _____ Phone: _____

Home Address: _____ Phone: _____
No. Street _____ *City* _____ *State* _____ *County* _____ *Area Code* _____ *Number*

Date of Birth: _____ Place of Birth: _____

Citizenship: _____ Marital Status: _____ Number of Dependents: _____

Health and/or Physical Disability: _____

Name of Parent or Guardian _____ Address: _____
Street _____ *City* _____ *State*
Number of Dependents on Family Income: _____
Occupation of Parent: _____ Employer: _____

GIVE A BRIEF STATEMENT CONCERNING YOUR REASON FOR WORKING PART TIME: _____

Do you have a scholarship or loan? _____ Specify and Name: _____ Amount $ _____

How much income must you earn? _____ Do you have a car at the University? _____

List below two references who may be contacted for a recommendation for you:

Name	Address	Occupation

EDUCATIONAL EXPERIENCE:

Name of high school from which you were/or are to be graduated: _____ Year: _____

Approximate high school average: _____ Honors won: _____

Other colleges attended: _____ and grade average: _____

When Did You/Or Will You Enroll At Southern Illinois University? _____ 19 _____
Term _____ *Year*

In what college, school or division, please check one:

Agriculture ____ Business ____ Communications ____ Education ____ Fine Arts ____ General Studies ____ Graduate ____
Home Economics ____ L.A.S. ____ Nursing ____ Special Institutes ____ Technology ____ V.T.I. ____

Major Interest: _____ Minor: _____ Undecided: _____

Current Grade Average at Southern Illinois University (if any) : _____

I have read the "General Instructions to Applicants for Student Employment" and am willing to abide by the Student Work Policies.

Signed: _____

NOTE: Please continue to fill out page two and the top of pages three and four.

6690-2.004-2

Please check jobs you are qualified to do or write in special skills you have which are not listed. If you have any questions, please ask counselor during your initial interview. Indicate years or months of training and experience in each job preferred.

		Training	Experience
CLASSIFICATION I.	Pre-Professional Jobs		
__04	Accompanist		
__05	Architect-		
	Drafting, Survey		
__06	Art Illustrator		
__07	Computer Operator		
__08	Electronics Worker		
__09	Guide for excursions,		
	trips, vacations		
__10	Guide for Sports		
	Instructional Aide		
__11	Agriculture		
__12	Art & Music		
__13	Eng. Speech & Drama		
__14	Foreign Language		
__15	Health & P.E.		
__16	Industrial Arts		
__17	Mathematics		
__18	Science		
__19	Social Studies		
__20			
__21			
__22			
	Laboratory Worker		
__23	Biological Science		
__24	Chemistry		
__25	Clinical or Hospital		
__26	Physics		
__27	Lighting Operator		
__28	Modeling		
__29	Nurse's Aide		
__30	Pharmacy		
__31	Photographer		
__32	Printer		
__33	Projectionist		
__34	Psychometrists		
__35	Public Address Oper.		
__36	Stage Equipment Oper.		
__37	Taxidermist		
__38	Dancing Teacher		
__39	Golf Teacher		
__40	Ice-Skating Teacher		
__41	Tutor		
__42	X-Ray Technician		
__43			
44			

CLASSIFICATION II. Clerical Jobs			
__45	Accounting & Bookkeeping		
__46	Business Machines		
__47	Cashier		
__48	Dictaphone Oper.		
__49	Justowriter		
__50	Filing		
__51	Good Handwriting		

		Training	Experience
__52	Key Punch		
__53	Lettering		
__54	Library Work		
__55	Manuscript Typist		
__56	Mimeograph Oper.		
__57	Multilith Oper.		
__58	Proof Reader		
__59	Receptionist		
__60	Sales		
__61	Shorthand		
__62	Statistical-		
	Calculator Oper.		
__63	Switchboard Oper.		
__64	Stenotype		
__65	Typing		
__66			
__67			

CLASSIFICATION III. Service Jobs			
__68	Baker		
__69	Bartender		
__70	Carpenter		
__71	Caterer		
__72	Cook		
__73	Food Service Worker		
__74	Janitor		
__75	Lifeguard		
__76	Meat Cutter		
__77	Painter		
__78	Police Worker		
__79	Sports Official		
__80	Waiter/Waitress		
__81			
__82			

CLASSIFICATION IV. Pre-Skilled & Semi-Skilled Jobs.			
__83	Bus Driver		
__84	Dry Cleaner		
__85	Work with Animals		
__86	Farm Worker		
__87	Landscaper, Gardner		
__88	Laundry Presser		
__89	Laundry Worker		
__90	Printing Press Worker		
__91	Seamstress		
__92	Shop Maintenance		
__93	Electronics Engineer		
__94			

CLASSIFICATION V. Temporary Jobs			
__95	Camp Counselor		
__96	Child Care		
__97	Entertainer		
__98	Entertainer, Musical		
__99			

Type of Work Most Desired: _____

Type of Work You Would Not Consider: _____

Freshman:
Class Schedule: Check hours when you <u>will be</u> available for work. (*if known*)

	FALL						WINTER						SPRING						SUMMER					
	M	Tu	W	Th	F	S	M	Tu	W	Th	F	S	M	Tu	W	Th	F	S	M	Tu	W	Th	F	S
8																								
9																								
10																								
11																								
12																								
1																								
2																								
3																								
4																								
5																								
6																								
7																								

Time Blocks for Additional Years:

Sophomore: _____   _____   _____   _____

Junior: _____   _____   _____   _____

Senior: _____   _____   _____   _____

Graduate: _____   _____   _____   _____

For Staff Use at Office of Student Work and Financial Assistance:

INTERVIEW RECORD

Initial Interview Date: _____ Complete Interview By: _____

Name of Counselor

Financial Need: A B C D E

Academic Potential: A B C D E

Social Maturity: A B C D E
(for student's age)

Remarks: _____

General Impression of Student on Initial Interview:

APPEARANCE: A B C D E
Neatness
Cleanliness
Appropriate Dress
Grooming
Complexion
Health
Other _____
Size _____

ATTITUDES: A B C D E
Co-operation
Responsibility
Personal-Social
Adaptability
Enthusiasm
Other _____

PERSONALITY: A B C D E
Pleasing
Emotional Control
Dynamism
Confidence
Leadership Potential
Other _____

Comments: _____
_____
_____
_____
_____

Name:_____ Date of Application_____ 19_____

Social Security Number:_____ Graduate: Graduate:

Classification: Freshman ___Sophomore___ Junior___Senior___V.T.I.___Special___Masters___Doctorate_____

 Year: 19_____19_____19_____19_____19_____19_____19_____19_____

EMPLOYMENT EXPERIENCE: List summer, part-time, or full-time employment you have done recently:

Employer	Address	Type of Work	Dates (Inclusive)

Have you worked on campus before? _____ Where?_____

 Number of Terms: _____ Type of Work:_____

For Staff Use at Office of Student Work and Financial Assistance:

Comments:_____

_____

Date	Record of Interviews and/or Job Referrals	Counselor

Title of Position:_____
(Example: File Clerk, Stenographer, etc.)

Describe the general nature of your job:

List the specific duties you perform:

Daily:	_____
Weekly:	_____
Monthly:	_____
Semi-Monthly:	_____
Annually:	_____
Very irregularly:	_____

To whom do you report?_____

From whom do you receive instructions?_____

How many employees do you supervise? _____
Give names and titles   _____
_____
_____

Education and Training:

In your opinion, what is the minimum schooling one should have for this job?
High School_____, College_____, Other_____
1 yr.   2 yr.   3 yr.   4 yr.

What special courses or training are needed?_____

What type of past experience is needed and how much?_____._____

What is the breaking-in time (that is, how long before you felt yourself to be
a competent employee)?_____

What did you have to learn on the job?_____

Working Conditions:

What is the most difficult part of your work?_____

Why?_____

Roughly, how much of your time each day is spent:
Sitting_____ Standing_____ Moving about_____

What are your working hours?_____ to _____

What are the most disagreeable features of your job, if any?_____
_____

What physical requirements are necessary for the performance of your job?_____
      (Example: Finger dexterity, strength, height, etc.)
_____

What standards of speed and accuracy are required?_____
_____

List any special or unusual working conditions:_____
_____

Machines, Supplies, and Equipment:

What machines do you operate, and roughly, how many hours per day?
      Daily_____   Hours_____
      _____   _____

Irregularly?   _____   _____
    _____   _____

What forms and reports do you originate? (List by title)_____
_____

What supplies do you use?
      Daily_____
      Irregularly_____

Responsibilities and Miscellaneous:

Indicate responsibility for:	Frequently	Sometimes	Never
Money or other valuables	_____	_____	_____
Supervision of employees	_____	_____	_____
Public Relations	_____	_____	_____
Decisions	_____	_____	_____
Judgment	_____	_____	_____
Planning	_____	_____	_____

State the nature of your responsibility for:·
  Public Relations_____
  Decisions_____
  Exercise of Judgment_____

Is your job changing?_____ (If so, how?)_____
_____

Describe any special features of your job not covered above that would help in
preparing a detailed description._____
_____
_____

JOB SPECIFICATIONS (DESCRIPTION)   **F**

(Written from Foregoing Job Analysis Questionnaire)

Job Title: Clerk Typist   Department: Accounting
Supervisor: John Doe

I. Duties

    A. Daily
        1. Types invoices from shipping orders; checks extensions
        2. Types purchase orders from requisitions received from purchasing
            department
        3. Files purchase orders alphabetically by company names
        4. Operates a small switchboard and acts as a relief receptionist
            fifteen minutes a day
    B. Occasionally
        1. Transcribes letters from a voice-recording machine
        2. Composes some routine letters and memos
    C. Periodically
        1. Posts checks to ledger twice a month
        2. Posts accounts payable at end of each month
        3. Types parts of annual accounting report at end of year

II. Equipment Used

    A. Standard Royal typewriter
    B. Electric ten-key Burroughs adding machine
    C. Alphabetical and date files for invoices, purchase orders, and a small
        number of letters, memos, etc.
    D. Dictaphone
    E. Switchboard

III. Special Skills and Knowledge

    A. Typing, special skill in numbers
    B. General knowledge in English and simple bookkeeping
    C. Some ability to greet business callers and handle a switchboard

IV. General Requirement of the Department

    A. Graduation from high school
    B. Good training in typing, English, and arithmetic (might be expressed as
        certain score requirements on college entrance examinations)
    C. No experience necessary. Department will train for job, except for typing

V. Physical Activities

    A. Sits at a desk most of the day
    B. Stands when filing
    C. Good eyesight and alertness needed for accuracy in numerical work

VI. Working Conditions

    A. Small room with other offices adjacent
    B. Other people frequently pass through office
    C. Fluorescent lighting

VII. Comments

    A. Work is varied
    B. No important decisions need to be made; individual simply follows
        instructions
    C. Deals with practically no one outside the office except during period
        on switchboard

Required Courses (38 - 44) for Major

Quarter
Credit
Hours

4   1. Educational Statistics

a. Study of the theory and techniques of measurement

b. Study of the standardized tests and other measuring devices
to reveal individual and group characteristics

c. Emphasize application and interpretation for counseling,
education, and research purposes

4   2. Counseling Theory and Practice

a. Systematic study of the assumptions and fundamental practices
of major approaches to counseling

b. Systematic study of major theories of counseling as they apply
to school situations

4   3. Financial Aid Counseling

a. Special attention given to the academic, social, and economic
needs of disadvantaged students

b. Particular emphasis given to the case study approach as it
applies to helping students from low income families

c. A study of the systematic approach to need analysis and
financial aid packaging for needy students

4   4. Vocational Counseling and Career Information

a. A study of the problems of college students as related to
careers and academic preparation

b. The importance of part-time student employment and summer
employment in career choice and employee attitudes

c. The procurement and distribution of occupational information

4   5. Principles of Guidance and Counseling

      a. This is an introductory course on student personnel services, a prerequisite for more advanced courses in counseling

      b. A survey of philosophy, principles, and organization of student personnel services in secondary and higher education

4   6. Higher Education in the United States

      a. An overview of American higher education, its strengths and weaknesses

      b. The development of private and public higher education, organization, functions, and issues

4   7. College Student Personnel Work: Operations and Policies

      a. Study of organization, functions, and undergirding policies of student personnel services

      b. Study of the various programs affected by private and public higher education today

4   8. The Administration of Multiple Programs of Student Financial Assistance

      a. Study of basic principles of administration as they pertain to institutional, state, and Federal financial aid programs

      b. Study of the organization structure and office procedures necessary for a functional operation

6 - 12   9. Internship in Higher Education

      (Internship to be done under the direction and supervision of the director of Student Financial Aids in conjunction with staff personnel in the Department of Higher Education)

      a. 12 credit hours (internship for three terms)
      The graduate student selecting this program would work for the financial aids office 20 hours per week for one academic year (9 1/2 months); however, for 16 hours per week, he would receive pay and for the remaining four hours would receive academic credit. Thus, the student would receive four hours of credit each term for three terms (12 hours). The arrangement for the graduate student could be on a salary level or on an hourly rate of pay

b. 6 credit hours (internship for two terms)
The graduate student electing this program would spend a
minimum of two hours daily in the financial aids office.
In this situation, the graduate student would consider
the financial aids office as a laboratory for learning.
He would be required to participate in a variety of learning experiences including counseling students and assisting with the routine operations of the office. The
graduate student would receive no pay, only academic
credit.

4   10. Student Work Program Administration and Operation

a. Study the employment interview, referral, and placement
process in work program operations

b. Identifications of special student work experiences that
relate to academic programs and the importance of job
descriptions and job analysis in effective job placement
of students for maximum educational values. (Includes
student jobs on campus, off campus, and cooperative
education.)

4   11. Philosophy of Higher Education

Critical examination of assumptions and aims, operations
and consequences, and basic concepts and symbols of
higher education from philosophic perspectives

4   12. The Community Junior College

a. A study of the nature and function of the junior college
in American higher education

b. A study of the relationship of the junior college to the
community and other educational institutions

c. An awareness of the special problems in curriculum design,
student services, faculty selection, and community services
which accompany the fast growing junior college

4   13. Careers in Higher Education

a. A study to explore employment possibilities in higher
education

b. A study to determine the special qualifications and
skills necessary to meet employment standards in
faculty and staff positions in colleges and universities

c. The importance of personnel selection in efficient program function

4 14. The Role of the Federal Government in Student Financial Assistance

    a. A course to acquaint the student with the various programs of financial aid and the requirements for student and institutional eligibility

    b. The impact of the "equality of educational opportunity" upon higher educational institutions as viewed by the Federal Government and the institution

    c. Regulations regarding forms, funding, and reports--Federal control?

4 15. College Students and College Culture

    a. A study of the nature of the student and the impact of the college on student development

    b. The nature of the college as a unique social institution

    c. The interaction between the student and his institution

2 - 6 16. The Research Study or Thesis

    Two to six hours of credit for a study that meets departmental requirements

8 17. Additional Electives

    Eight hours of academic credit may be selected from other graduate fields with the approval of the departmental chairman

Glossary

1. ACADEMIC HOURS: A term frequently used to indicate the academic credit and hours of recitation in a given course. (Illustration: A four-hour English course would normally require four hours per week recitation and satisfactory completion of four hours of credit.)

2. ACADEMIC PROBATION: A term used to indicate unsatisfactory scholastic achievement, usually an academic average below "C." In some institutions, it indicates a level of achievement so poor that the student is dropped from the college or university.

3. AMERICAN ASSOCIATION OF COLLEGIATE REGISTRARS AND ADMISSIONS OFFICERS: An association consisting of memberships, primarily registrars or admissions officers. However, financial aid is receiving more attention in the formal structure of the association. Not infrequently in smaller colleges, the commissions officer and financial aids officer are one and the same person.

4. AMERICAN COLLEGE PERSONNEL ASSOCIATION (ACPA): A division of the American Personnel and Guidance Association. The association maintains a commission on financial aid. The association also publishes a journal.

5. AMERICAN COUNCIL ON EDUCATION (ACE): A council of educational organizations and institutions. Its purpose is to advance education and educational methods through comprehensive voluntary and cooperative action on the part of American educational associations, organizations, and institutions.

6. ASSISTANTSHIP: Normally, a form of institutional employment reserved for graduate students and awarded by the department in which the student is academically enrolled.

7. AWARD: A form of financial assistance generally conferred in recognition of participation in a university-sponsored activity (music, theater, debate, athletics, etc.).

8. CAPABLE NEEDY STUDENT: A student who has the academic potential to perform college work as indicated by high school achievement records or college entrance tests, but who lacks the financial resources to attend college.

9. THE COLLEGE ENTRANCE EXAMINATION BOARD: A nonprofit national membership association of colleges, universities, public school systems, public and private secondary schools, and educational organizations. The College Board publishes a quarterly magazine as well as books and pamphlets in the field of education. (Publication Order Office: Box 592, Princeton, New Jersey 08540.)

10. COLLEGE SCHOLARSHIP SERVICE: This organization is devoted primarily to the financial aid activities of colleges and universities. CSS is noted for its pioneering work in family need analysis and has developed manuals and sponsored colloquiums for financial aid officers. CSS publishes a newsletter, *The Financial Aid News*.

11. COLLEGE WORK-STUDY PROGRAM: A form of student employment, primarily for students from low-income families. The employment may be for the institution or for an approved off-campus agency when the work is performed for a public or nonprofit organization. Students must be enrolled on a full-time basis and be listed in good academic standing. Students may work an average of fifteen hours per week while attending classes and may work forty hours per week during vacation periods. Hourly rates of pay for students range from the federal minimum hourly rate to $3.00 per hour. To be eligible to participate in the program, a student must have need for employment to defray college expenses. The College Work-Study Program is financed on a matching fund basis with the federal government contributing 80 percent and the institution 20 percent. (The United States Office of Education, Division of Financial Aids, administers the program.)

12. COOPERATIVE EDUCATION (Higher Education) : A term frequently used to identify an educational program in which the students alternate between college studies and full-time work experience, which is usually in some business or industry.

13. COOPERATIVE EDUCATION (Secondary Education) : A work-experience program which combines vocational instruction with a job in a business or industry. The work experience is usually jointly supervised by the employer and the school. In secondary schools the term "diversified occupations" refers to vocational instruction and work in a specific trade, business, or service.

14. COORDINATOR (Financial Assistance) : An administrative Job Title in common usage in institutions of higher education, identifying the person who is usually responsible for a part or the total program of student financial aid.

15. COUNSELOR (Financial Assistance) : A Job Title for financial aids personnel who devote their time to helping students who have problems which primarily stem from a lack of financal resources, necessary to attend or to remain in a college program.

16. COUNSELOR (Guidance) : A Job Title in common usage for personnel who assist students with problems relative to their social, educational, vocational, and personal needs.

17. DIRECTOR (Financial Assistance) : An administrative Job Title common in institutions of higher education to denote the person responsible for the total program of financial aid. (The title is especially common in the larger state universities.)

18. DIRECTOR (Guidance) : An administrative Job Title to identify the person responsible for a total program of guidance and counseling in elementary and/or high schools.

19. EDUCATIONAL OPPORTUNITY GRANT PROGRAMS: A federally sponsored program for college students with exceptional financial need. The program is administered by the United States Office of Education. The grant is in the form of a gift of $200 to $1000 per academic year, depending upon the exceptional financial needs of the students and the availability of other forms of financial assistance.

General eligibility requirements are: The student must show academic or creative promise; be enrolled on a full-time basis; be in academic good-standing; and be an undergraduate student.

20. FELLOWSHIP: A gift usually awarded to a graduate student for scholastic achievement; however, need is frequently given consideration.

21. FINANCIAL AID: A term broadly defined to include any and all forms of financial assistance for college students. (Such a program includes work, loans, grants, scholarships, awards, and fellowships.)

22. FINANCIAL AID APPLICATION: A form designed to obtain pertinent information concerning a student to be used in helping to determine the kind and the amount of financial assistance which a student may be eligible to receive.

23. FINANCIAL STATEMENT (Family). A form designed to obtain pertinent information regarding the financial resources of a student and his family with the purpose of establishing the degree of financial need of the student. The information is primarily used by financial aids officers in awarding scholarships, loans, grants, and student jobs.

24. GOOD-STANDING: The maintenance of that level of scholastic achievement determined by the faculty and administration which indicates satisfactory progress, usually a "C" average or above.

25. GRANT: A form of financial assistance conferred on the basis of demonstrated need for assistance.

26. GUARANTEED LOANS: A loan program primarily for students whose family's adjusted gross income is less than $15,000 annually. The federal government pays to the lender (bank, credit union, savings and loan association, etc.) the interest charge up to 6 percent a year while the student is in school and 3 percent interest during the repayment period. Students who enroll on a full-time basis generally are eligible to borrow $1,000 to $1,500 per year up to six years. The Guaranteed Loan Program has no forgiveness clause.

27. INSTITUTIONAL STUDENT EMPLOYMENT: Normally, part-time and full-time jobs an institution has under its jurisdiction and which are primarily allocated to students who enroll in the institution.

28. INTERNSHIP: A special type of work experience, usually for graduate students, conducted under the supervision of an academic department as part of the instructional program. The work experience is combined with study in the form of a practicum.

29. INTERVIEWER (Financial Aids): A Job Title for personnel who devote most of their time in interviewing and counseling financial aid applicants and explaining the financial aid programs available in a given institution.

30. INTERVIEWER (Student Employment): A Job Title for personnel who interview, analyze, refer, place, and follow up applicants in student job situations either on or off campus.

31. JOB: A job is usually thought of as consisting of a group of similar positions.

32. JOB DESCRIPTION: A job description is one or more statements concerning the duties, responsibilities, and qualifications of jobs in a given business or establishment.

33. JOB DESCRIPTION FORM: A form which lists the major duties, responsibilities, and qualifications which identifies a specific job or position in a particular business, industry, institution, or establishment.

34. JOB EVALUATION FORM: A form designed to rate the job performance and related characteristics of an employee in a work situation.

35. JUNIOR COLLEGE OR COMMUNITY COLLEGE: A higher educational institution which normally offers two years of education and training beyond high school in the areas of general education, vocational education, and adult education.

36. MIDWEST ASSOCIATION OF UNIVERSITY STUDENT EMPLOYMENT DIRECTORS (MAUSED): A regional association devoted primarily to student employment problems. The association publishes a newsletter, *The Mid-Western.*

37. MID-WESTERN ASSOCIATION OF STUDENT FINANCIAL AID ADMINISTRATORS (MASFAA): A regional organization concerned with all aspects of financial aid on both a regional and a national level. The association has an annual meeting, and it publishes a newsletter for members.

38. NATIONAL ASSOCIATION OF STUDENT PERSONNEL ADMINISTRATORS (NASPA): The association consists of individuals primarily concerned with student personnel administrators. The association maintains a commission on financial aid.

39. NATIONAL DEFENSE STUDENT LOAN PROGRAM: A United States Office of Education administered program of borrowing which had its beginning in 1958. Undergraduates may borrow $1,000 a year up to $5,000. Graduate students may borrow $2,500 per year up to $10,000. The repayment of the loan begins nine months after the student terminates his studies. Repayment period may extend over a ten-year period and draws interest at the rate of 3 percent per annun. A teacher forgiveness clause provides for as much as one-half of the loan to be forgiven at the rate of 10 percent for each year of teaching service. If a teacher elects to teach in selected schools located in areas of low-income families, he may qualify for the cancellation of the entire loan at the rate of 15 percent per year.

40. OFF-CAMPUS STUDENT EMPLOYMENT: Normally, the part-time and full-time jobs which business, industry, and governmental agencies allocate to college students. Students may be employed during the academic year or during vacation periods.

41. PLACEMENT DIRECTOR: An administrative job on the college level; the director usually coordinates the various activities of the placement office which includes student counseling, job listing, referral, placement, and following up of students and graduates. Also, works with employing agencies (business, industry, and schools).

42. PLACEMENT OFFICE OR BUREAU: An agency primarily concerned with the placement of its own graduates in full-time employment; some placement offices also find part-time employment for students on or off campus as well as in vacation employment.

43. PLACEMENT OFFICER: One who administers or assists with the administration of a placement office which provides a job placement

service for students and graduates; the officer usually counsels regarding job opportunities; the officer maintains contact with employers for the purpose of acquiring job listings.

44. POSITION: A position may be defined as the duties and responsibilities requiring the full-time service of one individual, or in the instance of students, a position may require the service of one or more part-time student employees.

45. REFERRAL CARD: A card or form issued in student employment offices which introduces the applicant to a prospective employer.

46. SCHOLARSHIP: A scholarship is a financial gift usually conferred on the basis of superior scholastic achievement. Need may be a factor in determining recipients for scholarships.

47. SOUTHWESTERN ASSOCIATION OF STUDENT FINANCIAL AID ADMINISTRATORS: A regional association composed of financial aid administrators and counselors from colleges and universities in the southwestern states.

48. STIPEND: A fixed amount of money usually provided to a student to compensate him for his service to his college or university.

49. UNDERGRADUATE SCHOOL: In general, the educational programs and curricula in a college or university which require 124 semester hours of satisfactory work before awarding the bachelor's degree.

50. U.S.O.E.: The United States Office of Education of the Department of Health, Education, and Welfare. Robert H. Finch, Secretary of H.E.W.; James Allen, Commissioner, Office of Education.

Bibliography

Books

American Student Information Service. *Earn, Learn, and Travel in Europe, 1965–66.* Luxembourg: Beurg-Bourger, 1965.

The American Workers' Fact Book. U.S. Department of Labor. Washington, D.C.: Government Printing Office, n.d.

Angel, Juvenal Londono. *How and Where to Get Scholarships and Loans.* New York: Regents Publishing Co., 1964.

————. *Students' Guide to Occupational Opportunities and Their Lifetime Earnings.* Modern Vocational Trends Bureau. New York: World Trade Academy Press, Inc., 1967.

Arthur, Julietta K. *Employment for the Handicapped.* Nashville, Tenn.: Abingdon Press, 1967.

Atherton J. C., and Mumphrey, Anthony. *Essential Aspects of Career Planning and Development.* Danville, Ill.: Interstate Printers and Publishers, 1969.

Ayers, A., Tripp, Philip, and Russell, John. *Student Services Administration in Higher Education.* Washington, D.C.: Government Printing Office, 1966.

Bier, William C., S.J., ed. *Woman in Modern Life.* New York: Fordham University Press, 1968.

Brubacher, John S., and Rudy, Willis. *Higher Education in Transition, an American History: 1936–1956.* New York: Harper & Brothers, 1958.

Callahan, Daniel, ed. *Federal Aid and Catholic Schools.* Baltimore: Helicon Press, 1964.

Career Information for Use in Guidance, 1966–67. U.S. Department of Labor. Washington, D.C.: Government Printing Office, 1968.

Career Opportunities. Career Information Service, New York Life Insurance Company. New York, 1966.

Cass, James, and Birnbaum, Max. *Comparative Guide to American Colleges: For Students, Parents, and Counselors.* New York: Harper & Row, 1965.

Characteristics of Workers in Selected Occupations. U.S. Department of Labor. Washington, D.C.: Government Printing Office, 1967.

College Aid for Students. U.S. Department of Health, Education, and Welfare Indicators. Washington, D.C.: Government Printing Office, 1965.

College Work-Study Program Manual. U.S. Office of Education, Bureau of Higher Education (OE-55054). Washington, D.C.: Government Printing Office, 1968.

The Counselor's Handbook: A Guide to the Student Work Program at Southern Illinois University. Carbondale, Ill., 1960.

Cox, Claire. *How to Beat the High Cost of College.* New York: Random House, 1965.

Current Issues in Higher Education. The Proceedings of the Nineteenth Annual National Conference on Higher Education April 19–22, 1964. Association for Higher Education, a Department of the National Education Association, Washington, D.C., 1964.

Dictionary of Occupational Titles, Part IV, "Entry Occupational Classification." Division of Occupational Analysis, War Manpower Commission. Washington, D.C.: Government Printing Office, 1944.

Dobbins, Charles, ed. *Higher Education and the Federal Government Programs and Problems.* Papers presented at the Forty-Fifth Annual Meeting in Chicago, Ill. on October 3–5, 1962. Washington, D.C.: American Council on Education, 1963.

The Economics of Higher Education, 1966 Colloquium. Princeton, N.J.: College Entrance Examination Board, 1967.

Educational Opportunity Grants: Program Manual of Policies and Procedures. U.S. Office of Education, Bureau of Higher Education. Washington, D.C.: Government Printing Office, 1967.

Emerging Patterns in American Higher Education. Edited by Logan Wilson. Washington, D.C.: American Council on Education, 1965.

Federal Aids for College Students. U.S. Department of Health, Education, and Welfare. Washington, D.C.: Government Printing Office, 1966.

The Federal Financing of Higher Education. 1968. Report of the Association of American Universities. Washington, D.C.: Association of American Universities, n.d.

Federal Government Programs for Colleges and Universities. Papers, Remarks, and Questions from Conferences of November 20–21 and December 11–12, 1961, of the American College Public Relations Association, Washington, D.C. Washington, D.C.: Government Printing Office, 1962.

The Federal Role in Education. Congressional Quarterly Service. Washington, D.C.: Government Printing Office, 1967.

The Federal Work-Study Concept: An Analysis. Report No. 3 of the Advisory Committee on National Student Financial Aid Programs of the College Scholarship Service. New York, 1963.

Final Report of the National Youth Administration Fiscal Years 1936–1943. The Federal Security Agency, War Manpower Commission. Washington, D.C.: Government Printing Office, 1944.

Financial Aid for Higher Education. Published by the Cooperative Program for Educational Opportunity under contract with the Educational Talent Section of the Division of Student Financial Aid, U.S. Office of Education. Washington, D.C.: Government Printing Office, 1968.

Fine, Benjamin. *How to Get Money for College.* Garden City, N.Y.: Doubleday, 1964.

Goldenthal, Allan B. *Your Career Selection Guide.* New York: Regents Publishing Co., 1967.

Granger, Russell H. *Collegian's Guide to Part-Time Jobs.* New York: ARC Books, 1968.

Growth of Labor Law in the United States. U.S. Department of Labor. Government Printing Office, 1962.

Guaranteeing an Opportunity for Higher Education to all Qualified High School Graduates: Should the Federal Government Participate? Washington, D.C.: Government Printing Office, 1963.

Guide to Grants, Loans, and Other Types of Government Assistance Available to Students and Educational Institutions. Washington, D.C.: Public Affairs Press, 1967.

Guide to Support Programs for Education. St. Paul, Minn.: Education Services Press, 1966.

Hall, R., and Craigie, S. *Student Borrowers, Their Needs and Resources.* Washington, D.C.: Government Printing Office, 1962.

Handbook for Financial Aid Officers. Iowa City, Iowa: American College Testing Program, 1969.

Handbook of Job Facts. Compiled by Norma L. Thiemann. 4th ed. Chicago, Ill.: Guidance Department, Science Research Associates, 1968.

Harbeson, Gladys E. *Choice and Challenge for the American Woman.* Cambridge, Mass.: Schenkman Publishing Co., 1967.

Harris, S., and Levinsohn, A., eds. *Education and Public Policy.* Berkeley, Calif.: McCutchan Publishing Co., 1965.

Higher Education. Compiled by the Bureau of Higher Education, U.S. Office of Education, Department of Health, Education, and Welfare. Washington, D.C.: Government Printing Office, 1968.

Hoppock, Robert. *Occupational Information.* 3rd ed. New York: McGraw-Hill, 1967.

How to Earn (a lot of) Money in College: The Student Guide to Employment. Cambridge, Mass.: Harvard Student Agencies, 1968.

Illinois State Scholarship Comission Report. Deerfield, Ill.: Illinois State Scholarship Commission, 1969.

Kauffman, Warren E., ed. *College Placement Annual, 1966.* Bethlehem, Pa.: College Placement Council, Inc., n.d.

Kesslar, O. *A National Catalogue of Financial Aids for Students Entering College.* Dubuque, Iowa: W. C. Brown and Co., 1967.

Knight, Douglas M., ed. *The Federal Government and Higher Education.* Englewood Cliffs, N.J.: Prentice-Hall, 1960.

Leith, Mynena A., ed. *Summer Employment Directory of the United States, Summer Jobs for 1966.* Cincinnati, Ohio: National Directory Service, 1965.

Lovejoy, Clarence E. *Lovejoy's Career and Vocational School Guide.* 3rd ed. New York: Simon and Schuster, 1967.

McGarry, D., and Ward, L., eds. *Educational Freedom and the Case for*

Government Aid to Students in Independent Schools. Milwaukee, Wis.; Bruce Publishing Co., 1966.

McKee, Richard C. *Financial Assistance for College Students.* U.S. Department of Health, Education, and Welfare, 1965–67. Washington, D.C.: Government Printing Office, 1968.

Man, Education and Work. Washington, D.C.: American Council on Education, 1964.

A Master Plan—Phase II for Higher Education in Illinois. Springfield, Ill.: Illinois Board of Higher Education, 1966.

Minter, W., ed. *Campus and Capitol: Higher Education and the State.* Berkeley, Calif.: University of California Press, 1966.

Monthly Labor Review. U.S. Department of Labor. Washington, D.C.: Government Printing Office, n.d.

Moon, Rexford G., Jr. *Student Financial Aid in the United States: Administration and Resources.* Princeton, N.J.: College Entrance Examination Board, 1963.

National Defense Student Loan Program: Manual of Policies and Procedures. U.S. Office of Education. Washington, D.C.: Government Printing Office, 1964.

National Scholarship Service and Fund for Negro Students. Annual Report, 1966–67. New York: National Scholarship Service and Fund for Negro Students, n.d.

1965 Handbook on Women Workers. U.S. Department of Labor, Women's Bureau. Washington, D.C.: Government Printing Office, 1965.

Occupational Outlook Handbook. Career Information, 1966–67 Edition. U.S. Department of Labor. Washington, D.C.: Government Printing Office, n.d.

Palmer, Robert A. *Summer Employment Guide: Wyoming, Colorado, Montana, New Mexico, Utah, and Arizona.* Denver, Colo.: University Publications, 1966.

Rivlin, Alice M. *The Role of the Federal Government in Financing Higher Education.* Washington, D.C.: Brookings Institute, 1961.

Sandman, Peter M. *The Unabashed Career Guide.* New York: Macmillan Co., 1969.

Sasscer, H., ed. *Conference on Federal Programs for Colleges and Universities.* Washington, D.C.: American Council on Education, 1964.

Seasonal Employment in the National Park Service. U.S. Department of Interior, National Park Service. Washington, D.C.: Government Printing Office, n.d.

Shartle, Carroll. *Occupational Information, Its Development and Application.* New York: Prentice-Hall, 1946.

Stress and Campus Response. Current Issues in Higher Education. San Francisco: Jossey-Bass, 1968.

Student Employment Division, National Employment Services Institute. *Summer Employment Guide—1967.* Garden City, N.Y.: Doubleday & Co., 1966.

Student Financial Aid and Institutional Purpose. Princeton, N.J.: College Entrance Examination Board, 1963.

Student Financial Aid and National Purpose. Princeton, N.J.: College Entrance Examination Board, 1962.

Student Financial Aid in Higher Education: An Annotated Bibliography. U.S. Office of Education, Division of Higher Education (OE-53006), No. 3. Washington, D.C.: Government Printing Office, 1961.

A Study of 1967–1968 Scholarship and Grant Recipients. A Joint Report/ Illinois State Scholarship Commission and Board of Higher Education. n.p., 1969.

Summer Employment Directory of the United States: Summer Jobs for 1968. 17th ed. Cincinnati, Ohio: National Directory Services, 1967.

Summer Vacation Jobs in Federal Agencies. U.S. Department of Labor, Pamphlet No. 68. Washington, D.C.: Government Printing Office, 1965.

Tennyson, Wesley Willard, Soldahl, Thomas A., and Mueller, Charlotte. *The Teacher's Role in Career Development.* St. Paul, Minn.: Department of Education, 1960.

Thorndike, Robert L., and Hagen, Elizabeth. *Ten Thousand Careers.* New York: John Wiley and Sons, 1959.

Tiedt, S. *The Role of the Federal Government in Education.* New York: Oxford University Press, 1966.

U.S. House of Representatives, Committee on Education and Labor. *A Guide to Student Assistance.* 91st Cong., 2nd sess., H. Doc. 91–221. Washington, D.C.: Government Printing Office, 1970.

U.S. Department of Health, Education, and Welfare, Office of the Assistant Secretary for Planning and Evaluation. *Toward a Long-Range Plan for Federal Financial Support for Higher Education (A Report to the President).* n.p., 1969.

West, Elmer D. *Financial Aid to the Undergraduate: Issues and Implications.* Washington, D.C.: American Council on Education, 1963.

Wilson, James W., and Lyons, Edward H. *Work-Study Programs: Appraisal and Report of the Study of Cooperative Education.* New York: Harper & Brothers, 1960.

Zapoleon, Marguerite Wykoff. *Occupational Planning for Women.* New York: Harper & Brothers, 1961.

Articles

Adams, Frank C. "Recommendations for a National Student Work Scholarship Program," *Journal of College Student Personnel* 4 (June 1963), 235.

Adams, Frank C., and Stephens, Clarence. "Summer Jobs," *Moderator* (March 1968), pp. 42–43.

Allen, D. J. "Financial Aid Updated," *National Association of Women Deans and Counselors Journal* 30 (Winter 1967), 57–62.

Austin, C. G. "On Financing Higher Education," *Journal of Higher Education* 38 (December 1967), 511–13.

Babbush, H. E. "College Work-Study Program," *California Education* 3 (December 1965), 13.

Beaumont, A. G. "Friendly Invaders," *Journal of College Placement* 25 (December 1964), 25–29.

Bjorklaind, C. "How to Build a Scholarships Program: South San Francisco Community Scholarship Association," *Journal of Secondary Education* 41 (April 1966), 174–79.

Bowman, J. L. "Dollars, Decisions and Diplomas: the Financial Aid Officer's Work," *American Education* 2 (May 1966), 30–32.

"Business of Financial Aid; Panel Discussion," *College and University* 37 (Summer 1962), 444–70.

Carnegie Foundation for the Advancement of Teaching. "Twenty-six Campuses and the Federal Government: Federal Support of Education and Training," *Educational Record* 44 (April 1963), 123–38.

"College Financial Aid Principles," *National Association of Secondary School Principals Bulletin* 46 (Summer 1962), 213–15.

"Colleges Increase Their Aid to Undergraduates," *School Life* 44 (May 1962), 17.

"College Provisions for Minorities," *School and Society* 97 (February 1969), 84–86.

Cranfill, C. "Scholarship Wasteland: Where Money for Education Goes Unused," *Educational Digest* 32 (May 1967), 38–39.

"Dollars for Scholars: Funds Given by each State PTA," *PTA Magazine* 61 (June 1967), 19.

Drexler, V. "Fundable Job Opportunities in College Business Departments," *Business Education World* 46 (April 1966), 26–27.

Dyer, G. W. "Should We Pay Students?" *Ohio Schools* 43 (May 1965), 25.

Eckberg, A. R. "Who Speaks for Student Employment?" *Journal of College Placement* 25 (December 1964), 69–70.

"Federal Money for Education—for Programs, Instruction, and Administration," *American Education* 4 (February 1968), 24–26.

"1,524 Institutions in 1962–63 Student Loan Program," *Higher Education* 18 (July 1962), 20.

"Functional Interrelationships Involving the Offices of Admissions, Financial Aid and Registrar: Panel Discussion." *College and University* 40 (Summer 1965), 418–49.

Hall, R. C. "National Defense Student Loan Program, Advance Report of a Survey of Student Borrowers, Fall 1960," *Higher Education* 17 (July 1961), 9–11.

———. "Occupational Plans of Student Borrowers Under NDEA," *School Life* 45 (January 1963), 26–29.

Hall, R. C., and Craigie, S. C. "Student Borrowers Under NDEA: Regional Contrasts," *School Life* 44 (November 1961), 16–18.

Hamilton, C. L. "College Costs and Financial Aids to Meet Them," *Illinois Education* 53 (October 1964), 83–85.

Harding, A. C. "Student Financial Aid," *NEA Journal* 57 (April 1968), 44–45.

Henry, Joe B. "Trends in Student Financial Aid," *Journal of College Student Personnel* (July 1969), pp. 227–31.

"Higher Education for the Talented Needy: Cooperative Program for Educational Opportunity," *School and Society* 94 (December 1966), 441–42.

Hockmann, W. S. "Scholarships in Recognition," *International Journal of Religious Education* 41 (July 1965), 18–19.

Hood, A. B. "Educational Loan Company; A Last Resort?" *Personnel and Guidance Journal* 40 (October 1961), 178.

"Institutions Report Loan Activity for 1960–61," *Higher Education* 18 (March 1962), 22.

Jacobson, R. F. "New Scholarships for Mature Women; AWARE Helps Women Return to College," *Junior College Journal* 38 (December 1967), 34.

Jensen, J. J. "Your Summer Job Program, a Success or Failure," *Journal of College Placement* 25 (December 1964), 61–62.

Jones, G., Jr. "Missing a Bet on Part-Time Jobs?" *Journal of College Placement* 24 (December 1963), 50–51.

Katzenbach, J. R. "Does Your Summer Job Program Recruit or Antagonize?" *Journal of College Placement* 23 (February 1963), 24–25.

Keene, Roland, and Adams, Frank C. "Capable High School Graduates Can Finance Their College Education," *Bulletin (of the National Association of Secondary School Principals)* (May 1961), pp. 24–27.

Kernan, E. R. "Student-Faculty Work Program," *School and Society* 91 (February 1963), 59.

Kimball, R. B. "Do Scholarships Help?" *Personnel and Guidance Journal* 46 (April 1968), 782–85.

Knapp, D. F. "Summer Work with Meaning," *Journal of College Placement* 28 (February 1968), 70–72.

"Loans to College Students," *School and Society* 95 (October 1967), 373.

MacGregor, A. "Part-time Work: Good or Bad?" *Journal of College Placement* 26 (February 1966), 127–28.

Miller, C. D. et al. "Student Patterns of Financing Education at a Land-Grant University," *Personnel and Guidance Journal* 45 (March 1967), 687–91.

Moon, R. C., Jr. "Borrowing for a College Education," *School and Society* 90 (Summer 1962), 254.

Moore, J. W., and Rioux, J. W. "Two Challenges of the Economic Opportunity Act: The Work-Study Program, and the Community Action Program are Ideal for Community College Participation," *Junior College Journal* 35 (March 1965), 17–18.

Morse, John F. "The Federal Government and Higher Education: General and Specific Concerns in the Years Ahead," *Educational Record* 47, no. 4 (Fall 1966), 429–38.

Mousolite, P. S. "Economic Opportunity Act of 1964; Title I-C, The College Work-Study Program," *American Association of College Teacher Education Yearbook* 18 (1965), 150–53.

Muirhead, P. P. "Federal Student Assistance Program," *Educational Record* 43 (April 1962), 129–31.

———. "Junior Colleges Must Assist in an Important Way to Discharge Society's Obligation to Put Higher Education within Financial Reach of All Qualified Students," *Junior College Journal* 31 (May 1961), 513–18.

O'Hearne, J. J. "Cash for College," *Texas Outlook* 52 (February 1968), 28–29.

Quattlebaum, C. A. "Enactments of the 89th Congress Relevant to Higher Education," *Educational Record* 48 (Summer 1967), 285–90.

Rivera, E. "Disadvantaged and the University Camp: Project APEX," *Teachers College Record* 67 (May 1966), 557–63.

"Scholarships and Financial Aid: Some Practical Considerations for the Administration of the Financial Aid Program: Panel Discussion," *College and University* 41 (Summer 1966), 423–26.

Scott, N. T. "Higher Education for Life: Linking Study and Work," *Times Educational Supplement* no. 2615 (July 1965), p. 21.

Sedacek, W. E. "Summer Job: It Should Offer More than a Paycheck," *Journal of College Placement* 24 (February 1964), 59–60.

Shapiro, E. "Long-term Student Loans," *Harvard Educational Review* 33 (Summer 1963), 360–78.

Silver, H. "Salaries for Students?" *University Quarterly* 19 (September 1965), 409–13.

Smith, P. M., Jr. "Realism of Counseling for Scholarship Aid with Freshman in the Negro College," *Journal of Negro Education* 33 (Winter 1964), 93–96.

Smith, S. L. "On-Campus Jobs Offer Advantages for College Secretarial Students," *Business Education World* 43 (May 1963), 22–23.

Stalmaker, J. M. "Evaluation and the Award of Scholarships," *National Society for the Study of Education Yearbook, 1968,* Part 2 (1969), pp. 102–14.

———. "Scholarship Aid for the Intellectually Able," *School and Society* 93 (May 1965), 264.

"Strengthening Negro Colleges," *School and Society* 95 (November 1967), 411.

"Student Borrowers: Their Needs and Resources," *Higher Education* 19 (October 1962), 12–14.

"Student Loan Program," *Higher Education* 19 (February 1963), 13.

"Support for Work-Study Projects," *School and Society* 95 (December 1967), 512.

Tragesser, E. F. et al. "Federal Loans and Scholarships in the Health-Professions," *College and University* 42 (Summer 1967), 479.

Trimble, L. T. "How to Get Money for College," *American Education* 3 (July 1967), 9–11.

Trimble, V. "Student Financial Aid: What, Where, How." *American Education* 5 (February 1968), 7–8.

Van Edmond, E. "Social Policy and Education: Aid to Students," *Review of Educational Research* 34 (February 1964), 96.

Van Straubenzee, W. R. "Case Against Loans for Students," *Times Educational Supplement,* no. 2713 (May 1967), p. 1689.

Ware, G., and Determan, D. W. "Federal Dollar, the Negro College and the Negro Student," *Journal of Negro Education* 35 (Fall 1966), 459–68.

Williams, N. "Part-time Jobs: Advantages and Disadvantages," *School and Community* 53 (January 1965), 36.

Wilson, M. S. "National Achievement Scholarship Program: Plan Offers

College Aid to Promising Negro Students," *Chicago School Journal* 46 (April 1965), 279–301.

Winfrey, J. K., and Feder, D. D. "Non-Instructional Services: Financial Aid, Employment and Placement," *Record of Educational Research* 35 (October 1965), 326–68.

Dissertations

Adams, Frank C. "A Classification System for Student Employment in State Universities in Illinois" (Ph.D. diss., Southern Illinois University, 1962).

DeJarnett, Raymond P. "A Pilot Study of Certain Work Experiences of Part-Time Student Workers as it Relates to Preparation for Teaching" (Ph.D. diss., Southern Illinois University, 1964).

Henry, Joe B. "Family Financial Power and College Attendance of High School Graduates in Two Ability Groups" (Ph.D. diss., University of Missouri, 1964).

Ideus, Harvey S. "The Relationships Between Wyoming Parents' Contributions to Freshman Student Expenses Attending the University of Wyoming and Selected Family Characteristics" (Ph.D. diss., University of Wyoming, 1965).

Reents, Harold "A Proposed Financial (Aid) Program for Public Junior Colleges in Illinois" (Ph.D. diss., Southern Illinois University, 1966).

Additional Sources of Information

Illinois Guidance and Personnel Association Quarterly. Southern Illinois University, Carbondale, Illinois.

The Journal of College Student Personnel. American College Personnel Association, A Division of the American Personnel and Guidance Association, Washington, D.C. University of Missouri, Columbia, Mo.

Journal of Cooperative Education. Cooperative Education Association. Drexel Institute of Technology, Philadelphia, Pa.

The Mid-Western. Midwest Association of University Student Employment Directors. Southern Illinois University, Carbondale, Ill.

The Personnel and Guidance Journal. American Personnel and Guidance Association, Washington, D.C.

Vocational Guidance Quarterly. National Vocational Guidance Association, A Division of the American Personnel and Guidance Association, Washington, D.C. Easton, Pa.

Index